Issues

A Course Book for Advanced Level English Language

Issues

A Course Book for Advanced Level
English Language

Peter Turner

Edward Arnold

© Peter Turner 1987

First published in Great Britain in 1987 by
Edward Arnold (Publishers) Ltd
41 Bedford Square, London WC1B 3DQ

Edward Arnold (Australia) Pty Ltd
80 Waverley Road, Caulfield East
Victoria 3145

British Library Cataloguing in Publication Data

Turner, Peter
  Issues: a course book for advanced level English language.
  1. English language — Composition and exercises
  I. Title
  808'.042   PE1413

  ISBN 0-7131-7600-8

Set in 10/11pt Times Compugraphic
Typeset by Colset Private Limited, Singapore
Printed and bound in Great Britain by Richard Clay Ltd, Bungay, Suffolk

Preface

The essential idea of this book is to provide a thematically integrated approach to advanced level English studies. It aims to cover the major social, political and cultural issues of the late twentieth-century, in a way which would be of value both for post GCSE English examination work, and for general and social studies discussion, with or without written work to follow.

The book is most specifically directed towards the A.E.B. 'A' and 'A/S' level English (Language and Literature) syllabuses, and the themes chosen are ones that appear frequently on the 'A' level exam essay paper. The discussion material may also be found to be of direct relevance to B.TEC Communications Levels II and III, and its approach may be valuable also for Sixth form and F.E. College Social/Liberal/General Studies sessions.

Each major chapter covers a single issue, providing a comprehension or precis exercise, a series of extracts designed to present a wide range of viewpoints and information, with suggestions for discussion and research and further written work, and lists of essay titles and additional stimulus material. Each thematic chapter also contains a final section dealing with problems inherent in some aspect of written work. A further chapter deals with four additional issues more briefly, providing overall, for 2 full-scale discussion and writing sessions per term over a 2-year course. There are also 3 shorter chapters specifically related to English language.

Most of the essay questions are taken from A.E.B. 'A' level English examinations; the remainder are from A.E.B. Use of English and 'O/A' level English language − Professional and Business Use papers.

Acknowledgements

The publishers would like to thank the following for their permission to reproduce the following extracts which are copyright:

W H Allen for Williams & Burkitt: *The Silicon Civilisation*; Allen & Unwin for Russell: *Authority and the Individual* and Ellis Cashmore and Troyana: *Black Youth in Crisis*; The Associated Examining Board for passages from examination papers dated June and November 1984; Associated Book Publishers (U.K.) Ltd for Ellis Cashmore: *A Dictionary of Race and Ethnic Relations* and Winnicott: *The Child, the Family and the Outside World*; Basil Blackwell for Oakley: *Subject Women* and Davis & Walton: *Language, Image, Media*; Jonathan Cape Ltd for Tweedie: *In the Name of Love* and de Beauvoir: *The Second Sex* translated by H M Parshley; Century Hutchinson Publishing Group Ltd for Husband (ed): *Race in Britain* and Hall and Whannel: *The Popular Arts*; Rex Collings for Wole Soyinka 'Telephone Conversation'; Comedia for Walker: *News Limited*; Constable Publishers for Cohen & Young: *The Manufacture of News*; Professor Cox for *Black Papers*; Curtis Brown Group Limited for B Inglis: *The Forbidden Game: a Social History of Drugs* © Brian Inglis 1975, reprinted by kind permission of Curtis Brown and for Daphne du Maurier: *The Birds* reprinted by kind permission of Curtis Brown Ltd on behalf of Daphne du Maurier © Daphne du Maurier 1952; Delacorte Press and A M Heath for Holt: *How Children Fail*; Andre Deutsch for Mailer: *Presidential Papers*; Sybil Eynsenck for her article; Victor Gollancz Ltd for Evans: *The Mighty Micro*, Friedan: *The Feminine Mystique* and Neill: *Summerhill*; Gower Publishing Company for Parker: *Friends of the Earth Guide to Pollution* and Briggs: *In Place of Prisons*; Grafton Books for Greer: *The Female Eunuch*; Her Majesty's Stationery Office for extracts from *Hansard*; Hamish Hamilton Limited for extracts from Davies: *The Creighton Report* and Radzinovicz: *The Growth of Crime*; Bernard Hasell for Baldwin: *Go Tell it on the Mountain*; Paul Harrison for his *Inside the Third World*, Penguin 1979; Hodder & Stoughton Educational for Macbeath: *A Question of Schooling*; Ellis Horwood Limited for Burns: *The Microchip: Appropriate or Inappropriate Technology?*; Kogan Page for Allen: *How To Save the World*; David S Lake Publishers for Holt: *The Underachieving School*; Longman Group Limited for Golding and Elliott: *Making the News*; Macmillan Accounts & Administration for Freedman: *Britain and Nuclear Weapons*; Manchester University Press for Whale: *The Politics of the Media*; New Internationalist for an article; Oxford University Press for Shallis: *The Silicon Idol: the Micro Revolution and its Social Implications*; Penguin Books Ltd for Whitehead: *Advertising* from Thompson: *Discrimination and Popular Culture* (Pelican Books, 1964, second edition 1973) copyright © Penguin Books, 1964, 1973, Blishen: *The School That I'd Like* (Penguin Education Special, 1969) copyright © Penguin Books and the contributors 1969, Brown: *Techniques of Persuasion: from Propaganda to Brainwashing* (Pelican Books, 1963) copyright © the Estate of J A C Brown, 1963 and Smith: *Racial Disadvantage in Britain: The PEP Report* (Pelican Books, 1977) copyright © PEP, 1977; Anthony Sheil Associates Ltd for Parker: *The Man Inside*; A D Peters & Co Ltd for Harris: *Gotcha! the Government and the Falklands Crisis*; Pluto Press for Fryer: *Staying Power*; SCM Press Ltd for David Bleakley: *In Place of Work . . . the Sufficient Society*, 1981; Martin Secker & Warburg Limited for Grigg: *The White Question*; Simon & Schuster and The Bodley Head for Spock: *Baby and Child Care*; Society for Education in Film and Television for an article by James Freeman; Stage 1 for an article by − de Chungara with Moema Viezzer; Syndication International Ltd for an article by Frank Conless from the Daily Mirror; Thames and Hudson Ltd for Hallam: *Domesday Book*; Times Newspapers Limited for an article by Dudley Doust; A P Watt Ltd for H G Wells: *Our World in 50 years time* and Friedan: *The Feminine Mystique* and *The Second Stage*; Wildwood House for Cottle: *Black People in Britain: the Voices of Britain's West Indians* and John Wiley & Sons Limited for Sherman: *New Revolution*.

I would like to thank in particular Nicky Day, whose help throughout has been invaluable. I would also like to thank my colleagues at Bournemouth and Poole College of Further Education for their encouragement, especially Bob Baker, Irene Bee, Andrea Etherington and Jim Watson, for their practical assistance. Thanks also go to my friends Julie Matthews, Mikki Nanowski and John Randall for their help and encouragement. Finally, I would like to mention the patient assistance of the people who typed the manuscripts: Gill Cooke, Gillian Davies, Trudy Hayter, Mary Morrison and Melinda Simons.

Contents

1

The Language Essay

This book is concerned with exploring some of the major issues of the 1980s, and is designed to provoke discussion of each of these issues for its own sake. It is also designed to help people pass advanced examinations in English language, and this first chapter is addressed to those whose primary concern is writing. The chapter is intended as a general guide to preparing and writing discussion essays.

Most people reading this will have passed 'O' level English Language and will be familiar with the requirements for discussion essays at that level. To pass, you will have had to demonstrate the ability to structure your ideas into coherent paragraphs, and to write, punctuate and spell with a fair degree of accuracy. *What* you write for 'O' level is of secondary importance. This is not true after 'O' level. Competence in the essentials of English will now be assumed. To excel at a higher level you will have to display sophistication in your arguments and a genuine grasp of the issues at stake in any question you answer.

Let us begin, then, with some general approaches to preparation for advanced English discussion essay writing. A study of past examination papers over the previous few years will give you a good idea of the kinds of topics favoured by the examination board with which you are concerned. You will probably find that most of the topics covered in this book feature in past examination papers. During your course you will almost certainly be involved in class discussions or debates which draw on the material contained in the chapters which follow, and jotting down ideas which interest you from these sessions is a start. But the material contained in the book is obviously not intended to provide the last word on any issue. To be adequately informed you must read further into the topic before the discussion takes place, and each chapter contains suggestions for preparatory reading.

Early on in your course, it would be advisable to make a list of the most important issues which recur in past examination essay questions. This should guide your reading. It is not enough, of course, if you are preparing for an examination which includes questions requiring analysis of current issues, simply to learn about the topics covered in this book. The examination paper you eventually sit may include none of them. Wider reading is therefore essential. A quality Sunday newspaper is a valuable source of information, and periodicals and good daily papers can also be useful. Simply *reading* informed analysis is bound to develop your own ideas and understanding, but newspapers and magazines are by nature ephemeral; before they reach the waste bin you are likely to have forgotten the details. If you cut out and keep useful articles and collect them, perhaps in the form of a scrapbook, then you will be able to *learn* some of their contents and to refer back to them as you would to books. You could draw up a list of twenty or more themes and make a collection of pieces relating to each.

If you follow this advice you should find at least one question on your examination paper about which you have prepared some material. But there is no guarantee. It is quite possible that none of the topics you have researched will appear in any form at all on your final examination paper. Will it matter? It may, or it may not. You cannot be expected to have a specialist knowledge of any subject area on the language essay paper, so a carefully thought out argument, with only a few "hard" facts to back it up, can form a perfectly adequate essay. Much depends on whether you have thought about the issue on which you choose to write before you start writing. Working out your ideas as you go along almost inevitably results in a laboured and unconvincing essay. Thus, breadth of reading and thinking is the only certain safeguard in examinations which are as unpredictable as general English essay papers.

Let's look at a hypothetical situation. You are faced with an examination paper which contains no topic on which you are specifically prepared. You, therefore, choose the question which interests you most. The question is about the virtues or vices of cars. Let's now go back a little to fundamentals.

You will almost certainly have been told to make notes and a plan before beginning an English essay. The same principle applies to more advanced essay work. But if you have only got an hour, or less, for an essay, you can't devote much of it to detailed planning. The examination for which you are now preparing, however, may well allow you more time for your essay. If you are advised to spend an hour and a half on the essay, for example, you can afford to spend up to twenty minutes on planning and making quite detailed notes. The examiner will expect to see them. Admittedly there can be no scheme for essay writing which suits everyone, but probably the most useful approach for most people is simply to sit and think about the subject, and jot down ideas as they come into your mind. They may or may not follow a logical pattern of development, and at the initial planning stage it does not matter. An overall approach to the topic will probably occur to you after a few minutes, and the more or less random notes can be organised into a paragraph scheme, once you have worked out a sufficient range of ideas. Some people seem to be able to write well-balanced and logically-developed essays off the top of their heads, but for the majority, detailed planning makes a crucial difference.

Here is an example of an essay planned and written in an hour and a half. You should perhaps be warned that the viewpoint it adopts is deliberately provocative!

"Cars are not a blessing but a curse!" What are your views?

Random Notes

2. Convenience – buses take longer in and between towns
                – annoyance of using buses when car breaks down

2. Re-organised public transport system

3. Using up world's scarce oil

3. Need to do without petrol-driven cars if oil disappears

3. Noise pollution

3. Lead pollution – Britain particularly bad/people living near Spaghetti Junction

4. Accidents – major cause of death
             – drain on Health Service
             – danger to cyclists/puts people off cycling

5. Garage bills and other costs

4. Motorways – pollution of environment
               – destroy countryside

3. Air pollution – carbon monoxide, especially Tokyo and Los Angeles

4. Destruction of towns – flyovers and bypasses
                    – motorways go right into cities

1. Intro: origins of car
      are cars a blessing?

4. Effects on people – adds to isolation
                – stress: traffic jams, rushing through traffic

5. Conclusion: Main advantage – speed and convenience
           Could cars be done away with?
           Effect on unemployment

Plan

1. Introduction: history of car

2. Advantages: convenience → re-organisation of transport system

3. Disadvantages: pollution and depletion of resources

4. Disadvantages: destructive effects on people and places

5. Conclusion: cost and summing up

In 1885 a German, Carl Benz, produced the first petrol-driven vehicle, which proved to be the forerunner of the modern motor car. Few people in those days realised what a monster had been spawned. If they had foreseen the extent to which the automobile has come to dominate life in the Western world a century later, would they have looked on Herr Benz's achievement with approval?

To many people, in the 1980s, a car has come to seem an indispensible part of daily life. The extent to which I myself have become dependent on my car is highlighted whenever it breaks down and I have to use buses. By the time I have walked to the bus stop, which is some distance from my house, and waited for twenty minutes in the pouring rain for a bus which leaves me with another twenty-minute walk at the other end, the car does indeed seem a blessing. In a town like Bournemouth, the public transport system is so run-down that cars tend to be the only comfortable and efficient mode of travel. Does this have to be the case?

Many people have felt that the days of the car are numbered, that the world's reserves of oil will be exhausted within a generation, and the petrol-driven car will have to be phased off the roads. What will happen then? The answer which many have suggested, a full-scale re-organisation of the public transport system, shows that the car is not necessarily such a blessing as we tend to assume. If everyone used buses instead of cars, then public transport could be run efficiently, with a regular, rapid network of routes in every town and city in the country, and with no traffic jams! There could be express buses, stopping only at major points along the route, even within cities. However, cars are fast and efficient, except in rush hours, so what, apart from slowing down the depletion of oil reserves, would mankind gain from the loss of the motor car? Is it really a curse?

You have only to travel to Tokyo or Los Angeles to realise the appalling effects of cars on the environment. Traffic police in Tokyo have to wear masks and carry oxygen, or they would collapse because the air is so polluted with carbon monoxide from cars. Cars produce other, more insidious types of pollution. Lead has been proved to be a major cause of brain damage. The petrol burnt in car engines contains lead, and studies in places where there are vast concentrations of automobiles, such as Spaghetti Junction in Birmingham, have shown that children in those areas suffer from nervous disorders to a significantly greater extent than those in rural areas. Noise pollution, caused by the ceaseless roar of engines and honking of horns, is a further cause of stress in major cities. Actual death from these causes, however, is rare. The car is, nevertheless, a major killer.

One of the principal causes of premature death in the Western world is from car accidents. Thousands of people are killed on the roads every year in England. Thousands more are injured and maimed, which results not only in indescribable suffering, but also in a serious drain on the resources of the National Health Service, with precious space in hospital wards taken up, for months or years, by the car's victims. Not only human life is destroyed by the ubiquitous car. Towns and cities are ruthlessly knocked about to build fly-overs and bypasses which destroy the character of our urban areas; motor-ways destroy the peace and beauty of the countryside.

Clearly the car has come to dominate human life to an unhealthy extent. Can the monster be killed off, without too much pain? Car workers will say no. Unemployment would soar if the motor industry folded up. But is the saving of jobs a strong enough reason for the destruction of human life and the environment? Without cars, more people would take to the roads on bicycles, with a resultant improvement in health. Indeed, many people who currently drive would ride bicycles if it were safer to do so. With an efficient public transport system, the only real blessings of the car — speed and convenience — would be rendered insignificant, and the death of the car would make the world altogether safer and less stressful.

* * * *

This would gain a high grade as a general English language essay, despite the fact that, as you can see, it contains little "hard" factual information. One of its advantages, of course, is that it contains no errors of spelling, punctuation or grammar! Perfection in the essentials of written English is not expected, even for an *A* grade at 'A' level, but an examiner will not give an essay a top grade without a high level of formal accuracy. However, our concern in this chapter is with content and presentation of ideas. Let's analyse the content.

How many "hard" facts does the essay actually contain? The opening sentence presents precise historical detail, and the argument of paragraph 4 is backed up by references to problems in particular cities. Are even these facts absolutely necessary? The first adds elegance to the opening. It gets the essay off to a stylish start, but has no particular value as information. What about paragraph 4? If you knew generally about the problems of atmospheric and lead pollution, but could not give any specific details, would the argument be weakened? Such facts certainly add colour and an air of authority to the arguments, as does the reference to "carbon monoxide", but the points could be made without them. The essential requirement is to have thought about the issues themselves. Paragraph 5, in fact, conspicuously fails to provide any precise facts and figures. The vague "thousands" is not particularly convincing; exact figures would add potency to the argument. But the analysis is still valid, despite the vagueness in the details.

The one crucial feature of any successful discussion essay is a coherent argument, and for this, obviously enough, you must have a definite viewpoint. The key idea of this essay is developed in paragraph 3 — it does not have to be stated immediately. A careful build-up to the central argument is always more effective than a bald statement of attitude at the beginning, which tends in any case to pre-empt the argument. You will, what is more, be expected to show that you realise that there are two sides to any argument, and at least passing reference to the opposing point of view is essential.

Paragraph 2, the first main paragraph after the brief introduction, develops one of the major arguments *in favour* of private cars. It leads, in the last sentence, directly into the central argument about the re-organisation of public transport. Thereafter, the essay concentrates on arguments against the use of private cars. There is nothing wrong with such heavy weighting of your argument. In fact, one common weakness of discussion essays is a lack of direction, presenting first one side of the case, then the other, and leading nowhere. Showing that you understand the opposition's case does not mean that you have to be unbiased, unless the question specifically asks you to "discuss arguments for *and* against" something. Careful organisation of your ideas into paragraphs, however, is essential. Let's look in more detail at the planning of essays.

If you look at the random notes for the essay above, you will notice numbers before each point. The numbers are written in *after* the paragraph plan has been worked out, and refer to the paragraph into which each point will fit. This is simply a convenient way of picking out the ideas which are relevant to a particular paragraph, swiftly working out the order in which they are to be used, and checking that you have not missed any points. You may find the technique useful if you have not tried it before.

As stated earlier, the actual paragraph plan will probably not fit into place in your mind until after you have started making random notes. Similarly, the plan may well be modified when you actually begin writing your essay. There is no need at all to feel that you must follow your plan. It is, after all, for your benefit. If you look again at the essay you will notice that it does not even contain the same number of paragraphs as the plan indicates. What in fact occurred when the essay was being written was that the argument about the re-organisation of public transport assumed a greater importance after the essay had been started than had been envisaged at the planning stage, and instead of being incorporated into the discussion of the advantages of private motorised transport, it earned a paragraph for itself. If the original paragraph scheme had been followed, paragraph 2 would have been twice as long as the others, which is, in any case, structurally unsatisfactory. New ideas will always come to you when you start writing, and as long as they are directly relevant to the paragraph on which you are working, they can be accommodated perfectly easily. If they are not immediately relevant, they can be added to the random notes and incorporated where they do fit in.

If you do think of new ideas as you go along, however, you may come up against the eternal bugbear of examinations – time. Trying to develop every idea that occurs to you can result in your running out of time before you have managed to follow through your prepared structure properly. Therefore, it is essential to *pace* yourself. Good ideas may have to be discarded if time is getting short; other ideas, which you would like to develop, may have to be stated much more briefly than they might be. The final sentence of paragraph 5, for instance, glosses very briefly over two ideas which could have been embellished and made much more compelling with examples. However, this would have been at the expense of an adequate conclusion, which is much more important.

Not all the random notes are included in the essay. The point about individual isolation and stress caused by queues of cars with single occupants was left out. The ideas are just as valid as many that *are* included, and might have been illustrated interestingly by referring, for instance, to a Ray Bradbury science-fiction story about a time in the near future when pedestrians in the Western world are almost unknown and everybody uses cars. But it would have taken too long to explain the point of the story. When ideas are flowing freely, self-discipline is sometimes required! No illustration of a single idea should, in any case, take up too much space, and more crucially, you should *never* include ideas just because you have thought of them. Your essay must have direction, and every idea must be plainly relevant to the theme of the paragraph in which it appears.

So, although there is no need to adhere rigidly to your original plan, it should provide a clear overall structure for your essay, and a reasonably full set of random notes to refer back to will almost certainly make the writing of the essay much easier. As well as achieving coherence within paragraphs, you should also try to dovetail neatly from one paragraph to the next. If you look once more at the essay, you will notice that the first three paragraphs all end with a question. As long as it is not overused, this can be a reasonably simple and effective technique by which to achieve links between paragraphs. The final sentence of paragraph 4 also leads, by a statement this time, directly into the theme of paragraph 5. Thus the argument develops with an air of naturalness and inevitability. The conclusion, though quite short, is firmly stated; this too is essential. It must also, however, like the introduction, be interesting, which a bald statement of opinion, or a brief rehash of some of the earlier arguments would not. Before the final statement of opinion in this essay, reference is made to an argument against the abolition of private cars, which was not mentioned earlier. There is no reason why you should not include new material in your concluding paragraph, provided it does not obscure the conclusion itself.

Finally, a couple of general questions that often arise about discussion essay writing. Should you refer to yourself and your own experience in a formal discussion essay? Again, if you look back at the essay, you will notice that paragraph 2 draws entirely on personal experience to elaborate the point. As long as you do not fall into the classic logical flaw of arguing from the particular to the general, a personal anecdote can add interest and variety to an essay (though it must be added here that some teachers disapprove of the use of the personal pronoun in any but a personal essay). Lastly, will it jeopardise your chances if you adopt an unconventional viewpoint with which the examiner is likely to disagree? The answer to this question is again illustrated by the essay. Most people, examiners included, would probably disagree with its viewpoint. Perhaps even the writer was playing devil's advocate to some extent, for the sake of producing an interesting discussion! This would certainly not prevent the essay from gaining a high grade. The examiner is not looking for the "right" answer, but for clarity of expression, of ideas and of organisation, and these are the qualities which you must strive to develop as you progress through your course.

2
The Craft of Précis

Précis, in one form or another, features in many examinations. The exercise generally involves either the straightforward reduction of a passage to about a third of its length, or the summary of specified sections or ideas within a passage, in a given number of words. Whilst anyone, as long as they are able to comprehend the passage in question, can give the rough gist of it, successful examination précis work requires the application of a fairly clear-cut technique which can be mastered through study and practice. The purpose of this chapter is to explain the technique.

The first stage in any précis work is to achieve as full as possible an understanding of the passage to be summarised. This will probably mean reading it through two or three times before even picking up your pen. On your initial reading, the sense of much of the passage may well be obscured by the presence of difficult words. You should learn not to be thrown into a state of panic by this! It will be possible, after a couple more readings, to understand what the writer is saying, without necessarily knowing what is meant by every word he or she uses.

On the second reading you should be looking for the theme of the passage as a whole. Until you have worked this out, you cannot hope to begin your précis. Once you are sure of the theme, after your second or third reading, you should think of it constantly while you are working, one by one, at the separate thoughts contained in the passage.

The next stage — that of working out a first draft — can be tackled in various ways. The simplest is to read through the passage once more, this time underlining sentences and phrases which you feel to be important to the argument, and then begin writing a draft in continuous sentences, without making notes, and with the word limit in mind. Unless you are very lucky, of course, your first draft will require pruning or expanding before you write it out again as a final draft. Some people advocate deliberately keeping your first draft short, and building it up to the word limit in the second, whilst others favour the inclusion of everything of major or minor relevance in the first draft, and cutting down in the second. It is purely a matter of personal preference. A more time-consuming general approach is to make full notes of the points to be included, before writing them out in sentences. You will discover soon enough whether you can manage to complete a set of notes and two drafts within the time limit, and which general technique suits you better. The second draft should be your perfected answer, as nearly as possible in the number of words stipulated.

One further general point needs to be made before analysing specific précis techniques. It is absolutely essential to tackle the passage in terms of *ideas* rather than sentences. If you attempt to summarise the passage sentence by sentence you are certain to end up with an incoherent and inaccurate answer. You must try to work out each idea, and its relevance, in terms of the overall line of argument of the passage, and only on that basis will you succeed.

Now to the rather more complicated question of how, and what, to summarise. The easiest way to illustrate the "do's and don'ts" of précis writing is to study a finished answer, and to analyse it in terms of technique. Here is a passage for summary. It contains 379 words, and has to be reduced to 125. The theme is the validity of précis!

The art of writing a concise, well-balanced, comprehensive and accurate précis demands clarity both of thought and of written expression. It is not a question of reflecting on a writer's ideas in the light of one's own, nor of interpreting those ideas; it is, instead, a question of reproducing the ideas
5 with precision, and in summary form. It is an exercise in condensation. There can be little doubt, however, that many students, on undertaking a précis exercise, will wonder why they are expected to fritter away their time on a task which seems to them frustratingly tedious and futile; they will ask themselves, with a sigh, "What is the point of slavishly re-writing what
10 someone else has already said, when I could be producing something new and original of my own?" It must seem to many like sitting in front of a portrait by Rembrandt or Van Gogh, and being asked to copy it in outline form, without colour, light and shade, or atmosphere, when their artistic instinct cries out to be allowed to draw on the master's work as the inspiration for an
15 original creation. They are apt to consider the whole business stultifying, the very antithesis of creativity. And in one sense their criticism is valid: by précising a writer's work one is taking away much of its essence, draining it of its colour, its tone, its subtlety, its imaginative vitality. It is rather like describing a "cordon bleu" meal by mentioning only the ingredients.
20 Yet in another sense the criticism is profoundly unfair. There are many aspects of the study of English language in addition to creative writing. And précis is by no means irrelevant to the demands of "real life". In business, in fact in all walks of professional life, it is frequently necessary to summarise factual information and the arguments presented by others; indeed, we are
25 constantly engaged in verbal summary of television programmes, film plots, conversations and comical incidents in the normal course of our daily lives. The conciseness and precision of expression which comes with précis practice is thus of no small value both as a necessary attribute of articulate men and women in its own right, and as a skill which is of practical value in work and
30 in life.

Here is a specimen summary of the passage:

Effective précis requires clear thinking and writing, involving accurate summary of another's ideas. Almost certainly, however, many students find the exercise monotonous, and question the value of mere reproduction

rather than originality, comparing it to the sterile task of copying an old
5 master's painting in outline. The criticism is partially valid, since a précis
destroys much of the flavour and artistry of the original. In another way,
however, it is unjust. English language involves more than merely creative
writing, and précis has relevance to life. In all professions précis is often a
necessary requirement, and in normal life we constantly summarise things
10 seen and heard. Précis practice develops brevity and clarity of expression,
and is therefore extremely useful in enhancing conversational and professional skills.

124 words

Let us now analyse the passage and specimen answer in terms of précis
technique.

A couple of readings of the passage will reveal the theme to be the
drawbacks and virtues of précis. Having established that, we can begin
working through the passage, selecting ideas which have a direct bearing
on the development of the argument, and discarding those which are
unimportant.

The first main point is contained in the first three sentences, which
establish a definition of précis and what it involves. The opening sentence
contains a list of the features of effective précis and a further list of what
it demands, and is thus clearly relevant. This raises our first problem –
what to do with lists. There are three possibilities: to copy them out in
full; to select some items from the list and ignore the others; or to find a
generalised phrase which covers the essential features which the items in
the list have in common. The first solution is unsatisfactory in two ways:
it will use up too many words, and it is not summary at all, but copying,
and if you copy whole phrases from the passage you will lose marks. The
second solution is also unsatisfactory: selection from a list, even with the
addition of "etc" (which should always be avoided) is not summary
either, since it includes only *part* of what is being said. So we are left with
the third solution. One of the most difficult, but essential, features of
précis is, in fact, just this: finding accurate generalisations to cover all the
items in a list. The word used in the sample answer to cover the first list
– "effective" – is perhaps a little imprecise, but "effective précis" is
essentially what the writer is talking about. The second list in the opening
sentence ("of thought and of written expression") necessitates a phrase
which covers both ideas, since a single generalisation like
"communication" would be imprecise. We have therefore already broken
our first rule, since we have not really generalised the list! This should
sound a note of caution. Rules of précis should not be applied
automatically; judgement and common sense must come into play as well.

The first part of the second sentence in the passage, up to the semi-
colon, is a negative statement, telling us what précis is *not*; it is then
followed by a statement of what précis actually is. Only the second part
of the sentence need be included in our answer. As a general rule, you
should always make positive rather than negative statements, and the
latter can normally be left out. The brief third sentence (line 5) is merely a

restatement of the point just made, and can be ignored. You should never repeat ideas. Note that these opening three sentences in the passage have been summarised in a single sentence in the specimen answer, the ideas being linked together with a present participle ("involving"). This is good précis technique, giving continuity and fluency to your writing, and avoiding sequences of short sentences. You will be marked partly for the style and coherence of your answer, so this is important.

The long fourth sentence introduces a new main idea − students' response to précis − and is thus essential to the argument. The key phrase in the first half of the sentence (up to the semi-colon) is "tedious and futile", and this must be brought out. The first word ("tedious") is covered in the sample answer by the word "monotonous", and the idea of précis being "futile" is used to create a link with the ideas contained in the second half of the sentence. This linking technique again adds to the sense of continuity and fluency. Notice that in the sample answer the phrases "almost certainly" and "many students" are used. In the interests of brevity, the words "almost certainly" and "many" could have been left out. But this would have created the impression that *all* students *definitely* dislike précis, which would have distorted the meaning of the passage. You should try to explain what the passage is saying *exactly*. Note also that the phrase "many students" is lifted directly from the passage, in contradiction to what was said earlier about copying phrases. Again, common sense is needed in interpreting the "rules". It is clearly impossible to find a more concise phrase than "many students", and alternatives, such as "a large number of students", or "a significant proportion of those involved in learning situations" actually use *more* words than the original, which is the opposite of précis! The copying of words and even short phrases will not be penalised if there is no obvious alternative which does not either distort the meaning of, or involve the use of more words than, the original.

The second half of the fourth sentence (lines 8−11) includes an imaginary question. In the specimen answer (lines 2−5) this is turned into a statement. Since the object of a précis is to summarise ideas, you should never pose questions, but always turn them, if they contain relevant ideas, into statements. The final phrase of the question ("something new and original of my own") is otiose; the words "new" and "of my own" are redundant. You should always be careful to avoid using unnecessary words.

The fifth sentence (lines 11−15) raises what is probably the most problematic aspect of précis technique. It develops a comparison, designed to illuminate the point just made, and, in general, comparisons, illustrations and examples should be left out in a précis. Yet once again the rule is not absolute, and you will see from the sample answer (lines 4−5) that the comparison has been included. This is because the idea of copying a painting in outline, without colour, etc. leads on directly to the idea which follows (lines 16−19) of destroying the colour, etc. of a piece of writing by précising it. It is for you to decide whether an illustration or example actually forms a link in the argument, or whether it is there *simply* to reinforce a point already made. Lengthy examples will generally not warrant inclusion. You will notice that the final sentence of the first paragraph is another comparison, and it *is* left out in the sample answer, since it falls into the category of mere reinforcement. Note the way that the list in line 18 has been summarised. In this case two distinct generalisations have been used ("flavour and artistry") since "colour" and "tone" are different in kind from "subtlety" and "imaginative vitality", and thus a single generalised word or phrase would not accurately convey all four listed aspects of the writer's art.

The first sentence of the second paragraph introduces an alternative viewpoint about précis. The key phrase here is "profoundly unfair". This has been summarised by the word "unjust" (line 7) which fails to indicate the *degree* of unfairness, but it gets across the essential point, and is probably adequate. A phrase like "deeply unjust" would have been more precise, but some degree of precision has to be sacrificed if too many words have been used in the first draft. The second and third sentences (lines 20–22) are essential and they are already so concise, and contain terminology so specific, that they cannot be much reduced in overall length. The next sentence (lines 22–26) contains three lists, all of which are dealt with by varieties of generalisation in the sample answer; the third one, after the semi-colon, again requires two separate generalisations ("things seen and heard"). Note that the word "things" is normally frowned on as poor style, but it results in a simple and effective generalisation here, and is probably acceptable. The final sentence makes the concluding point, and can be summarised quite straightforwardly.

A further point will have emerged from this analysis – that the ideas should generally be summarised in the order in which they appear in the passage. Once more, however, this is not a cast-iron rule, and slight variations in the order in which closely related ideas are recorded can actually increase the impression of a tightly constructed argument. As well as summarising a series of points which go to make up an argument, you are, when writing a précis, constructing an argument of your own, and the various points must be connected in a logical manner.

Summary of précis techniques

1. Use your own words as far as possible.

2. Keep, as far as possible, to the arrangement of ideas of the original passage.

3. Include only the points made in the passage; do not introduce any ideas of your own.

4. Leave out negative statements, or make them positive.

5. Do not write questions, but turn them into statements if they are relevant.

6. Do not include spoken words or quotations, but report the idea contained in them if it is relevant.

7. Do not include repetitions of ideas or phrases, and be as concise as possible in your wording.

8. Leave out examples, comparisons and details if they merely illustrate a point which is being made and do not contribute anything new to the main argument of the passage.

9. Try to find generalisations for the ideas contained in lists of words and phrases.

10. Use linking words and constructions, such as "nevertheless", "consequently", "despite", "although", "however", "therefore", "thus", "since", and present participles ("-ing" verbs) to provide balance and continuity.

Additional points

There are a few more details which are worth mentioning:

1. You will almost certainly be asked to count the number of words you have used, and record the total. Don't forget to do this, and try to be accurate. If your passage looks as if it might be longer than you have indicated, the examiner will certainly count the words himself. You can probably afford to be up to ten words over the allowed maximum without losing more than a couple of marks, but if you are only two or three words over, it should be easy enough to save a mark by simple techniques like combining sentences with the use of a present participle. If you are many words *under* the limit, on the other hand, the chances are that you have missed some relevant points, and you should expand your précis.

2. If you are asked to supply a title for the passage, try to keep it short (no more than ten words at most) and try to think of a phrase which represents an encapsulation of the theme of the passage as a whole. You are *not* expected to include the title in your final word count.

3. There is no point in wasting words by using reported speech, with phrases like "the writer said/says that . . .". Simply summarise what is said without any kind of introduction.

4. It is generally considered appropriate for the précis to be written as a single paragraph, but if you split it into separate paragraphs at suitable points it is extremely unlikely to be held against you. It is probably best not to follow the paragraphing of the original passage in your précis, since this is likely to result in some extremely short paragraphs.

5. It is best not to use abbreviations of any sort, since a précis is a piece of formal prose, and abbreviations are a rather unfair short-cut to word saving.

6. When your précis is complete, you should check carefully for spelling and punctuation errors, since marks will be allocated for technical accuracy.

Passages for Précis

1. Write a summary of the following passage in not more than 115 words. The passage contains 342 words.

Most of us will agree that previous training is desirable before we approach the arts. We mistrust untrained appreciation, believing that it often defeats its own ends. Appreciation ought to be enough. But unless we learn by example and by failure and by comparison, appreciation will not bite. We shall tend to slip about on the surface of masterpieces, exclaiming with joy, but never penetrating. "Oh, I do like Bach," cries one appreciator, and the other cries, "Do you? I don't. I like Chopin." Exit in opposite directions chanting Bach and Chopin respectively, and hearing less the composers than their own voices. They resemble investors who proclaim the soundness of their financial assets. The Bach shares must not fall, the Chopin not fall farther or one would have been proved a fool on the aesthetic stock exchange. The objection to untrained appreciation is not its naïveté but its tendency to lead to the appreciation of no one but oneself. Against such fatuity the critical spirit is a valuable corrective.

It is desirable to know why we like a work, and to be able to defend our preferences by argument. Our judgement has been strengthened and if all goes well the contacts will be intensified and increased and become more valuable.

I add the proviso "if all goes well" because success lies on the knees of an unknown God. There is always the contrary danger; the danger that training may sterilise the sensitiveness that is being trained; that education may lead to knowledge instead of wisdom, and criticism to nothing but criticism; that spontaneous enjoyment, like the Progress of Poesy in Matthew Arnold's poem, may be checked because too much care has been taken to direct it into the right channel. Still it is a risk to be faced, and if no care had been taken the stream might have vanished even sooner. We hope criticism will help. We have faith in it as a respectable human activity, as an item in the larger heritage which differentiates us from the beasts.

E M FORSTER

Now study the following specimen answer in the light of the rules of précis already analysed. Notice in particular how the ideas are linked together.

Most people recognise the usefulness of critical training in the arts, feeling that, although appreciation should be sufficient, it will remain superficial unless backed up by analytical study, and that untrained appreciation tends to lead to mere self-assertion, rather than real involvement in the arts. The capacity to explain our preferences in the arts to ourselves and others is valuable, since generally it deepens our awareness of art.

Critical training may, however, lead to desensitisation, so that while we learn to understand and evaluate artistic works, our natural pleasure in them is dulled through an over-concentration on correct interpretation. But this is a necessary risk, and critical evaluation is one means of developing our humanity.

115 words

2. Write a summary of the following passage in not more than 165 words, (the passage contains 533 words). Give it a brief title, and indicate the number of words at the end. You are advised to spend about 50 minutes on this exercise.

What is the normal child like? Does he just eat and grow and smile sweetly? No, that is not what he is like. A normal child, if he has confidence in father and mother, pulls out all the stops. In the course of time he tries out his power to disrupt, to destroy, to frighten, to wear down, to waste, to wangle, to appropriate. Everything that takes people to the courts (or to the asylums, for that matter) has its normal equivalent in infancy and early childhood, in the relation of the child to his own home. If the home can stand up to all the child can do to disrupt it, he settles down to play, but business first, the tests must be made, and especially so if there is some doubt as to the stability of the parental set-up and the home (by which I mean so much more than house). At first the child needs to be conscious of a framework if he is to feel free, and if he is to be able to play, to draw his own pictures, to be an irresponsible child.

Why should this be? The fact is that the early stages of emotional development are full of potential conflict and disruption. The relation to external reality is not yet firmly rooted; the personality is not yet well integrated; primitive love has a destructive aim, and the small child has not yet learned to tolerate and cope with instincts. He can come to manage these things, and more, if his surroundings are stable and personal. At the start he absolutely needs to live in a circle of love and strength (with consequent tolerance) if he is not to be too fearful of his own thoughts and of his imaginings to make progress in his emotional development.

Now what happens if the home fails a child before he has got the idea of a framework as part of his own nature? The popular idea is that, finding himself "free" he proceeds to enjoy himself. This is far from the truth. Finding the framework of his life broken, he no longer feels free. He becomes anxious, and if he has hope he proceeds to look for a framework elsewhere than at home. The child whose home fails to give a feeling of security looks outside his home for the four walls; he still has hope, and he looks to grandparents, uncles and aunts, friends of the family, school. He seeks an external stability without which he may go mad. Provided at the proper time, this stability might have grown into the child like the bones in his body, so that gradually in the course of the first months and years of his life he would have passed on to independence from dependence and a need to be managed. Often a child gets from relations and school what he missed in his actual home.

The antisocial child is merely looking a little further afield, looking to society instead of to his own family or school to provide the stability he needs if he is to pass through the early and quite essential stages of his emotional growth.

D W WINNICOTT

Controlled conditions   30·XI·89

3. Write a summary of the following passage in not more than 200 words (the passage contains about 600 words). Your summary should be in clear, connected English and the number of words used should be indicated at the end. You are advised to spend about one hour on this exercise.

Propaganda is to many a suspect word and a suspect activity. It smacks of trying to make people do things against their will, of under-hand methods, of sharp practice, of deceit, of trickery.

No doubt propaganda has been and is guilty of all these charges. After all, a form of activity which seeks to influence people's minds and attitudes and, if possible, action is bound at times to lead its practitioners astray. Whether their work gains in effectiveness as a result, is another question. For when truth itself becomes a commodity which is in short supply or non-existent, it can become a more powerful method of propaganda than any other. In times of confusion many people would rather know what is happening than be fobbed off with cleverly contrived explanations or interpretations.

Propaganda and psychological warfare are as old as the history of mankind itself. The weak have always sought to make themselves out stronger than they were. Sometimes they were successful and sometimes they were not. The Byzantine Empire, in its efforts to prolong its existence, resorted to such devices as having the emperor on his throne raised as if by divine intervention and lowered again while the stuffed lions which served as the arm-rests of his throne belched forth fire and smoke and uttered terrifying roars as the ambassadors from foreign lands lay prostrate before him. It also, from time to time, organised for the diplomatic corps, military parades in which the Imperial Guard — as soon as it had disappeared from sight of the reviewing stand — hastily changed uniforms and re-appeared again, seeking to give the illusion of being but a fraction of an army numbering hundreds of thousands.

Since all foreign diplomats, indeed all foreigners, were kept under strict surveillance in ancient Byzantium such ruses may have been effective for a time. They could not prevent the ultimate collapse and disappearance of the Byzantine Empire.

Armour and uniforms have always been designed to give pride, courage and confidence to the wearer and to strike terror in the heart of the enemy. When primitive warriors put on warpaint, it was not only to protect themselves by magic symbols but to intimidate the enemy by showing him plainly that they meant business — death and destruction.

One of the most effective devices of dual-purpose propaganda was the use of drums by Red Indian tribes before attacking a white settlement or wagon train. The drums aroused the fighting spirit of the Red Indian warriors while their sound gnawed away at the nerves of the white settlers who knew not when the drums would stop, but knew that once they did, the attack was due to begin soon.

The Christian churches, indeed all proselytising religions, have never regarded propaganda with disfavour. On the contrary, they have always felt it an obligation to propagate their faith with all the power at their command. The great political ideologies take a similar view.

In any case, whether or not we look upon some manifestations of propaganda with distaste, propaganda has become an essential element in the relations between and within states. Wars are no longer the business of professional armies nor politics the exclusive preserve of relatively small oligarchies. This century has seen two world wars. They have in every sense been "total", drawing in and absorbing the energies of every section of the warring nations. Their attitudes, their moods, played a vital part in the way in which they acted and conducted themselves. And in shaping those attitudes, those moods, their own propaganda and that of their enemies exerted a key influence.

CHARLES ROETTER

4. Write a summary of the following passage in not more than 200 words (the passage contains about 560 words). Your summary should be in clear, connected English and the number of words used should be indicated at the end. You are advised to spend about one hour on this exercise.

Since the beginning of recorded time the dream has occupied a prominent position in every culture and has exercised a profound effect, not only on the individual but also over religions and history. Defined as divine messenger, prophet, muse, problem-solver, route to the group unconscious, guardian of sleep, fulfiller of wishes, or signpost to psychological and physical ills, the dream has apparently opened a door into the unknown that could be of service to humanity. Its sister, the nightmare, enjoys equal significance for quite other reasons. Her unsolicited visits are so miserable that human beings have always wondered what purpose could be served by this grim invader of sleep.

The nightmare respects neither age nor youth: a sixteenth-century writer on paediatrics gave it ninth place in a list of fifty-two childhood maladies. Anyone who has tried to comfort a small child in the toils of a bad dream will agree that this is one of the nightmare's most pitiless and cowardly onslaughts.

The nightmare recognises no boundary of time or culture. It hounds both the sophisticated and the primitive. It scourges the healthy and the sick, the sane and the mentally deranged. It links the past with the future, for it comes unbidden to mock the outward self-assurance of the twentieth-century urban dweller (holding fast to the panacea of technology) just as it visited his prehistoric forebears when all that was inexplicable was to be feared and darkness contained a multitude of terrors. No doubt it will continue to stalk our descendants even if they build themselves plastic castles on other planets for, like the dream, the nightmare is a universal and involuntary human experience.

Although frequently claimed to encompass the fears and dilemmas of a person's earliest years, the nightmare may also enshrine those terrors and problems of humankind's childhood that lie at the heart of so many myths. Certain images, therefore, do not arise from the individual's conditioning but spring out of the vast cosmic sea of the shared unconscious.

The paperback dream manuals, available at any bookstand, are the mass-produced descendants of Babylonian and Assyrian clay tablets, describing dreams and nightmares and giving interpretations, that date back to 5000 BC. What we know of ancient terrors has been garnered from these earliest writings on religion, magic and medicine; but we can be certain that, because of basic human physiology, similar nightmares were experienced long before any form of writing had been evolved to record them.

In those last isolated outposts where communities are totally ignorant of Western society, anthropologists have noted dreams and nightmares that are fundamentally the same. The real difference, however, is one of attitude. We may smile at the idea of South American Indians panicking and almost deserting a village because one of their number saw enemies stealthily approaching in a nightmare, but that is because we no longer allow the phenomena within a dream the same validity as actual events in the external world. For the child, the primitive and the superstitious, the drama in a dream is happening, or soon will, and therefore any warning or prophecy contained in it must be observed. After aeroplane and train crashes there are always those who claim to have seen it happen in a nightmare. Some have changed their plans and lived. Others have ignored their dreams and perished.

SANDRA SHULMAN

3

The World in Crisis: Population Explosion and Poverty

More than half the people in the world are living in serious poverty, under-nourished, or at best malnourished, and hence prevented from having any hope of achieving their full potential. One in every three is living in absolute, abject poverty[1]: underfed and, as a consequence, lacking in vitality and highly prone to disease, ill-housed, most probably underemployed and illiterate. Many millions of people in Latin America, Asia and Africa are destitute: every day, on average, fifteen thousand people in the world starve to death.

The purpose of this chapter is to explore the crisis of world hunger, and perhaps provoke some discussion of tentative solutions. The passage for comprehension is a "utopian" solution to the world crisis in general. Then follows a glimpse of individual lives of some of the world's poor. The remainder of the chapter presents the two main schools of thought on the crisis of world hunger: first, that the root of the problem is the "population explosion", and secondly, that it lies in the unequal distribution of the world's food and resources. Each of these views will be explored largely through selections from works by two influential writers.[2]

Comprehension

Read the following passage and answer the questions below it. You are advised to spend about one hour on this comprehension.

Instead of progress there is crisis everywhere. There is no government, not even the American, which has now the manifest fixity of the "Great Powers" of the 1880s. There is a growing scepticism whether any existing government is as necessary as it ought to be. All contemporary governments
5 have been outgrown − physically and mentally − by the needs of mankind. The abolition of distance, foretold 50 years ago, is achieved. That has made all the governments in the world misfits. Seventy-odd sovereign govern-ments, all acting independently and competitively, all jammed together by

1. According to the International Labour Office, quoted in Paul Harrison, *Inside the Third World*, pp. 405−6.
2. It is perhaps worth mentioning that this chapter is closely related to the one which follows, on the environmental crisis. The two chapters can be taken together, and treated at length, over two or three sessions, as a single topic: "The World in Crisis". Some of the essay questions and the debate suggestion at the end of Chapter 4 invite this treatment.

that abolition of distance, are trying to carry on the affairs of our race, which now, under the new conditions, would be far more conveniently and successfully dealt with as one world business. Human life has become a world-wide thing, but governments remain cramped and partial things.

More and more people are coming to realise this. Yet none of us knows clearly how to change over to a more comprehensive and securer way of
15 running the world.

While we puzzle over the riddle, armaments go on, and the old — and now utterly stupid — tradition of malevolence between sovereign governments and their "peoples" is maintained. International politics still consist largely of idiotic attempts on the part of these seventy-odd governments, amid which our affairs are entangled, to get the better of their rivals, to maintain a flaming prosperity within their borders while restricting and injuring the welfare of all other peoples.

The old game goes on because the world lacks the mental energy to call it off. So we are all drifting through needless and wasteful economic war
25 towards actual military war. Some years ago I wrote that the salvaging of civilisation was a race between education and catastrophe. Nowadays I am forced to add a qualification. Catastrophe indeed travels briskly; tariffs strangle trade; gold — the life blood of trade — is being hoarded against some fresh day of reckoning; armaments increase; the friction between states intensifies. The new air war is being prepared. The new gas war is being prepared. But education has not even started yet. There is no race. It looks like a walk-over for catastrophe.

In the schools of Britain, America, France, Germany, Italy, Japan today the school-teachers are still doing the fundamental work of mental
35 armament. There are few exceptions. And the hundreds of millions of "modern democracy" show as much ability to protect their minds from sub-jugation and arrest the advancing disaster, which will enslave, torture, mutilate, and destroy the greater proportion of them, as a trainload of hogs bound for Chicago.

Gladly would the prophet prophesy pleasant things. But his duty is to tell what he sees. He sees a world still firmly controlled by soldiers, patriots, usurers, and financial adventurers; a world surrendered to suspicion and hatred, losing what is left of its private liberties very rapidly, blundering toward bitter class conflicts, and preparing for new wars.
45 The economic machine is stalling in every country in the world. The decline is going on under our eyes. Production is diminishing, trade is declining; presently we shall find even our present educational and hygiene services too costly for our existing methods of payment. Few people realise yet how flimsy are the liberties and securities, the plenty and the leisure, we still enjoy.

The prophet must say what he sees. It is as if I was watching a dark curtain fall steadily, fold after fold, across the bright spectacle of hope with which the century dawned. The way toward a great world state of power, freedom, and general happiness is still plainly open to mankind. We have been
55 brought to the very borders of the Promised Land of Progress. And the amount of visible human determination to cross those borders and escape

from the age-long sequences of quarrelling, futile insufficiency, wars, and wasted generations that fill the bloodstained pages of history, is contemptible.

There is no inevitability in the approaching catastrophe. I confess I see no signs whatever of any such awakening as might save us, but who can tell what may be happening among the young, among the intelligent and wilful, outside one's range. It would need nothing superhuman to avert the decline. We are not being beaten in an honourable struggle; we are loitering and
65 rotting down to disaster. A few thousand resolute spirits, the tithe of a tithe of the misdirected heroism that went to waste in the Great War, a few hundred million dollars for a world campaign for the new order, might still turn the destinies of mankind right round toward a new life for our race.

It needs only that the governments of the United States, Britain, France, Germany, and Russia should get together in order to set up an effective control of currency, credit, production, and distribution; that is to say, an effective "dictatorship of prosperity" for the whole world.

The other sixty-odd states would have to join in or accommodate themselves to the overruling decisions of these major powers. It is as simple a
75 business as that, which our presidents, potentates, statesmen, kings of finance, and so forth, do not even realise they could carry through with human decay and disaster plain before them!

They just fumble along. The bands play and we "troop the colours". The party men twaddle about debts and security. They cant patriotism. They love their countries so that they would rather see them starve than let them co-operate with nasty foreigners. They do their best to reassure the world — and do, it seems, succeed in reassuring the world — that this skimped, anxious, dangerous life we lead is the best that can be done for us. These rulers and leaders and statesmen of ours get in front of the cameras at every possible
85 opportunity to put their fatuous selves on record, while Death, the Ultimate Creditor, and Collapse, the Final Stabiliser, add up their inexorable accounts.

But given that wave of sanity, that sudden miraculous resolve to stop this foolery, and what sort of world might we not have before another half century has passed?

Everyone alive might be by then a citizen of the whole world. All of us would then be free to go where we would about this fascinating and some-times so lovely planet, which would have become our own. For most of our lives we should be released from toil. All the necessities of the human
95 population — food, abundant transport, clean, fresh, and beautiful housing and furniture, adequate health services, education, social security — could be supplied now under modern conditions by something between twelve and twenty years of not too arduous work on the part of everyone. The town, the countryside would be undergoing constant revision and improvement: the world city would be constantly more gracious and pleasant; the world garden constantly more beautiful. The layout of industry could be as exciting as a game.

These are not the assertions of an "imaginative writer"; they are possibilities proved up to the hilt by economists and by the scientific examination of

105 these matters. Some fifteen or twenty years of growth, education, and
preparation there would have to be for everyone, and the rest of life would
be free for creative work, for graceful living, for movement and experience.

There is no need why any human being now should be underclad or ill-
clad, badly housed or sickly. The whole world could be run as one concern
and yield a universal well-being.

And it is no good mincing matters when it comes to saying why we have
not this universal well-being at the present time. Most of our rulers and
directors are, to put it plainly, narrow-minded, self-centred, mentally
indolent, pompous, and pretentious creatures of the past; and we others are
115 fools enough to tolerate their mismanagement. These ruling and controlling
people have got enough for themselves, they stick to the controls like
barnacles, they live in relative comfort and immense dignity, chiefly engaged
in the defence of their own conceit, and the mass of us lacks the spirit, will,
and understanding to call them to account.

A thousand million human beings are leading lives of want, limitation,
humiliation, and toil, scores of millions are in immediate danger of the futile
tortures of war, and these dull, self-protective folk in control of things do
nothing of what they might do and pose for our respect and admiration with
infinite self-complacency.

125 But in another fifty years after that renascence – if, after all, it should
occur – things will be different. For an ignorant world we shall have a
soundly educated world, aware of its origins, capable of measuring and
realising its possibilities, and controlling its destinies.

Every human being born into that world of plenty will learn from the
beginning of the varied loveliness of the life before it, and of the expanding
drama of human achievement in which it has to play its part. Its distinctive
gifts will be developed. It will be taught another history than that of kings
and conquerors and armies. It will do its fair and definite share in the
productive or other necessary service of mankind, and for the rest it will be
135 released to accomplish whatever possibilities it has of innovation, happiness,
and interesting living.

That wide fine life is within reach of mankind; it is there for the taking.
But mankind is not taking it. The curtain is falling. When the Promised Land
is cut off forever, "Homo sapiens" will be readily convinced there never was
a Promised Land. The last thing we human beings will produce is concerted
effort; only under the spur of greed or panic do we produce that. We shake
our heads sagely at the "dreamers". As long as possible we will go on living
the close, ignoble lives of thieves, bullies, and drudges to which we are
accustomed. We will snuffle our satisfaction that we are not in any
145 "fantastic Utopia". *Perfect social + political system*

And when presently the rifles are put into our hands again, we shall kill.
The whips will be behind us and the "enemy" in front. The Old History will
go on because we had not the vigor to accept the new.

H G WELLS (1931)

Note: Your answers should be *in your own words* as far as possible.

(a) Explain what the writer means when he says "the abolition of distance . . . has made all the governments in the world misfits" (lines 5–7). (6 *marks*)

(b) Explain the phrase "tradition of malevolence" (line 17) as used in the passage. (2 *marks*)

(c) What does the writer mean by saying that "the salvaging of civilisation was a race between education and catastrophe" (lines 25–26), and why does he feel that "it looks like a walk-over for catastrophe" (line 32)? (6 *marks*)

(d) Explain briefly the meaning of *two* of the following phrases, as used in the passage:
   (i)   tariffs strangle trade   (line 28);
   (ii) financial adventurers   (line 42);
   (iii) the Ultimate Creditor   (line 86). (4 *marks*)

(e) What, according to the writer, would be needed to reverse the drift towards catastrophe? (6 *marks*)

(f) Explain briefly, in your own words, the writer's final vision of how life might be in fifty years' time. (6 *marks*)

(g) According to the writer, what normally spurs mankind to "concerted effort"? (2 *marks*)

(h) Write a brief comment (about 8 lines) on any one idea in the passage with which you strongly agree or disagree. (8 *marks*)

(*Total:* 40 *marks*)

Themes for Discussion

Some of the issues raised by H G Wells in this passage are perhaps of sufficient importance to warrant fuller discussion and analysis. Three of these issues are selected here. The first is of particular relevance to the world of the 1980s, the second has been relevant since the dawn of mankind, and the third is of at least academic relevance to you, as a student.

1. The world economy

Is Wells' idea of a world government, or a "dictatorship of prosperity", possible, or desirable? What factors continue to prevent it from happening?

Which countries are currently most in debt to the west? What are they, and the creditor nations, doing about it?

What is the IMF, and what does it do to help bring about world prosperity?

2. *War*

Wells talks about the "now utterly stupid tradition of malevolence" between nations. Is war always "utterly stupid", or are some wars essential?

Are there any circumstances in which it is right to be a conscientious objector?

What international wars are being fought at the moment? What civil wars are being fought in which other nations have significant military or economic involvement?

For what reasons were wars generally fought in the past? Are the motives of warring nations today fundamentally different, on the whole?

3. *Worldwide education*

In what sense can it be argued that only "education" can save the world from "catastrophe", as Wells says?

How many people in the world are still illiterate? How might their lives be improved if they became literate? Is literacy always desirable?

Does it make any real difference to you if you read essays and works of fiction by creative writers such as H G Wells, or is literature simply "art for art's sake"?

Preparing for discussion

Discussion, if it is to be more than a matter of "sounding off" ideas, or "letting off steam", needs to be informed. A fully effective discussion of some of the issues raised above will probably require at least some of the students in the class to do more than merely read the H G Wells passage. Here are some suggestions for preparing for such a discussion:

1. Read through the discussion questions and think about them before the class.

2. Look out for and collect items from newspapers and magazines on the discussion topics.

3. Be prepared to introduce this material into the class discussion.

4. In the case of very specific questions, such as the role of the IMF, and the situation of debtor and creditor nations, interested students, with advance warning of the discussion, should be prepared to undertake private research, and to report their findings to the class when the discussion takes place. It should be possible to find passages from books, magazines and newspapers, or to jot down details from television and radio programmes, which are relevant to the issue which they are researching. Students who specialise in, or have studied other disciplines than English — economics, history and sociology in the case of the three themes suggested above — should be in a particularly

strong position to provide factual information to help with the discussions.

Creative essay

Write an essay of about 450 words on one of the following titles:

(a) What do you imagine the world will be like 50 years from now?

(b) Write the essay on "the condition of humanity" which H G Wells might have written if he had been alive today.

Life in the Third World

For millions of Third World families, even when the husband has a regular income, life can be a perpetual struggle to preserve a degree of dignity and the semblance of a decent, happy life. In the following extract, Domitila Barrios de Chungara, the wife of a tin miner in Bolivia, describes her family's circumstances:

Our houses are very small, that is, we have a little room measuring four by five or six metres. That little room has to be living room, dining room, pantry, and bedroom. In some houses there are two little rooms, and one of them is the kitchen; they also have a little corridor. This is what the company housing is like, only the four walls, without any water or sanitary installations. And that's how we have to live, with our children, all crowded together. In my case, we set up three beds in the room; that's all that will fit. That's where my seven children sleep, that's where they do their homework, that's where we eat, that's where the kids play. In the little back room I have a table and a bed where I sleep with my husband. The few things we have just have to be piled one on top of the other, or hung from the ceiling, in the corridor. And the babies, well, some of them have to sleep in the beds and some of them under the beds. Wherever . . . .

For some hours during the day and all through the night we have electric light in the camp which the company gives us.

We also have drinking water. But not in the houses. In the neighbourhoods there are public water pumps. You have to line up to get water.

So you see, we don't have too many comforts. For example, we don't have a bath in the house. Of course, there are public baths, but there are ten to twelve showers for everyone, for so many people, and these showers are for the whole camp. So the showers are open on alternate days; one day for the women and one day for the men. The showers only work when there's oil. Because the water is heated by oil.

Not only that, but there are only sanitary facilities, latrines, in the houses of the company's technical personnel. There aren't any in the workers' houses. There are public latrines but only about ten of them, for a whole neighbourhood. For a whole neighbourhood! They get dirty very fast and there's no running water. In the mornings the company workers assigned to the job clean them; but afterward, all day long they're very dirty. And if there's no water, they're dirty for several days. Even so, we have to use them. Just like they are.

There are plenty of problems with water, especially in the non-company villages. They suffer there more than we do. They have to stand in long lines. They have to come from very far away to get their water. And in these villages they don't have electric light like us. Their life is really hard.

BARRIOS DE CHUNGARA

For the landless peasant's family the struggle is often a hopeless one. Here the English journalist and writer Paul Harrison illustrates the cycles of despair through which such people travel. The passage describes a family he met in Brazil:

Francisco's mother Fatima is small for her age. She is visibly weak, distant, yet easily irritated by the children. Years of pregnancy and menstruation, along with an iron-poor diet of maize, have made her chronically anaemic. Her husband Jaime is a landless labourer, with a low, erratic income barely enough to keep them all alive and clothed. No one eats enough, and when there's not enough to go round Fatima goes without, even when she's pregnant. And that is frequently, as the couple use no form of contraception. They have had ten children, six of whom survived to adulthood.

Fatima went through several periods of undernourishment while Francisco was in her womb. There were times when Jaime could not get regular work and everyone went hungry. Fatima also had several attacks of stress and anxiety when Jaime beat her. Francisco probably suffered his first bout of growth retardation, both mental and physical, before he even saw the light of day.

He was born underweight, and his brain was already smaller than normal size. For the first few months he was breast-fed and suffered few infections, as he was partly protected by the antibodies in his mother's milk. Then he was weaned onto thin gruels and soups, taken off the breast and put onto tinned evaporated milk, thinned down with polluted water from the well. His diet, in itself, was inadequate. Then he started to get more and more infections, fever, bronchitis, measles and regular bouts of gastro-enteritis. With well-fed children these pass within a few days, but in his case they went on for weeks and sometimes a month or more. In these periods he could tolerate no milk and few solids, and so was given weak broths, tea or sugar water. By now he was 25 per cent underweight. Because of poor nutrition, he was even more susceptible to infection, and each time he was ill, he lost his appetite and ate even less. Then he got bronchitis which developed into pneumonia.

But Fatima borrowed money off a relative, went to town and got antibiotics for him.

So he survived. But malnutrition made him withdrawn and apathetic. His mother got no reward from playing with him, so he received little of the stimulation his brain needed to develop properly. As he grew older, infections grew less frequent, but by the time he went to school, aged eight, he was already a year behind normal physical development and two years behind mentally. The school, in any case, was a poor one, with only three classes, no equipment, and a poorly qualified teacher. As Francisco was continually worried about whether and what he was going to eat that day, he was distracted, unable to concentrate, and seemed to show little interest in schoolwork. The teacher confirmed that he was a slow learner, and could not seem to get the hang of maths or reading and writing. As the family was poor, they did not want to keep him on at school. He was doing so badly anyway that there seemed no point. He did a year, then was away for three years helping an uncle who had a farm, then did another year, then left for good, barely able to read or write more than a few letters. He soon forgot what little he had learned. So, like his father, he began tramping round the local ranches asking for work. Without any educational qualifications or skills, that was all he could ever hope for. And because so many were in the same boat, pay was low. When he was twenty-two he married a local girl, Graciela, aged only fifteen. She too had been undernourished and was illiterate. She soon became pregnant and had to feed another organism inside her before she herself had fully developed. Graciela had heard about family planning from a friend, but Francisco would not let her use it and anyway she was not sure she wanted to. So by the age of only twenty-five, Graciela already had five children and had lost two. The children had every prospect of growing up much as Francisco and Graciela did, overpopulating, underfed, in poor health and illiterate.

HARRISON

At the very bottom of the pile are the destitute. Paul Harrison met many people without work or hope in the Indian city of Calcutta. He describes some of them:

And there are the street dwellers . . . .

The street dwellers are variously estimated to number anything from 40,000 to 200,000. You see them curled up on a straw mat or a piece of cardboard by the odd aluminium pot. Along the staid colonial shopping arcades, under the subways, camped on a roundabout by the gigantic pylons of Howra bridge. A random line of them under a high wall by the riverside warehouses of Strand Road: a family of three living in a tiny shelter of torn khaki canvas slung over bamboo poles, not more than four feet square. A woman dreaming on her charpoy string bed, baby at her side with a tattered shirt over its face, pots, pans and boxes stuffed under the bed. A large family of eight under an awning, their tea cups neatly hanging from a string tacked to the wall. All this in full gaze of passers-by and a noisy flow of traffic. Street life is by definition, a life lived in public.

Each of these faces hides a personal disaster: a fifteen-year-old boy whose parents died of cholera four years earlier. His uncles neglected him so he left his home village for Calcutta, and he earns two rupees a day collecting rags and scrap paper. A twenty-five-year-old woman whose husband deserted her, so she had to move out of their bustee room. Now she lives on the pavement near the railway station, working as a domestic servant in the daytime and at night as a prostitute. A widow of forty with five children: when her husband died she couldn't work the family smallholding and bring up the children, so she fell into debt and had to pay it off by selling house and land. Now she lives on a platform at Ballygunge railway station where she has to pay protection money to thugs to stop them driving her away. She supplements her meagre servant's pay by begging.

HARRISON

Suggestion for writing

Write a story, or a brief biography, about the life of either the fifteen-year-old boy or the twenty-five-year-old woman in Calcutta referred to above.

The Population Explosion

Two writers who argue that the population explosion is the fundamental problem to be tackled, before world hunger and want can be eased, are the American environmentalists Paul Ehrlich and Gordon Rattray Taylor. The extracts are taken from Erhlich's *The Population Bomb*, published in 1971, and Taylor's *The Doomsday Book*, published in 1972.

What "the population explosion" means in simple terms is that the world's population is expanding at a rate vastly greater than at any previous period in human history and at a faster rate than resources and living space are likely to expand.

Recent figures are contained in Robert Allen's book, *How to Save the World*, published in 1980:

"In the next 20 years the world population is expected to increase by almost half, from just over 4,000 million to just under 6,000 million. Yet at present rates of destruction these people will have to make do with a third less farmland and only half the present area of productive tropical forest."

What this means in human terms is graphically suggested by Ehrlich on the front cover of the paperback edition of *The Population Bomb*:

"While you are reading these words four people will have died of starvation. Most of them children."

The principal reason for the explosion in world population is the vast increase in the proportion of people surviving infancy:

Around 1800, when the standard of living in what are today the DC's (Developed Countries) was dramatically increasing due to industrialisation, population growth really began to accelerate. The development of medical science was the straw that broke the camel's back. While lowering death rates in the DC's were due in part to other factors, there is no question that "instant death control", exported by the DC's, has been responsible for the drastic lowering of death rates in the UDC's (Under-Developed Countries).[3] Medical science, with its efficient public health programmes, has been able to depress the death rate with astonishing rapidity and at the same time drastically increase the birth rate.

EHRLICH

The fact that so many more people are surviving infancy results in an increasing proportion of the world's population being at or near child-rearing age, which in itself accelerates the "population explosion".

It is already the case that in the under-developed world, about half the population is under fifteen years of age.

TAYLOR

A rapidly expanding population in the "Third World" has many repercussions in addition to malnourishment and starvation amongst the poor:

More people with more technology spells more pollution, more environmental distortion and less privacy. Much of the damage will come from attempts which will necessarily be made to feed the ever-increasing number of mouths, and to house their owners. The crash of falling timber, as forests are felled, will be echoed by the thunder of explosives, as canals and harbours are blasted into existence.

It is obvious that this process cannot continue for ever: when will the poison-point come? Some maintain the world could support 15,000 million people, one or two have put the figure as high as 30,000 million. The earlier figure could come in the lifetime of those now living, so the question is not an academic one.

TAYLOR

Think what it means for the population of a country to double in 25 years. In order just to keep living standards at the present inadequate level, the food available for the people must be doubled. Every structure and road must be duplicated. The amount of power must be doubled. The capacity of the transport system must be doubled. The number of trained doctors, nurses, teachers and administrators must be doubled. This would be a fantastically difficult job, say, even in the United States — a rich country with a fine agricultural system, immense industries, and rich natural resources. Think of what it means to a country with none of these.

EHRLICH

The problems of providing schools and teachers become immense . . . In some African countries, already, despite unprecedented programmes of school-building, the percentage of children receiving education is falling: children are born faster than schools can be put up to receive them.

TAYLOR

3. Referred to later in this chapter as "Developing Countries".

In developing countries, cities are growing at a terrifying rate . . . . The extreme instance of city growth is expected to be Calcutta, which is currently expanding by 300,000 a year: Kinglsley Davis estimates that it is headed for a population of between 36 and 66 million by the end of the century, when population growth and agricultural modernisation are allowed for, though its growth is due more to its central role in the area than to these factors. Already it is in a state of social disorganisation. The Metropolitan Planning Commission says that it sees "no prospect" of housing the population over the next 25 years. At the moment, open-sided sheds are being built to provide some sort of shelter. Twenty or thirty people share a single cold tap. Sewage runs in open gutters in the streets, and at times of river-flood may be washed anywhere. People wash their clothes and themselves in the polluted water. Other parts of the city, of course, are highly civilised — but the disorganised sector is growing. Traffic problems are already acute, especially at the main bridge across the river, crossed by half a million pedestrians every day, in addition to animals and motorised traffic. It is inconceivable that the city can continue to operate at a level of 30 million inhabitants or more.

New York, with a much longer experience, finds it hard enough to function at 12 million. Cities like Calcutta can hardly avoid becoming jungles, in which crime cannot be controlled, in which health standards cannot be maintained and in which people die on the pavement without the fact even being remarked . . . .

In short, it seems certain that the mushrooming cities of the immediate future will be plagued by crime and mental disturbance of various kinds.

TAYLOR

Whilst population growth in developed countries like Britain has slowed to zero with the help of easily available birth control methods, the same methods in countries like India have had negligible effects, despite the fact that India has had an official birth control programme for thirty years. The main reason is poverty:

Large families are a response to high death-rates in infancy and childhood. In many oriental countries the figure is 10 or 12 children born, of whom formerly only 2 or 3 would survive. Now that death rates have been cut dramatically, people begin to attempt to limit their families, but not by the full amount required. Custom is important, and a family of two seems ridiculous in a culture geared to twelve. Experience shows that it takes several generations for people to make a full response. The first generation cuts back from 10 to 7 or 8; the next to 5 or 6 and so on. But the period we are looking at is little more than one generation . . . .

Unfortunately, it is not the case that, when people are poor, they try to restrict the family to a size they can afford. Sometimes they hope their position will improve; sometimes they see their children as an asset, able to work in the fields or support them when they are old. There is thus little hope that the provision of contraception will, of itself, make much impact. The prime need is to convince people that *two* is the best family size.

TAYLOR

Writers such as Ehrlich and Taylor see hope only in controlling the world's birth-rate.

Basically, then, there are only two kinds of solution to the population problem. One is a "birth-rate solution", in which we find ways to lower the birth-rate. The other is a "death-rate solution" in which ways to raise the death-rate – war, famine, pestilence – *find us* . . . .

Men do not seem to be able to focus emotionally on distant or long-term events. Immediacy seems to be necessary to elicit "selfless" responses. Few Americans could sit in the same room with a child and watch it starve to death. But the death of several million children this year from starvation is a distant, impersonal, hard-to-grasp event. You will note that I put quotes around "selfish" and "selfless". The words describe the behaviour only out of context. The "selfless" actions necessary to aid the rest of the world and stabilise the population are the only hope for survival. The "selfish" ones work only towards destruction . . . .

Remember, above all, that more than half of the world is in misery now. That alone should be enough to galvanise us into action, regardless of the exact dimensions of the future disaster now staring "Homo Sapiens" in the face.

EHRLICH

Discussion suggestion

Assuming that the "population explosion" *is* a serious world problem, you might discuss how the "birth-rate solution" could be made more effective. You could consider such options as:

wider early education about birth control and family limitation;

free distribution of the pill or other birth-control devices, and education in their use;

free abortion on demand;

financial or other penalties for families which have more than, say, two children;

government encouragement or enforcement of late marriage;

compulsory sterilisation.

Some of these suggestions may seem grotesque, but all have been tried out somewhere in the world. Whether you find them acceptable or offensive, you should be able to explain why. Wider reading by one or more selected students will, of course, assist the discussion.

Note-taking

As well as jotting down interesting points brought up in class discussion, it can be a useful exercise to make summary notes of relevant articles and extracts which you have read. It is much easier to remember information and ideas if you have made notes on them.

As a preliminary exercise in note-taking, you could try listing, in note-form, the main general points covered in the preceding section, (The Population Explosion), under the following five headings:

Meaning	**Reasons for failure of policies**
Causes	**Future prospects**
Effects	

Distribution of Resources

Over the past decade, a shift of emphasis in the analysis of world poverty has been noticeable. Writers on population and global politics tend now to stress the unequal distribution of wealth more than overpopulation as the principal cause of starvation and malnourishment.

This alternative analysis of world poverty is again represented by extracts from two books by influential writers: *How the Other Half Dies*, by the American writer, Susan George, published in 1976, and *The Creation of World Poverty*, by the British writer, Teresa Hayter, published in 1981.

Rich and poor: the global situation

The extent of world poverty and destitution today, and the contrast between rich and poor countries, is suggested by Teresa Hayter:

Wage rates in underdeveloped countries are often one-twentieth to one-thirtieth of those in the richer countries, for the same type of work . . . .

Today the World Bank says that, "excluding the centrally planned economies", there are about 800 million people, or almost 40 per cent of the population of the so-called developing countries, who live in "absolute poverty": "a condition of life so characterised by malnutrition, illiteracy and disease as to be beneath any reasonable definition of human decency". In some countries one child in four dies before the age of five. Millions of people live in houses or huts made of corrugated tin, cardboard boxes and other "impermanent" materials. They have no running water and no toilets. Electricity is a luxury. Health services are rarely within walking distance, and have to be paid for. Primary education may be available and free but often children are needed for work. There is generally no social security or unemployment pay, and many people, some 300 million, according to the ILO (International Labour Organisation), are without any kind of employment.

HAYTER

Susan George also quotes from a statement by a representative of the World Bank (the major world lending organisation):

World Bank figures show that "on average the one billion people in the countries with per capita incomes below $200 consume only about 1 per cent as much energy per capita as the citizens of the United States". The Bank's Mr McNamara also hopes that "once the people of the United States understand that they, with 6 per cent of the world's population, consume about 35 per cent of the world's total resources, and yet in terms of economic assistance as a percentage of GNP rank 14th among the 16 developed nations . . . [they will not] turn away in cynicism and indifference".

GEORGE

The moral implications of this are starkly suggested by Rene Dumont, quoted by George:

> "The rich white man, with his overconsumption of meat and his lack of generosity for poor people, behaves like a veritable cannibal – an indirect cannibal. By consuming meat, which wastes the grain that could have saved them, last year we ate the children of the Sahel, Ethiopia and Bangladesh. And we continue to eat them this year with undiminished appetite."[4]

The root of the problem: overpopulation or unequal distribution of resources?

The following extracts typify much recent writing on the question:

Many calculations show that food supplies in the world as a whole are more than adequate, actually and potentially, to feed a population much larger than the existing population . . . . Rapid population increases cause particular problems at particular times, but it is the case that in many countries with the greatest problems of malnutrition *overall* food supplies have been increasing faster than the increase in population. This is so for nearly all countries in South and East Asia, including India. The most likely explanation for probably increasing impoverishment in rural areas is not to be found in population increases, but rather in an increasingly unequal distribution of income.

HAYTER

This is not intended, of course, to suggest that the "population explosion" is unimportant:

Even taking for granted that current knowledge and technology are equal to the task of providing a decent diet for every human being now on earth or for a much larger number – given a radically different world order – it would not be ecologically desirable to decimate the last natural forest in order to provide arable land and food for tens of billions of people.

GEORGE

4. Rene Dumont, "Population and Cannibalism" (UN Development Forum).

Division between developed and developing countries

It is easy, and consoling, to assume that the developed Western nations have no responsibility for the plight of the other half of humanity, that "charity begins at home", and that it is somehow their own fault that the world's poor and destitute have to wage a bitter struggle simply to survive; that they should sort out their problems for themselves.

Writers such as George and Hayter point out, however, that the imbalance between rich and poor nations owes a great deal to the process of colonisation which began five centuries ago:

One of the results of colonial policy in dependent territories seems to have been, in many cases actually to produce hunger where it did not exist before, as self-sufficient farming gave way to cash crop production for export to the colonial nation, and local industries were deliberately held back and destroyed in the interests of the export of raw materials to and of finished products from the controlling power.

GEORGE

As early as the seventeenth century, when the British began enacting the protective Navigation Acts, colonies were prohibited by law from turning to any industry which might compete with the industry of the mother country. For example, the North American colonists were forbidden to manufacture caps, hats, woollen or iron goods. They were expected to send the raw materials for these products to England to be manufactured and then to buy them back from England.

HAYTER

Hayter quotes from a report by Lord Cromer, governor of Egypt from 1883 to 1907, which provides a startling illustration of the way in which colonialism benefited the ruling country to the detriment of the ruled. Explaining Britain's policy of running down Egyptian industry and forcing Egyptian industrial workers back into agriculture, Lord Cromer stated proudly, looking back on his career:

"The difference is apparent to any man whose recollections go back some ten or fifteen years. Some quarters (of Cairo) that formerly used to be veritable centres of varied industries — spinning, weaving, ribbonmaking, dyeing, tentmaking, embroidery, shoemaking, jewellery making, spice grinding, copper work, the manufacture of bottles out of animal skins, saddlery, sieve making, locksmithing in wood and metal, etc — have shrunk considerably or vanished. Now there are coffee houses and European novelty shops where once there were prosperous workshops".

The destructive effects of cash crop plantation are vividly illustrated by a quotation from the Latin America writer, Eduardo Galeano:

"Early chroniclers told of travelling across all of Cuba in the shade of giant palms and through leafy forests abounding in mahogany, cedar

and ebony. Cuba's precious woods may still be admired in . . .
Madrid, but in Cuba the sugarcane invasion sent the best virgin forests
up in smoke. In the same years it was destroying its own timberlands,
Cuba became the chief purchaser of United States timber. The
extensive plunder-culture of sugarcane meant not only the death of the
forest but also, in the long run, the death of the island's famous
fertility. With forests surrendered to the flames, erosion soon did its
work on the defenceless soil and thousands of streams dried up."[5]

Why mass poverty continues in the post-colonial era

For most of the nations of Latin America, colonial exploitation ended in
the early nineteenth century, whilst most countries of Africa and Asia
were ruled by European governments until the 1950s and 1960s. Though
almost all of them are now independent, however, desperate poverty on a
mass scale persists, as we have seen.

This can partly be explained by the positions in which the developing
countries were left after independence. The general pattern in Third-
World ex-colonies is that local élites and landowners, left behind (and
often originally created) by the colonial country, are still in control and
still largely dependent on cash crop and raw material export for their
income, instead of concentrating on producing food for consumption by
their own people.

Third World governments and people are thus still at the mercy of
fluctuations in the worldwide market for their commodities:

The fluctuations in commodity prices can be dramatic. They are accentuated
by speculation on commodity markets, many of them in London, which are
of course outside the control of the underdeveloped countries. In the
mid-70s, the price paid for sugar dropped from 64 cents a pound to 6 cents a
pound in 18 months.

HAYTER

The system by which the great majority of the land is owned by a small
number of rich landowners makes the life of the rural poor precarious in
the extreme:

In India peasants have become deeply indebted to landowners and traders
who are able to force them to sell their crops cheaply in order to obtain
further credit. Such traders hoard food and sell it in times of scarcity at
prices that peasants cannot afford.

A K Sen[6] gives evidence to show that the famines in Ethiopia in 1973 and
1974, which were responsible for the deaths of between 50,000 and 200,000
people, were not the result of overall food shortages in Ethiopia as a whole,

5. Eduardo Galeano, *The Open Veins of Latin America: Five Centuries of the Pillage of a
    Continent.*
6. A K Sen, *Ingredients of Famine Analysis.*

but of a terrible decline in the purchasing power of people in the areas affected by the famines . . . .

Massive unemployment, underemployment and migration from impoverished rural areas into cities have become the most obvious features of current forms of underdevelopment.

HAYTER

This migration from the countryside into the cities accounts, in part, for the situation in cities like Calcutta, described earlier.

Recent changes in relations between developed and developing countries

Since the mid-1970s, the World Bank, and groups of Western politicians such as those who produced the "Brandt Report", have become conscious of some of the factors outlined above, and called for a more responsible attitude from the governments of developed countries towards developing countries.

Susan George quotes Robert McNamara, former president of the World Bank, who argued that the governments of the developed countries must not only increase their aid, but also link it to land reform and redistribution in the recipient countries if it is genuinely to help the poor.

> "The average citizen of a developed country enjoys wealth beyond the wildest dreams of the one billion people in countries with per capita incomes under $200 . . . . We must . . . give as much attention to promoting the inherent potential and productivity of the poor as is generally given to protecting the power of the privileged . . . . Land reform is not exclusively about land. It is about the uses and abuses of power and the social structure through which it is exercised."

Yet as Hayter points out, loans continue to be given regardless of whether they benefit the poor or not. She quotes the example of Brazil:

Brazil is one of the biggest recipients of World Bank loans, but its record on income distribution is one of the most notoriously bad. Between 1960 and 1977, according to Brazilian official sources, the share of national income of the poorest half of the population fell from 17 per cent to 13 per cent, while the share of the richest one per cent rose from 12 per cent to 18 per cent, or more than the poorest half receive.

HAYTER

In fact, aid is rarely given to underdeveloped countries with the aim simply of helping the poor, and with no strings attached. Hayter quotes a statement by Hubert Humphrey, who was later to become Vice-President of America, made in 1957, which puts the issue of aid with unusual frankness:

> "I have heard . . . that people may become dependent on us for food. I know that was not supposed to be good news. To me, that was good news, because before people can do anything they have got to eat. And

if you are looking for a way to get people to lean on you and be dependent on you, in terms of their co-operation with you, it seems to me that food dependence would be terrific.''

The developed world has recently begun to affect the economies of the underdeveloped countries in another significant way, through the operations of multinational companies which, according to Hayter, "today control between a quarter and a third of all world production". Increasingly, "labour-intensive" manufacture is being located in underdeveloped countries, "in order to take advantage of the extreme cheapness of labour there''. Once again the benefits generally are not experienced by the poor; the profits go to the shareholders of the companies and the élites in the countries where they are operating.

A partial, short-term solution to the problems of third-world poverty put forward by writers like George and Hayter is that of "intermediate technology'', a term invented by Ernst Schumacher, meaning small-scale, low-cost technologies which can be developed independently of Western expertise and financing, producing goods of immediate use to the local community. George feels that the governments of underdeveloped countries should make it *public policy* to seek out and produce intermediate, low-cost solutions to their problems involving maximum participation on the part of the rural poor themselves.

Conclusion

The argument of writers who consider that the redistribution of resources is a more pressing need than population control is summed up by Susan George:

So long as thoroughgoing land reform, regrouping and distribution of resources to the poorest, bottom half of the population does not take place, Third World countries can go on increasing their production till hell freezes and hunger will remain, for the production will go to those who already have plenty – to the developed world or to the wealthy in the Third World itself. Poverty and hunger walk hand in hand.

Written or Oral Comprehension

A good way to check whether you've fully understood and assimilated material you have read is to test yourself on it. You could try *briefly* answering the following questions, *without* looking at the book, either in the form of a written test, or as a series of oral questions round the class. Try to explain the ideas in your own words rather than learning parrot-fashion "definitions".

1. What is "absolute poverty"?
2. List six ways in which "absolute poverty" is revealed in practice.
3. What is the explanation given for "increasing impoverishment in rural areas"?

4. How did "cash crop production" help to widen the gap between rich and poor nations?

5. What generally happened to the raw materials, and the industries, of colonised countries?

6. How do "fluctuations in the worldwide market" affect the economies of Third World countries?

7. What are the two main results of "the system by which the great majority of the land is owned by small numbers of landowners"?

8. Explain the term "strings" as applied to aid to developing countries.

9. What is the normal policy of Multinational Companies towards developing countries?

10. What is the meaning of the term "intermediate technology"?

Themes for Discussion

What do you imagine happens to Third World families in which the breadwinner has no regular paid employment?

Do you think that Robert McNamara was being over-optimistic when he expressed the hope that "the people of the United States . . . will not turn away in cynicism and indifference" when they realise the problems of the Third World? Do you think the people of the US or Britain are generally aware of these problems *yet*? If not, why not? Does it matter?

Do you think that developed countries such as Britain and the USA are still, in any respects, to blame for Third World poverty?

Why do you think so little progress has been made towards land reform and income redistribution in most Third World countries since independence?

Is there anything that Western governments and aid agencies can, or should, do to encourage reforms?

Are there any signs of Third World countries converting back from cash crops to staple food production?

Are there any signs that Third World governments are attempting to diversify their economies to counter the effects of market fluctuations in their dominant export commodity?

Do you think that the general situation of the poorer half of the world's population has improved or worsened in the last 25 years? Will it have changed for better or worse by the end of the century?

Suggestions for debate

If the issues in this chapter are to be tackled by means of formal debate rather than informal discussion, here are two debate motions:[7]

---

7. A further debate topic, taking in the issues of Chapters 3 and 4 as a whole, is suggested on page 52.

(*i*) "Charity begins at home."
  We should solve the problems in our own country before we start worrying about the problems of others.

(*ii*) Enforced sterilisation is the only answer to the problems of countries like India.

Essay Titles

Essays on global problems are frequently fairly general, so that an answer might well be concerned equally with the material contained in the next chapter, on environmental issues, as with population and poverty. You may wish, therefore, to write an essay only after dealing with *both* chapters.

Here are two titles which relate specifically to this chapter:

(a) "We must share the world's resources more fairly than we have done in the past, even if we reduce the standard of living in the Western World."

(b) The arguments for and against the United Kingdom making money available to the underdeveloped and developing countries.

Bibliography

Books

Barrios de Chungara, Domitila, with Moema Viezzer. *Let me speak!: Testimony of Domitila, a woman of the Bolivian mines*, Stage 1, 1979

Brandt, Willy, et al. *North–South, a programme for survival: report of the Independent Commission on International Development Issues*, Pan Books, 1980

Ehrlich, Paul R. *The Population Bomb*; Ballantine, Friends of the Earth, 1971

Galeano, Eduardo. *Open Veins of Latin America: Five Centuries of the Pillage of a Continent*, Monthly Review Press, 1973

George, Susan. *How the Other Half Dies: the real reasons for world hunger*, Penguin 1976

Harrison, Paul. *Inside the Third World: the anatomy of poverty*, Penguin, 1979

Hayter, Teresa. *The Creation of World Poverty*, Pluto Press in association with Third World First, 1981

Lappé, Frances Moore, and Collins, Joseph. *Food First*, Abacus, 1982

Schumacher, E.F. *Small is Beautiful: a study of economics as if people mattered*, Abacus, 1978

Taylor, Gordon Rattray. *The Doomsday Book*, Panther, 1972

World Bank. *The Assault on World Poverty: problems of rural development, education and health*, Johns Hopkins University Press for the World Bank, 1975

Periodicals

New Internationalist

Additional Materials

Various resources, ranging from free pamphlets to photopacks, slides, videos and films, are available from the major organisations concerned with alleviating hunger and poverty in the Third World.

Catalogues, resources and suggestions can be obtained from the following:

CAFOD (the Catholic Fund for Overseas Development)
2 Garden Close
Stockwell Road
LONDON SW9 9TY

CWDE (Centre for World Development Education)
128 Buckingham Palace Road
LONDON SW1W 9SH

Christian Aid
PO Box No 1
LONDON SW9 8BH

Oxfam
274 Banbury Road
OXFORD OX2 7DZ

Speakers can often be booked to visit schools and colleges to show videos and films, and discuss the issues.

Advice on Writing: Tackling a Comprehension

For comprehension there are no clear cut rules to be learnt and applied, as there are for précis. Success depends on precise understanding and expression of ideas contained in a passage. This cannot be taught; it can only be developed by practice.

Nevertheless, a few general points are worth making about answering comprehension questions. As with précis, a preliminary reading, to achieve some sense of what the passage is about, must come first. The questions can then be read, and borne in mind when re-reading the passage, as often as necessary, to clarify the ideas.

Most comprehension questions will refer to a particular idea or ideas in the passage, frequently with line references, and explanations will be asked for. Generally the answer will be found in the lines surrounding the quoted phrase or idea. This is not always the case, however, and some questions will refer to an idea which is developed in more than one paragraph. Care must be taken to check whether an idea is developed in this way before attempting an answer.

In either case, *all* of the relevant details should generally be included in your answer. You may find it helpful to underline the phrases in the passage which are relevant to the question. You must then explain these points, in your own words as far as possible, as exactly as you can. On occasions you will find that words or phrases are so specialised or precise as to be impossible to re-express without altering the sense, in which case it is acceptable to copy them, but this is unlikely to happen very often. You should always check the number of marks allocated to each question, as this will give a fairly clear idea of the amount of detail required in your answer.

In the case of questions which ask for explanations of vocabulary used in the passage, a brief answer is all that will be required. There is no need to explain the context of the word or phrase, and your answer should not contain many more words than are contained in the phrase itself.

If you are asked to *comment* on an idea in the passage with which you agree or disagree, it is best to choose a relatively major idea and you should make sure that you can express the idea precisely yourself before commenting on it.

Finally, if you are asked to comment on the *style* of the passage you should attempt to deal with the following matters:

diction – whether the vocabulary is generally abstract or concrete, simple or complex, with examples

tone – whether the passage is essentially serious or light-hearted or humorous, with illustrations if there are any variations in the tone

imagery – whether the passage contains any figures of speech, either of sound or of meaning (see Chapter 12 for explanations of the main figures of speech); if so, you should quote and comment on the techniques

sentence-construction – whether the sentences are simple or complex, or a combination of the two, with illustrations and comments on the varieties of construction.

There is no particular need to tackle the questions in order, and if you find yourself getting bogged down on a particular question it is best to leave it. As with all examination work, it is essential to learn to pace yourself so that you can complete the exercise in the time allocated.

4

The World in Crisis: Environmental Destruction and Pollution

Poverty and overpopulation have an immediate effect on the day-to-day lives of hundreds of millions of people in the developing world. The destruction of the world environment, by contrast, has a less obvious impact on human life; yet in the long run it may prove to be the greatest threat of all to humanity.

The subject of environmental decay is vast and complex, requiring, for an adequate understanding, a study of ecology, which is a far more ambitious task than can be undertaken here. All that can be attempted in a brief survey is to indicate some of the problems which are considered by experts to pose the greatest threat to our environment, and to summarise some of the solutions which have been put forward.

The chapter begins with a passage for précis, taken from Barry Commoner's book *Science and Survival*.

Précis

Write a summary of the following passage in not more than 200 words (the passage contains about 575 words). Your summary should be in clear, connected English, and the number of words used should be indicated at the end. You are advised to spend about one hour on this exercise.

Urban pollution involves many cost/benefit decisions. For example, smog levels cannot be reduced without supplanting urban automotive traffic with electric-powered mass transit systems, or possibly by introducing new types of vehicles. The first of these actions would impose a massive economic burden on cities that are already unable to meet their social obligations; the second course would mean a serious disruption of one of the mainstays of our economy, the automobile industry. In the same way, the government's decision in 1970 to close the biological warfare arsenal at Pine Bluff, Arkansas, was protested by the local chamber of commerce, which expressed a readiness to accept the possible environmental hazard — and to enjoy the benefits of the 200 jobs associated with the arsenal — for the sake of "deterring" an enemy with the threat of bacterial attack.

We come then to a crucial question: who is to be the Solomon of modern technology and weigh in the balance all the good that comes of it against the ecological, social costs? Or, who will strike the balance between the concern of the prudent manager of a nuclear power plant for economy and the concern of a mother over the health of her child?

Confronted by decisions on nuclear power, radiation, nitrate levels, photochemical smog, bacterial warfare, and all the other technicalities of environmental problems, it is tempting to call in the scientific expert. Scientists can, of course, evaluate the relevant benefits: how many kilowatt hours of electricity a nuclear power plant can deliver and at what price, or the yield of corn to be expected from nitrogen fertilizer. They can also evaluate the related risks: the radiation dose to people in the vicinity of the power plant and the hazard to infants from nitrate levels exacerbated by fertilizers. These evaluations can be derived from appropriate scientific theories, principles, and data.

However, no scientific principle can guide the choice between some number of kilowatt hours of electric power and some number of cases of thyroid cancer, or between some number of bushels of corn and some number of cases of infant methemoglobinemia. These are value judgments; they are determined not by scientific principle, but by the value that we place on economic advantage and on human life or by our belief in the wisdom of committing the nation to mass transportation or to biological warfare. These are matters of morality, of social and political judgment. In a democracy they belong not in the hands of "experts", but in the hands of the people and their elected representatives.

The environmental crisis is the legacy of our unwitting assault on the natural systems that support us. It represents hidden costs that are mounting toward catastrophe. If it is to be resolved, these costs must be made explicit and balanced against the benefits of technology in open, public debate. But this debate will not come easily. For the public has little access to the necessary scientific data. Much of the needed information has been, and remains, wrapped in government and industrial secrecy. Unearthing the needed information and disseminating it to the public is, I believe, the unique responsibility of the scientific community. For to exercise its right of conscience, the public must have the relevant scientific facts in understandable terms. As the custodians of this knowledge, we in the scientific community owe it to our fellow citizens to help inform them about the crisis in the environment.

BARRY COMMONER

How to Save the World

The most thorough analysis of the environmental crisis is contained in *World Conservation Strategy*, published by the three major international conservation agencies.[1] This vast document is summarised for the general reader in a book called *How to Save the World* by Robert Allen, and it is from this book that the extracts which follow are taken.

---

1. International Union for Conservation of Nature and Natural Resources (IUCN); United Nations Environment Programme (UNEP); World Wildlife Fund (WWF)

How pollution is related to poverty and overpopulation

Much habitat destruction and over-exploitation of living resources by individuals, communities and nations in the developing world[2] is a response to relative poverty, caused or exacerbated by a combination of rising human numbers and inequities within and among nations. Peasant communities, for example, may be forced to cultivate steep, unstable slopes because their growing numbers exceed the capacity of the land and because the fertile, easily managed valley bottoms have been taken over by large landowners. Similarly, many developing countries have so few natural resources and operate under such unfavourable conditions of international trade that often they have very little choice but to exploit forests, fisheries and other living resources unsustainably . . . . Every country should have a conscious and deliberate population policy to avoid as far as possible the development of such situations, and eventually to achieve a balance between numbers and environment. At the same time it is essential that the affluent constrain their demands on resources, and ideally reduce them, shifting some of their wealth to assisting the deprived. To a significant extent the survival and future of the poor depends on conservation and sharing by the rich.

The worst environmental problems

Loss of soil:
The bottom is dropping out of the world's breadbasket. Prime farmland is being obliterated by roads and buildings. Croplands and grazing land are being mutilated on a huge scale by farming methods that more resemble mining than good husbandry. Wild and traditional crop varieties, the main weapons against pests and diseases that could wipe out harvest after harvest, are vanishing . . . .

Not only is farmland disappearing at an alarming rate, but much that remains is being heavily degraded by bad farming practices. As much as one-third of the world's cropland will be destroyed in the next 20 years if current rates of land degradation continue.

Spreading deserts:
The creation of new desert areas is happening on a colossal scale. All over the world people are busy making life more difficult than it already is. They are turning semi-desert into desert and desert into extreme desert, transforming the barely productive into the unproductively bare . . . .

The vulnerable areas are the drylands. Drylands, where rainfall is low and evaporation and transpiration are high, cover about a third of the earth's land surface. They are extremely prone to desertification (the process by which land becomes desert) unless used with care and skill, and they represent the most extensive ecological problem area on this planet.

It is estimated that almost 80 million people are immediately threatened by

2. Referred to earlier as the "underdeveloped countries" or the "Third World"

a desertification induced drop in productivity of the land on which (directly or indirectly) they depend. Regions already in the grip of desertification or at very high risk cover 20 million square kilometres (9 million square miles), or an area twice the size of Canada . . . . Most of it is in Africa and Asia.

Deforestation:
Forests are the prime example of natural areas that contribute heavily to human welfare by acting as environmental buffers . . . . Removal or degradation of watershed forests and pastures can cause great human suffering. Without the sponge-like effect of their vegetation, which retains moisture and releases it slowly, the flow of water becomes erratic, leading to both floods and water shortages. The increased rate of water run-off causes additional damage by stripping the soil away, depriving agriculture of nutrients while clogging reservoirs, irrigation systems, canals and docks with silt, and smothering coral reefs . . . .

Badly organised timber operations are degrading the forests as effectively as expansionist agricultural and settlement schemes. In a given forest section, only a few species . . . may be considered of commercial value. Yet to reach them, 75 per cent of the surrounding canopy is destroyed. The *apparently* endless supply discourages caution . . . .

In many parts of South America . . . large tracts of forest are being burned down and converted into ranchland. The beef is raised cheaply enough to satisfy demand in the United States, Canada and Europe, but it is a destructive business; the pasture is invaded by scrub so rapidly that after a few years it becomes uneconomic to maintain and is abandoned.

    We are at the point now where what goes now is gone forever. Once destruction is widespread, tropical rain forests can no longer be reconstructed . . . .

Destruction of tropical rain forests may have serious climatic effects well beyond the tropics. Tropical forests contain in their wood, leaves, litter and humus, an enormous store (estimated to be 340 thousand million tonnes) of carbon. Carbon is burned when fossil fuels are destroyed and it accumulates in the atmosphere . . . . The likely consequence of the accumulation of carbon dioxide in the atmosphere is that the global climate will become warmer, and that the warming will be greater at the poles than between them. Nobody knows the effects of this uneven warming, but it is quite possible that one of the effects would be a general drying of the wheat areas of North America. Another possible effect is an increase in sea level if the western ice sheet in Antarctica were to melt, as it did in earlier geological times during a similar warm period.

Overfishing and sea pollution:
The world's most valuable wild animals are almost certainly shrimps. Their closest rivals are cod and herring. The total annual value of exports of fresh and frozen shrimps from developing to developed countries is already close to $1000 million . . . .

Unfortunately use of fisheries is often not sustainable and their contribution to national diets and incomes is likely to diminish . . . . At least 25 of the world's most valuable fisheries are seriously depleted. Many more are now so fully exploited that they can expect to become depleted within a decade or so, because of the effects of exploitation either alone or in combination with those of pollution and habitat destruction . . . .

Over-exploitation is waste: the substitution of relatively small short-term gains for much bigger medium or long-term losses. A sobering measure of this wastage is the conversion over the years of poor people's food into rich people's food. There was a time in the UK, before over-exploitation and pollution did their work, when oysters and fresh salmon were a mono- tonously common feature of the poor person's diet. This is no longer the case and both are now beyond the pocket of the average family. Now the cod . . . seems to be going in the same direction.

Why immediate action is necessary

Current attempts by a quarter of the world's people to carry on consuming two-thirds of the world's resources and by half of the people simply to stay alive are destroying the means by which all people can survive and prosper. Everywhere fertile soil is either built on or flushed into the sea; otherwise renewable resources are exploited beyond recovery, and pollutants are thrown like wrenches into the machinery of climate. As a result, the planet's capacity to support people is being irreversibly reduced at the very time when rising human numbers and consumption are making increasingly heavy demands on it . . . .

Unless concerted action is taken immediately, there will be a further decline in the planet's capacity to support its population. Subsequent generations will be left a sorry heritage. The decision is not one we can postpone or ignore. Doing nothing is itself a decision to allow the world to be a much less fruitful and promising place than that into which we were born.

ALLEN

The *World Conservation Strategy* contains a wide range of suggestions for international action to "save the world", far too diverse to attempt to summarise. Here is an illustration of the type of action which it proposes, taken, again, from Robert Allen's book:

Proposals for action

Governments should first of all make a decision to give precedence to agri- culture and other uses for high quality land. They can enforce that decision by prohibiting the sale of farmland, dropping government assistance for projects that would encourage conversion of farmland, and promoting the use of lower quality land as sites for urban development . . . . People need incentives to conserve. The best possible incentive for the farmer is demon- stration that soil conservation brings big enough benefits, such as higher average yields for lower overall costs, quickly enough to make it worth the effort and expense. Every country, therefore, should have a soil conservation service with sufficient technical staff to help with as many demonstration projects as may be needed and professional staff to provide the technical workers with expert back-up.

If, however, it is clear that the benefits from conservation will be too gradual for the farmer alone to support the costs of conservation, other incentives, such as low-cost credit or tax concessions for installing and maintaining drains, retaining tree cover and re-cycling farm wastes, should be given. Land reform is often another indispensible incentive. People cannot be expected to look after land they do not own and from which they may be expelled without notice. "Land to the tiller" is a cardinal maxim, and it must not be just the land the wealthy do not want.

ALLEN

Discussion points

Why are the four environmental problems outlined here currently considered the most serious? What are the chief threats posed by each?

Is there anything that Britain or the western world generally can do to assist in the achievement of any of the solutions suggested by Robert Allen?

Other Aspects of Atmospheric Pollution

Atmospheric pollution is in several ways a serious threat to the global environment. Most potentially catastrophic is the concentration of carbon dioxide in the atmosphere, producing the so-called "greenhouse effect", described in the extract on "deforestation" above. This concentration of CO_2 is also caused by the burning of fossil fuels to provide energy. Further global aspects of atmospheric pollution are discussed by Brian Price in *Friends of the Earth Guide to Pollution*:

In the past decade, a number of pollution problems of international, if not global, significance have been identified or at least postulated.

The first of these problems, or potential problems, was originally discussed in 1974 following research into the chemistry of the atmosphere. Scientists became worried that the continued release of gases called chlorofluorocarbons (CFCS) would lead to damage to the layer of ozone which surrounds the earth. (CFCS are widely used in aerosol spray cans and in refrigerators.) Damage could occur since, under the influence of sunlight, CFCS break down to give chemical species called free radicals. These free radicals can then attack ozone and destroy it, following which free radicals can be regenerated. Thus one molecule of a CFC can destroy several molecules of ozone.

This would be of purely academic interest were it not for the fact that the ozone layer is vital to the maintenance of life on earth. Ozone absorbs certain types of ultraviolet radiation emitted by the sun and thereby acts as a filter. The particular wavelengths in question are dangerous to life, causing skin cancer and possibly mutations. Thus any damage to the ozone layer is likely to be reflected in an increase in skin cancer rates in people exposed to the increased radiation. Smaller organisms such as plankton could be seriously damaged, even killed outright, while possible long-term effects include damage to the world's climate.

The situation is complicated somewhat by the fact that it takes a very long time for CFCS released at the surface of the earth to rise through the atmosphere as far as the ozone layer — perhaps as long as thirty or forty years — and they may remain active for several decades. This means that the effects of most of the CFCS released to date have still not been felt, since they are still in transit and nothing can be done to prevent any damage they may cause.

The account given so far is a simplified one — it has to be since atmospheric chemistry can be very complex. However, not all scientists accept that there is a risk to the environment from the use of CFCS. There is a dispute over whether or not other substances in the atmosphere will soak them up and protect the ozone layer. There is also doubt about the significance of any reduction in ozone concentrations, which anyway vary quite markedly from time to time and from place to place; and it has also been suggested that other materials, such as nitrogen oxides, pose a greater threat to the ozone layer.

At this point the argument becomes more political than scientific. There are those people who believe that the uses of CFCS should continue until a definite hazard is proven, while others believe that they should be banned immediately since we cannot afford to wait for definite proof as it takes so long for the materials to reach the upper atmosphere.

New information about the chemistry of the atmosphere appears every year and other chemicals likely to affect the ozone layer are being identified. As some of them are likely to be used in larger amounts in the near future, CFCS may become relatively less significant. Equally, some chemicals may increase the amount of ozone in the upper atmosphere. The fact that our knowledge of atmospheric chemistry is growing does not necessarily mean that we can afford to wait and see if there is a hazard to the ozone layer. More than a few scientists would argue that preventive measures are essential now . . . .

The second issue in air pollution to be discussed here is also a global one. It concerns the likely effect on the world's climate of an increase in the amount of carbon dioxide in the atmosphere. As with CFCS and the ozone layer, it may be too late to take remedial action once a hazard is proved, yet the results of not taking action could be very serious . . . .

The effects of the third air pollutant discussed here are not predicted to occur at some distant date: they are visible here and now. This pollutant is sulphur dioxide (SO_2) which, together with associated sulphates and acids, is responsible for serious ecological damage in Europe and North America. Sulphur dioxide is produced whenever sulphur is burned, and sulphur is present in nearly all fossil fuels. It is also emitted by smelters, steelworks, brickworks and many other industrial plants. The effects of sulphur dioxide on people, although still not fully understood, are well documented since sulphur dioxide is a toxic component of smogs such as the one which killed four thousand people in London in 1952.

The more insidious ecological effects of sulphur dioxide, and the "acid rain" in which it and its relations fall, were much more difficult to determine but a number of points are now clear. Firstly, large numbers of lakes in Southern Sweden and Norway are devoid of fish life as a result of acidic sulphur compounds deposited in them from the atmosphere . . . .

Similar effects have been reported in Canadian and American lakes . . . .

The other serious effect of acid rain is damage to forests in West Germany, where serious reductions in forest productivity have been attributed to acidic sulphur compounds . . . .

Sulphur dioxide has been identified as one of the major "transboundary" pollutants, since SO_2 released from power station chimneys is carried long distances before it falls to earth, often in another country. Most of the acid rain causing problems in Norway and Sweden originates from other parts of Europe . . . .

The problem of sulphur dioxide pollution is likely to increase as the consumption of fossil fuels rises. It is possible to remove sulphur from most fuels before burning them and chimney gases can be washed to remove SO_2, but both processes can be costly and produce other wastes which have to be disposed of . . . .

Most environmentalists would agree, however, that the most effective way of reducing sulphur dioxide emissions in the short term is to institute energy conservation measures and use fuels more wisely. After all, if twice as much heat can be obtained from a given amount of fuel, then the sulphur emissions from the production of that heat are effectively halved . . . .

Sulphur dioxide is not the only chemical involved in the production of acid rain. Others, such as nitrogen oxides, are also involved and it may be just as important to reduce emissions of these substances if acid rain is to be prevented.

The effects of pollution are not always immediate and obvious. They may take a long time to occur and a long time to detect in the midst of many other complex processes. By the time their effects are proven it may be too late to prevent them from getting worse. There is, of course, a conflict between the need to develop new chemicals for the benefit of humanity and the need to protect humanity from these chemicals' adverse effects. However, where a substance is likely to cause serious pollution problems it may be preferable to treat it as "guilty until proven innocent" — we may not be able to afford the luxury of absolute proof of guilt.

PRICE

The people most directly and immediately affected by pollution are the Third World poor. A glimpse of the impact of atmospheric pollution at its worst is provided in the following article by Sue Branford, which appeared in a 1985 edition of *The Times*:

Sirens, similar to those used in Britain during the Second World War, are being installed in the town of Cubatao on the coast of Brazil to warn the population, not of an imminent air raid, but of a more insidious enemy – toxic chemicals and inflammable oil derivates.

Cubatao is a town of 100,000 about 35 miles from the industrial metropolis of Sao Paulo. Conveniently situated about eight miles from the port of Santos, Cubatao has taken on dirty servicing tasks for Brazil's industrial sector.

Using largely imported crude oil, it produces fertilizers, petrochemicals and oil derivates, as well as steel products.

This concentration has turned Cubatao into probably the most polluted city in the world.

Cubatao achieved temporary international notoriety in February 1984, when petrol leaked from one of the huge pipes taking oil derivatives over the mountain to Sao Paulo. The petrol went up in flames in the middle of the night, setting fire to a large shanty-town. An unknown number of people, possibly as many as 1,000, were killed.

Since the fire, there have been other leaks of toxic or inflammable products. The most serious, of ammonia, led to the evacuation in the middle of the night of another shanty town, perched outside the gates of one of the factories. It is hoped that the system of sirens, to be used with loudspeakers, will reduce the level of panic.

BRANFORD

Research and Discussion

One way of organising a discussion of such a wide-ranging issue as pollution is for individual students or small groups to choose an aspect of the subject on which to research, and report briefly to the rest of the group. Students who have studied geography and biology might well take a lead in this research.

Research might be useful on:

1. river pollution
2. lead pollution
3. noise pollution
4. insecticides and the ecological balance
5. nuclear waste and radiation

Discussion points

Do you think we should wait until a link between aerosols and destruction of the ozone layer, sulphur dioxide emissions and "acid rain" etc., has been *proved* before taking action?

If not, what specific actions would be suitable for overcoming the problems outlined here?

Do you know of any other cities in which pollution is particularly severe?

A research "potpourri"

As a way of developing conciseness and confidence in public speaking, each student might deliver a 2–5 minute prepared speech on a different one of the following topics:

> bilharzia (or schistosomiasis); Club of Rome; DDT; food chains; "greenhouse effect"; "Green Revolution"; kwashiorkor; "New Ice Age"; Strontium 90; World Wildlife Fund.

Attacking Pollution

Here is a five-point plan proposed by Gordon Rattray Taylor to deal with pollution in general, taken from *The Doomsday Book*:

First, [pollution] must be recognised as a world problem. Not just a worldwide problem, in the sense that every country should tackle its own pollution, but an international problem in the sense that the wastes of each country affect, or may affect, the climate and health of other countries or even the whole world . . . . An international organisation is needed . . . .

Second, it is essential to increase by many orders of magnitude the scale and scope of research into these problems . . . .

Thirdly, we need a decisive educational effort . . . . This does not mean a few vague lessons on ecology, but a planned attempt to give the student a sense of man's place in the scheme of things . . . .

Fourthly, there is the actual attack on pollution activities . . . . A much tauter structure for pollution control is needed.

Fifthly and finally, though one could lengthen the list, I put the need to reconsider far more thoroughly the setting of acceptable standards of purity, including freedom from radioactivity, for water, air and soil.

A glimpse of what might be possible was afforded when in July 1968 the *New York Times* published a paper by Andrei D Sakharov, the father of the Russian H-Bomb, entitled: "Progress, Co-existence and Intellectual Freedom". Departing entirely from the conventional attitude expected, he argued that civilisation is emperilled by the threat of nuclear war, famine, degenerating mass culture and "bureaucratic dogmatism" . . . . In such circumstances, he said, "Only universal co-operation . . . will preserve civilisation". He pinpointed the problem of hunger and over-population, proposing a 15-year tax equal to 20 per cent of national income on developed nations to help in stabilising the situation. The silence which greeted this suggestion could be heard round the world.

RATTRAY TAYLOR

Discussion points

How many of Gordon Rattray Taylor's proposals are achievable in the near future? What steps would be needed to achieve them?

What do you think of Andrei Sakharov's proposal?

Suggestion for debate

The following debate motion assumes that Chapters 3 and 4 are treated as a single topic:

> For the next decade, the rich nations should devote 20% of their Gross National Product to solving the problems of poverty and pollution in the Third World which they have helped to create.

Essay Titles

(a) "I have often heard it said that posterity must look after itself. I can think of no more callous viewpoint."

(b) "It is lack of confidence, more than anything else, that kills a civilisation. We can destroy ourselves by cynicism and disillusion just as effectively as by bombs."

(c) The importance of international co-operation.

(d) "Science solves problems and occasionally creates them." What do you consider is the major scientific problem today and how do you think it can be solved?

(e) The successes and failures of technology.

(f) How can we avoid an energy crisis?

(g) How far has science liberated man?

(h) Many people are concerned to protect our environment. Do you support the conservationists or do you think they overstate their case?

Bibliography

Books

Allen, Robert. *How to Save the World: Strategy for World Conservation*, Kogan Page, 1980
Bugler, Jeremy. *Polluting Britain: a report*, Penguin, 1972
Carson, Rachel. *Silent Spring*, Penguin, 1965
Chandler, William U. *Energy Productivity: Key to Environmental Protection and Economic Progress*, Worldwatch Institute, 1985
Commoner, Barry. *Science and Survival*, Viking Press, 1967
Elsworth, Steve. *Acid Rain*, Pluto Press, 1984
Mabey, Richard. *The Pollution Handbook: the ACE/ Sunday Times clean air and water surveys*, Penguin, 1974
Mellanby, Kenneth. *Pesticides and Pollution*, Collins, 1981
Price, Brian. *Friends of the Earth Guide to Pollution*, Maurice Temple Smith, 1983
Taylor, Gordon Rattray. *The Doomsday Book*, Panther, 1972

Periodicals

The Ecologist
New Internationalist

Audio-visual materials

Several commercial companies produce good videos, film-strips and tape-slide materials on the environmental crisis. Here are some companies from which catalogues can be obtained:

Audio-visual Productions,
Hocker Hill House
Chepstow
GWENT NP6 5ER

Diana Wyllie Ltd
1 Park Road
Baker Street
LONDON NW1 6XP

Concord Films Council
201 Felixstowe Road
Ipswich
SUFFOLK

Visual Publications
The Green
Northleach
CHELTENHAM GL54 3EX

Advice on Writing: Essay Writing – Use and Misuse of Information

Many students fare badly in the discussion essay through lack of ideas and information. The possession of an encyclopaedic knowledge of facts and factors relevant to a question, on the other hand, is no guarantee of success. You have still got to know how to use that information effectively to produce a well-structured, coherent and relevant essay.

One of the most ruinous pitfalls in language essay writing is, in fact, irrelevance. Though it is uncommon for post 'O' level students of English to miss the point of a question completely, there are nevertheless many snares into which you can fall – with possibly fatal consequences – while *seeming* to be answering the question.

Let us look at a question for which the material contained in Chapters 3 and 4 would be ideally suited, and see what can go wrong! Read through the following essay plan, and try to work out its failings as an embryonic answer to the question:

"The world will not live in harmony so long as two-thirds of its inhabitants find difficulty in living at all."

Paragraph 1 – Introduction:
  Living conditions in developed countries compared with those in Third World countries

Paragraph 2 – Poverty:
  "absolute poverty" in Third World
  unequal distribution of resources in Third World countries, e.g. Brazil
  imbalance in affluence between developed and developing countries

Paragraph 3 – Population explosion:
  causes: developments in medicine and lack of birth control
  effects: doubling of populations requiring doubling of resources
  description of situation in Calcutta to illustrate horrors of poverty and
    population explosion

Paragraph 4 – Effects of poverty and population explosion on
environment:
  deforestation
  spreading deserts and soil erosion
  overfishing and sea pollution

Paragraph 5 – Conclusion:
  Gap between rich and poor nations is widening. Adequate birth control
    policies and redistribution of resources in Third World countries
    needed if starvation and malnutrition not to increase further

All of this is relevant, *potentially*. But an essay based on this plan would
not score very high marks. The points outlined are simply not related
sufficiently closely to the question. Had the question been more general,
had it been worded, for instance: "While a third of the world's
population lives in comparative luxury, two thirds find difficulty in living
at all", the plan would have been perfectly adequate. The core of the
question, however, lies in the phrase about the world living "in
harmony", and unless the analysis of the global imbalance of wealth is
specifically related to this idea, the essay will merely skirt round the
central issue.

A useful exercise would be to try to relate this plan more closely to the
title, making any additions and alterations necessary, but retaining as
many of the points as possible. Alternatively, you could ignore the above
plan altogether, and write one of your own.

A still more damaging failing in language essay writing can spring from
the attempt to twist a question to fit material which you have learnt. An
ingenious student can often manage this successfully, but skill and
confidence are needed for such adaptation to be convincing.

A case in point might be the question about "the major scientific
problem today" in the list of essay titles. The "scientific problem"
treated could be pollution, and the entire essay could be successfully
based on it. The question "The successes and failures of technology", on
the other hand, demands broader treatment, and a too heavy
concentration on the issue of pollution would result in a seriously
unbalanced essay.

The worst extreme of this type of failing is the attempt to use learnt
material to answer a question for which it is simply unsuitable. To take an
instance: the question reads "Liberty must be limited in order to be
possessed". A student who was absolutely determined to write about the
global crises might just about manage to work the essay round to this
issue. But it would require some very skilful jugglery, and the result would

probably seem rather forced. Just as a brain-teaser, you might try to see if it could be done.

The question was obviously designed to provoke discussions of the need for law and order, or of the dangers of anarchy, or of the degree to which the curtailment of individual liberty is justified in a state or an institution, or alternatively as the title of a story. An attempt, for instance, to show how two-thirds of the world live in such poverty and misery that the concept of "liberty" is meaningless to them, followed by a discussion of what should be done to alleviate world poverty, *without* attempting to discuss the question of the curtailment of the liberty of those for whom the word *does* have meaning, would be considered largely irrelevant, and would fail.

One final point, while on the topic of irrelevance. Though rare at a more advanced level, total misreading of the question can happen. In the nerve-wracking conditions of an examination, it is possible for the most capable student to read a question wrongly. It would only require an anxious brain to register the word "problems" for "problem" in the question on science referred to above, for an answer to be rendered totally irrelevant. A "mercy" mark would be awarded, if this happened, but it would be nowhere near enough to pass! Careful reading of the question, careful thought about its implications, and frequent re-reading of the question in the light of what you are writing are essential, if you want to avoid falling into the most maddening and wasteful trap of all.

5

Education

What is education for? At the time when Forster's Education Act introduced universal education to Britain in 1870 the answer was simple. The act was a response to the requirements of an increasingly industrialised society for an educated workforce. No such certainty about the purposes of education exists today. The nurturing of interests and aptitudes for life and leisure, as well as for employment; the development of social and personal awareness; the goal of social cohesion: all these take their place beside the original concentration on literacy, numeracy and skill learning, in the thinking of modern educationalists.

The chapter begins with a comprehension passage reflecting doubts which were beginning to be expressed early in the century about the goals and methods of British education, and the discussion passages which follow explore the aims, methods and institutions of Western education from a variety of modern viewpoints.

Comprehension

Read the following passage, and answer the questions which follow it. You are advised to spend about one hour on this exercise.

Authority in education is to some extent unavoidable, and those who educate have to find a way of exercising authority in accordance with the spirit of liberty.

Where authority is unavoidable, what is needed is reverence. A man who is
5 to educate really well, and is to make the young grow and develop into their full stature, must be filled through and through with the spirit of reverence. It is reverence towards others that is lacking in those who advocate machine-made cast-iron systems: militarism, capitalism, Fabian scientific organization, and all the other prisons into which reformers and reaction-
10 aries try to force the human spirit. In education, with its codes of rules emanating from a Government office, its large classes and fixed curriculum and overworked teachers, its determination to produce a dead level of glib mediocrity, the lack of reverence for the child is all but universal. Reverence requires imagination and vital warmth; it requires most imagination in
15 respect of those who have least actual achievement or power. The child is weak and superficially foolish, the teacher is strong, and in an every-day sense wiser than the child. The teacher without reverence, or the bureaucrat without reverence, easily despises the child for these outward inferiorities. He thinks it is his duty to "mould" the child: in imagination he is the potter

20 with the clay. And so he gives to the child some unnatural shape, which hardens with age, producing strains and spiritual dissatisfactions, out of which grow cruelty and envy, and the belief that others must be compelled to undergo the same distortions.

The man who has reverence will not think it is his duty to "mould" the
25 young. He feels in all that lives, but especially in human beings, and most of all in children, something sacred, indefinable, unlimited, something individual and strangely precious, the growing principle of life, an embodied fragment of the dumb striving of the world. In the presence of a child he feels an unaccountable humility — a humility not easily defensible on any rational
30 ground, and yet somehow nearer to wisdom than the easy self-confidence of many parents and teachers. The outward helplessness of the child and the appeal of dependence make him conscious of the responsibility of a trust. His imagination shows him what the child may become, for good or evil, how its impulses may be developed or thwarted, how its hopes must be
35 dimmed and the life in it grow less living, how its trust will be bruised and its quick desires replaced by brooding will. All this gives him a longing to help the child in its own battle; he would equip and strengthen it, not for some outside end proposed by the State or by any other impersonal authority, but for the ends which the child's own spirit is obscurely seeking. The man who
40 feels this can wield the authority of an educator without infringing the principle of liberty.

It is not in a spirit of reverence that education is conducted by States and Churches and the great institutions that are subservient to them. What is considered in education is hardly ever the boy or girl, the young man or
45 young woman, but almost always, in some form, the maintenance of the existing order. When the individual is considered, it is almost exclusively with a view to worldly success — making money or achieving a good position. To be ordinary and to acquire the art of getting on, is the ideal which is set before the youthful mind, except by a few rare teachers who have
50 enough energy of belief to break through the system within which they are expected to work. Almost all education has a political motive: it aims at strengthening some group, national or religious or even social, in the competition with other groups. It is this motive, in the main, which determines the subjects taught, the knowledge offered and the knowledge withheld, and
55 also decides what mental habits the pupils are expected to acquire. Hardly anything is done to foster the inward growth of mind and spirit; in fact, those who have had most education are very often atrophied in their mental and spiritual life, devoid of impulse, and possessing only certain mechanical aptitudes which take the place of living thought.

BERTRAND RUSSELL (1916)

Note: Your answers should be *in your own words* as far as possible.

(*a*) Explain in your own words what the author means by his use of the word "reverence" in the passage.   (8 *marks*)

(*b*) Explain the author's use of the terms "machine-made cast-iron systems" and "prisons".   (3 *marks*)

(c) Explain the metaphor of the potter, as used in the passage. (4 *marks*)

(d) What do you think the author means by "an embodied fragment of the dumb striving of the world"?   (2 *marks*)

(e) What, according to the writer, are the main concerns of the majority of educators?   (5 *marks*)

(f) Convey the meaning of the final sentence in your own words.

(4 *marks*)

(g) Give the meaning of the following phrases as they appear in the passage:
   (i)   "the spirit of liberty" (line 3);
   (ii)   "reformers and reactionaries" (lines 9 – 10);
   (iii) "a dead level of glib mediocrity" (lines 12 – 13);
   (iv)   "brooding will" (line 36).   (8 *marks*)

(h) Discuss the extent to which you consider the author's comments on education to be still valid today.   (6 *marks*)

(*Total:* 40 *marks*)

The Views of Students

The reflections of a large number of students in British schools on different aspects of their education were collected by Edward Blishen and published in 1969 in a book called *The School That I'd like*. Here are some extracts:

Three cheers for the GCE and this product of the examination system: a stuffed puppet, reeling off facts and dates and predigested ideas, at the pull of a string, wondering if it was worth it and if this really is intelligence.

Boredom. Twenty-eight pairs of vacant eyes regarding with a hollow stare the woman at the front of the room who does the churning. Twenty-eight minds too apathetic to think, and twenty-eight bodies, too lethargic to do anything except scrawl over desks and carve names, with infinite care, on the lids.

This is education. This is the way in which a child's enthusiasm for learning is quelled to a point of non-existence. Is it surprising that so many escape after 'O' level, the climax of the whole ludicrous system?

ELIZABETH, 16

Teachers and pupils are bogged down, from thirteen and fourteen onwards, in the heavy mire of accumulation of often undigested and unrelated knowledge which can be spewed out as a turgid mark-gaining mess during the examination. The whole school week becomes geared to the GCE and all extra-curricular activities are forced to prostrate themselves in front of this almighty God.

This, surely, is not our ideal British education?

KENNETH, 17

In secondary education today the emphasis is on passing 'O' and 'A' levels. Half-educated children emerge from school clutching their exam certificates, having been filled to capacity with information about T S Eliot and Plato. They believe themselves to be "educated". To some extent they are, I suppose. But are they better equipped to understand and live with their fellow human beings? Moreover, has their education encouraged them to think creatively and originally? Isn't this what education should be about?

ANTHONY, 18

But what is the main purpose of schools — to educate young people so that when they go out into the world they will be prepared for it? But are they? We learn our mathematics, English, physics, etc., but what do we learn about sex, marriage and things like this? These are just as important, but we don't learn very much about them.

DAVID, 15

We ought to be taught the meaning of local government and how elections work. We should be told of the difference between the different parties, and the people they represent. We should also be taught about other countries' politics and have discussions on which is the best method used to govern the countries.

RUTH, 13

I hope that all the schools of tomorrow will primarily have much more freedom and variety than those of today. By freedom I mean much more time to work individually on subjects or aspects of subjects the people find interesting; and by variety I mean more flexibility in the weekly programme of lessons.

GILLIAN, 14

Themes for Discussion

What is your view of the British public examination system? Do you think that 'A' level courses are an effective way of developing specialist knowledge and interest?

Do you think your education has encouraged you "to think creatively and originally"? Which aspects of your education have been the most creative and stimulating?

Do you think your education has taught you to think sufficiently about adult life? Is it important "to learn about sex, marriage and things like this" at school?

Do you feel that you should have learnt more about politics and current affairs at school. Is it right for teachers to deal with controversial political issues in the classroom?

What changes would you have liked to see in the curriculum of your secondary education?

Teaching and Learning: Purposes and Methods

Guidelines for the future of secondary education in Britain were set out in
The Newsom Report: Half Our Future, published in 1963. Here is a key
passage from this seminal government report:

Skills, qualities of character, knowledge, physical well-being are all to be
desired. Boys and girls need to be helped to develop certain skills of communication in speech and in writing, in reading with understanding, and in
calculations involving numbers and measurement. These skills are basic, in
that they are tools to other learning, and without some mastery of them the
pupils will be cut off from whole areas of human thought and experience.
But they do not by themselves represent an adequate minimum education at
which to aim.

All boys and girls need to develop, as well as skills, capacities for thought,
judgement, enjoyment, curiosity. They need to develop a sense of responsibility for their work and towards other people, and to begin to arrive at
some code of moral and social behaviour which is self-imposed. It is important that they should have some understanding of the physical world and of
the human society in which they are growing up.

Since Newsom a bewildering variety of views have been expressed as to
how these objectives can be attained, and even as to the possibility of
attaining them within the limitations of the normal classroom. The four
extracts which follow reflect the spectrum of opinion.

The first two passages can be said broadly to represent the more
"traditional" viewpoint. Both appeared in *The Black Papers on
Education*, edited by C B Cox and A E Dyson. The latter two sets of
extracts represent more 'progressive" educational thinking. They are
taken from books by Americans: the psychologist, Dr Benjamin Spock,
and the educationalist, John Holt.

1.
The importance of discipline

No one would wish to return to the days when junior school children were
rigidly confined to their rows of desks and learnt long lists of largely
unrelated facts. But what is happening now? The restrictions of the old 11 +
have almost disappeared, but the resulting freedom has been used in a multiplicity of ways. The children moving on to secondary schools present a
bewildering problem even among the brightest groups.

Some at eleven can write fluently and imaginatively, paying due attention to
paragraphing, punctuation and spelling with none of their enthusiasm
dampened. Others, of comparable intelligence, write illegibly, have no idea
of arrangement of work and are thoroughly frustrated.

According to some present day psychologists, all teaching of young
children must be child-centred: the teaching must grow from the child's
interests and not be limited by any time-table division. Freedom of

expression is all important and the method of conveying it is relatively unimportant. So far so good, but at what point should the child learn that correctness and accuracy have their place? All may be well at the junior school stage, but the freedom of the look and say method of teaching, of the outpouring of ideas without arrangement or plan has disastrous results at a later stage. For instance, when learning a foreign language, one incorrect letter may well alter the whole meaning of a sentence.

Some of my friends in junior schools tell me that marking and correcting is a thing of the past as it may bring a sense of failure to a child. So one sees mistakes becoming firmly implanted in the child's mind. Many schools arrange projects for their children and some begin through this to learn the excitement of independent research and the joy of exploring in the library. Others undertake the work but do little more than copy passages from the encyclopaedia and stick cut out pictures in their books.

It is interesting to find that the children who, by the age of eleven, have mastered the skills of the three R's have gained a freedom which enables them to extend their horizons without the frustrations felt by those who at this stage realise the limitations imposed on them by the lack of disciplined thought . . . .

Attitudes and behaviour in the country as a whole, of course, exert great pressure on our young people, but the schools must take a share of the blame. At the very heart of the problem is the need for self-discipline, for freedom within certain defined limits, for the security resulting from a realisation of cause and effect, from having certain decisions imposed and being able to enjoy the peace and security that comes from an ordered life.

The world is a noisy, chaotic and restless place, yet in schools we see the same lack of quiet encouraged. It is putting a great strain on young children to leave them constantly to make decisions with rarely any time in the day when they are quiet and listening. This feeling was expressed in a delightfully naive manner by a little 11-year-old, beginning life in an ordered secondary school, who said she liked her new school because discipline was allowed.

A child who has always followed his own inclination finds it hard to sit down and learn his French and Latin verbs or his tables and yet, this knowledge acquired, he has the freedom to make rapid progress towards the exciting discoveries awaiting him at a more advanced stage. How comforting it is to know that, whatever distress there may be among the nations, two and two still make four.

The child who has been free to wander in his junior school much as he pleases, fails to see at a later stage why he should not wander further afield. Many children who come before juvenile courts have committed their offences during school hours, although the truancy is rarely known at the school. The boy has been present for registration and then has disappeared . . . .

Many of my colleagues who are working in secondary schools would agree that the children who are the most well-balanced and who make the steadiest progress, are those who come from the junior schools where the children have had plenty of opportunity for independent, free study, but who have learnt the importance of listening and concentrating and who have found the satisfaction which comes from doing something, at whatever standard, really well.

It is generally accepted that the home is the strongest influence on a child's development so the child from the inadequate home, more than any other, needs security, an ordered school-life, sensible discipline and quiet.

C M JOHNSON

2.
Discovery methods

Children manifest wide differences in developmental sophistication; some barely ever emerge from the stage of concrete operations; others enter on the stage of formal operations (implying the ability to handle certain sorts of abstractions) at a remarkably early age. It is these very bright children who often show considerable boredom with the leisurely informal pace of discovery methods – who yearn in fact to be told the answers to the questions they are asking because the answers will enable them to rush on to the next step in their eager intellectual enquiry. If discovery methods are used with these, they should be of the much more tightly structured type that Socrates used with the slave boy, when he led him from stage to stage by carefully framed questions; and indeed, the Socratic question is one of the best techniques by which a teacher can enable a child to make a discovery on his own; but, of course, it needs to be a very precise question, put by a teacher who knows exactly where he is going.

Discovery methods constitute an important but limited addition to the vocabulary of teaching. They are probably particularly useful for arousing interest – their function as motivators should not be underestimated; and with a child population many of whom are uninterested in school, this is not a factor to be despised. Furthermore, they can introduce children to a range of possibilities well beyond that of the old formal methods – they can make the world seem a more interesting place. Again, they help children to learn how to learn, without always having a teacher standing over them demanding a set piece in a set time. Children learn to rely on their own initiative to find out things, look up in books, etc.

But this enthusiastic picture needs to be curbed by a careful and thorough understanding on the part of the teachers as to exactly what they are aiming to accomplish, otherwise all the children acquire are a set of bits and pieces, orts and greasy relics, soon forgotten if ever really appreciated. The essence of their successful usage lies in their taking their place in a definite pedagogic scheme designed to aid initiation into complex learning structures which the teacher should have at his full command. To put it bluntly, he must work out for himself where he is going. He may find that "discovery" methods possibly work best in subjects the basis of which is empirical (like the sciences, in their early stages) or whose development is logical (like mathematics). He must know that "discovery" can and should be made from books – but that their use needs careful practice and a trained ability to glean relevant material from their contents. He should realise that in some subjects – such as literature – the main emphasis will still remain on his own personal charisma − on his ability to read well and feelingly in a class situation, for instance; and indeed that his power to excite interest and attention will always be fundamental. He will need to remember that instruction and planned repetitive work will still have vital roles to play, so that processes can be thoroughly explained, grasped and internalised by practice. He will even on occasions find that rote learning has a part to play − in the learning of spellings and tables, for instance. The point is that "discovery methods" need to be collated with carefully presented and meaningful but quite formal instructions; and that the effectiveness of the Socratic question depends on his pedagogic skill and not on some spontaneous inner ripening on the part of the child.

There is, in fact, no one way. Subject matter differs enormously in nature and demands quite different sorts of pedagogic devices for its efficient transmission. And effective learning is the most important function of the school − it is the only institution in our society explicitly set up for such a purpose, and if it is not accomplished there it will not be accomplished anywhere else. Used competently, with an awareness of their place in the general armoury of tools at the teachers' disposal, these new (not so new, as we have seen) methods have a great deal to offer. Used incompetently, as a gimmick or a fashion, they are probably more disastrous to learning than an exclusive reliance on the old formal methods.

G M BANTOCK

3.
What a school is for

The main lesson in school is how to get along in the world. Different subjects are merely means to this end. In the olden days, it used to be thought that all a school had to do was make children learn to read, write, add up and memorise a certain number of facts about the world. You learn only when things mean something to you. One job of a school is to make subjects so interesting and real that the children want to learn and remember.

You can go only so far with books and talk. You learn better from actually living the things you are studying. Children pick up more arithmetic in a week from running a school shop, giving change, and keeping the books than they learn in a month out of a book of cold figures.

It's no use knowing a lot if you can't be happy, can't get along with people, can't hold the kind of job you want. The good teacher tries to understand each child in order to help each pupil overcome weak points and develop into a well-rounded person. The child who lacks self-confidence needs chances to succeed. The trouble-making show-off has to learn how to gain the recognition he craves through doing good work. The child who doesn't know how to make friends needs help in becoming sociable and appealing. The child who seems to be lazy has to have her or his enthusiasm discovered.

A school can go only so far with a cut-and-dried programme in which everyone in the class reads from page 17 to page 23 in the reader at the same time and then does the examples on page 128 of the arithmetic book. It works well enough for the average child who is adjusted anyway. But it's too dull for the bright pupils, too speedy for the slow ones. It gives the boy who hates books a chance to stick paper clips in the pigtails of the girl in front. It does nothing to help the girl who is lonely or the boy who needs to learn co-operation.

How school work is made real and interesting

If you start with a topic that is real and interesting, you can use it to teach all manner of subjects. Take the case of a class in which the work of the year revolves around Indians.[1] The more the children find out about Indians, the more they want to know. The reader is a story of the Indians, and they really want to know what it says. For arithmetic they study how the Indians counted and what they used for money. Then arithmetic isn't a separate subject at all but a useful part of life. Geography isn't spots on a map, it's where the Indians lived and travelled and how life on the plains is different from forest life. In science study the children make dyes from berries and dye cloth, or grow corn. They can make bows and arrows and Indian costumes.

The "open classroom" means that several activities are going on at the same time in a classroom and that each child is free to participate in the one which appeals most at that time. This philosophy may seem much too permissive to be effective, to parents accustomed to the traditional classroom. But the method has been used extensively in Britain and the United States and it produces highly satisfactory results in the hands of competent teachers. Classroom order can be maintained. Each child gets round to all the necessary subjects in time and makes good progress. The great advantage is that the children, instead of developing the attitude we all developed – of waiting for the teacher to tell them what to do and how – take the initiative in learning, go at their own pace, keep a positive sense of discovery and joy about it, and seek individual help from the teacher as they need it.

The teachers in a good school know well that every child needs to develop self-discipline to be a useful adult. But they have learned that you can't snap discipline on to children from the outside, like handcuffs; it's something that children have to develop inside, like a backbone, by first understanding the purpose of their work and feeling a sense of responsibility to others in how they perform it.

How a school helps a difficult child

A flexible interesting programme does more than just make school work appealing. It can be adjusted for the individual pupil. Take the case of a girl who had spent her first two years in a school where teaching was done by separate subjects. She was a girl who had great difficulty in learning to read and write. She had fallen behind the rest of the class. Inside, she felt ashamed about being a failure. Outwardly she wouldn't admit anything except that

1. North American Indians. The project outlined here is designed for American school pupils.

she hated school. She had never got on too easily with other children anyway, even before her school troubles began. Feeling that she was a duffer in the eyes of the others made matters worse. She had a chip on her shoulder. Once in a while she would show off to the class like a smart-alec. Her teacher used to think that she was just trying to be bad. Of course, she was really attempting, in this unfortunate way, to gain some kind of attention from the group. It was a healthy impulse to keep herself from being shut out.

She transferred to a school that was interested in helping her not only to read and write but to find her place in the group. The teacher learned in a conference with her mother that she used tools well and loved to paint and draw. He saw ways to use her strong points in the class. The children were all painting together a large picture of Indian life to hang on the wall. They were also working co-operatively on a model of an Indian village. The teacher arranged for the girl to have a part in both these jobs. Here were things she could do well without nervousness. As the days went by, she became more and more fascinated with Indians. In order to paint her part of the picture well, in order to make her part of the model correctly, she needed to find out more from the books about Indians. She wanted to learn to read. She tried harder. Her new classmates didn't think of her as a dope because she couldn't read. They thought more about what a help she was on the painting and the model. They occasionally commented on how good her work was and asked her to help them on their parts. She began to warm up. After all, she had been aching for recognition and friendliness for a long while. As she felt more accepted, she became more friendly and sociable.

Linking school with the world

A school wants its pupils to learn at first hand about the outside world, about the jobs of the local farmers and businessmen and workers, so that they will see the connection between their school work and real life. It arranges trips to near-by industries, asks people from the outside to come in and talk, encourages classroom discussion.

DR BENJAMIN SPOCK

4.
The importance of active involvement

Sit still! Be quiet! These are the great watchwords of school. If an enemy spy from outer space were planning to take over the earth, and if his strategy were to prepare mankind for this takeover by making men's children as stupid as possible, he could find no better way to do it than to require them, for many hours a day, to be still and quiet. It is absolutely guaranteed to work. Children live all of a piece. Their bodies, their muscles, their voices, and their brains are all hooked together. Turn off a part of them, and you turn them off altogether . . . .

A child is most intelligent when the reality before him arouses in him a high degree of attention, interest, concentration, involvement − in short, when he cares most about what he is doing. This is why we should make schoolrooms and schoolwork as interesting and exciting as possible, not just so that school will be a pleasant place, but so that children in school will act intelligently and get into *the habit* of acting intelligently. The case against boredom in school is the same as the case against fear; it makes children behave stupidly, some on purpose, most because they cannot help it. If this goes on long enough, as it does in school, they forget what it is like to grasp at something, as they once grasped at everything, with all their minds and senses.

The child who wants to know something remembers it and uses it once he has it, the child who learns something to please or appease someone else forgets it when the need for pleasing or the danger of not appeasing is past. This is why children quickly forget all but a small part of what they learn in school. It is of no use or direct interest to them; they do not want, or expect, or even intend to remember it. The only difference between bad and good students in this respect is that the bad students forget right away, while the good students are careful to wait until after the exam. If for no other reason, we could well afford to throw out most of what we teach in school because the children throw out almost all of it anyway . . . .

The alternative − I can see no other − is to have schools and classrooms in which each child in his own way can satisfy his curiosity, develop his abilities and talents, pursue his interests, and from the adults and other children around him get a glimpse of the great variety and richness of life. In short, the school should be a great smorgasbord of intellectual, artistic, creative, and athletic activities, from which each child could take whatever he wanted, and as much as he wanted, or as little.

About the future of work, two things seem clear. There is likely to be less and less of it; what there is, is likely to seem less and less like work . . . . Men will tend more and more complicated machines; the proof that the job is going right will be that nothing is happening; only on the rare occasion when something goes wrong will they have something to do; usually it will be someone else's job to make sure that something doesn't go wrong again . . . .

If so, more and more people will face two problems: how to justify, make meaningful their own lives, and how to fill up their time. The answer in both cases is to do something that seems very much worth doing. An important part of the business of education will be the finding of that something. Schools, therefore, will be places where children − and adults − may have time and opportunity to *do* a great many things, so as to find out which seem most worth doing. I emphasise the *do*. Very little of a child's time in school today is spent in *doing* anything; most of the time he is, or is supposed to be, either taking in information or, to prove that he has taken it in, spewing it back out. Sprinkled around here and there may be a tiny bit of art, or crafts, or sport, or drama, or music, or dance, but very few children are given enough time, *in school*, to work seriously on any of these things. If they do work seriously on them, it is outside of school, and their parents usually have to pay . . . . Thus we have a huge vacuum in the minds and spirits of most children, and create a splendid market for mass entertainers and sensation peddlers of all kinds. The kinds of serious extracurricular interest that now occupy, and fill, and make worth living, the lives of a minority of people, will have to be found and enjoyed by all.

JOHN HOLT

Themes for Discussion

Do you agree with Johnson that learning is best carried out in an environment of order and strict discipline and comparative silence, or do you agree with Holt that enforced silence is counter-productive, and that children learn best when allowed to talk and move around the classroom?

What is meant by "child-centred" education? What do you think is the most common result of it: to promote selfishness and lack of self-discipline, as Johnson claims, or to promote happiness, self-confidence and co-operation, as Spock suggests?

Bantock claims that project-style "discovery methods" of learning generally result in students picking up "bits and pieces" of knowledge which are "soon forgotten"; Holt claims that formal class teaching, in which the class spends a good proportion of its time listening to and undertaking tasks imposed by the teacher, results in children quickly forgetting all but "a small part of what they learn in school". Which style of teaching have you found more valuable?

Do you agree with Bantock that "discovery methods" work best in conjunction with structured learning such as "the trained ability to glean relevant material" from books?

Can you see any advantages in the kind of "open classroom" approach advocated by Spock, in which the teacher becomes an adviser, and where a significant proportion of the time is spent outside the classroom itself?

Do you agree with Holt's scenario of the future of employment? How, and to what extent, should schools concentrate on "education for leisure"?

Theory into Practice: Three Schools

The extracts which follow are taken from three books in which quite different schools are described in detail. One or the other of the first two schools described will probably seem familiar to you, since they are chosen to represent the principal alternative styles of state secondary schooling in Britain in the 1980s. This fact is likely to make balanced assessment of the merits of the rival systems difficult for you, since most people tend automatically to support the type of school they themselves went to (or in some cases to react violently against it!) Nevertheless the discussion-points which follow are designed to make you think about some of the major issues concerning schooling in Britain, and you should try to be objective, while of course drawing on your personal experience.

The description of Highbury Grove School is written by its former

Headmaster, Dr Rhodes Boyson, and is taken from an essay entitled
"Civilised Authority", which appeared in an educational anthology called
A Question of Schooling, edited by John E C MacBeath, published in
1976. The school is fully described in Dr Boyson's own book
Oversubscribed: The Story of Highbury Grove.

Creighton School is described in a series of extracts from a book on the
school called *The Creighton Report: A Year in the Life of a
Comprehensive School*, also published in 1976, by the teacher-turned-
journalist, Hunter Davies, who spent a year teaching in the school to
provide him with the material for his book. Let us look at these two
schools first.

Highbury Grove School

The School
Highbury Grove was a single-sex Comprehensive school in North London,
which had 1400 boys at the time of writing. The essential features were:
banding of pupils on the basis of examinations, a closed sixth, the house
system, partial pupil control over subject choice, corporal punishment and
sixth form involvement in discipline, school prizes, regular school
assemblies, and emphasis on competition.

The Theory
My view is that man came into society for security. Outside, to quote
Thomas Hobbes, life is "solitary, poor, nasty, brutish and short". This
society, especially where it has liberal and civilised values, has to be
protected . . . . Neither civilisation, nor learning which is its flowering, is
natural and spontaneous, but arises from nurture, carefully analysed respect
for the past and controlled discipline . . . .

I also do not believe that man is perfectible in this life. He carries,
however, the primitive genes of struggle and pride and competition with
him.

School is a preparation for life, not life itself. Those headteachers and
teachers who are either not at home in the real world outside or in revolt
against it will do little good with children, most of whom are only waiting to
enter the real adult world.

The Practice
I thus saw Highbury Grove when I opened it in 1967 as both a traditional and
a meritocratic school . . . .

I believed that Highbury Grove should offer an academic education within
a cheerful but a strictly disciplined framework to every one of its 1400 boys. I
also believed that it was the duty of every teacher to teach and not to be an
elder brother. All teachers were appointed to departments under the firm
control of the heads of departments, who were responsible for the syllabus,
the discipline and the curriculum of the department. Every year I would
analyse the external examination results of all departments and these would

be available to all staff, and also to parents and boys who wished to see them. This was the discipline of external accountability, for we were dealing with the future life chances of boys in a none too prosperous area.

The boys were divided into three bands or streams at the age of eleven. There were three A bands, three B bands and two C bands. The division was made purely on academic ability. All A bands in a year went to a subject at the same time; all B bands went together; and all C bands went together, so that each department could further divide pupils according to their academic ability if they so wished. I did insist, however, on a common syllabus with the same number of lessons in each subject over the whole year group. This meant that pupils could easily move bands at the termly or half-yearly examinations. The syllabus in each subject was, however, taught at different depths in each band since the A bands could move easily to a more intellectual approach. Nonetheless, some 17 per cent of pupils were moved to a different band in a typical three-year course from eleven to fourteen. There was thus considerable mobility.

Some departments wished to non-stream or non-band their pupils. I agreed provided their external examination results at the end of the fifth year did not suffer.

In the fourth and fifth years, however, the boys had all to take English and mathematics while they chose a minimum of five additional subjects. These subjects were chosen by the boys after consultation with their parents, house masters and the careers masters . . . . We did not expect all boys to be equally able but we had faith that every boy, even the most backward, would achieve something worthwhile. To let academically gifted boys sit examinations which are useful to their future while denying the right of less able boys to sit at least some external examinations is to play a confidence trick upon them.

Motivation is a great help to study, and up to the raising of the school-leaving age in 1973 we always let it be known that staying on at school into the fifth year was a privilege which had to be earned and that boys would be removed if they did not do their best or if they created disciplinary problems. It is of interest that the external fifth-year results in 1974 were considerably down on the previous years, because with the raising of the minimum school leaving age there were boys who did not want to be in school who poisoned the whole atmosphere of the fifth.

We similarly made entry into the sixth form dependent upon academic merit and a good general attitude. The sixth form, like the school, should not be a waiting room for life but a place of intense study and concentration. Boys whose performance fell below this aim were removed and their absence was seen to increase the stimulus of other pupils.

The structure of the school was clear to staff and boys. I took all school assemblies three times a week. Assembly was a time for morale raising, and I tried every day to have some piece of information which would bring delight and self-congratulation to the school. I was flanked by my deputy heads; the house captains and vice captains sat alongside; the staff stood on one side of the hall; the tutor prefects on the other; and the boys in their tutor groups were in lines. The structure was clear. Assembly was for a hymn, a prayer, a reading, uplift announcements — and then away. I also held back houses with their tutor prefects and tutor masters to inspect the boys' uniform and to make sure that all boys and staff were on their toes.

The boys were under six housemasters and a sixth-form master. Each housemaster was completely responsible for his 200-plus boys and only taught half the week so that he had time to prepare his work properly. Once a week boys had assembly in houses, where they also ate daily and where all leisure and evening activities were centred.

Sports also played a great part. I believe that boys are competitive creatures. We would field up to eight soccer teams on a Saturday and they knew that it was their task not just to play good football but to win. We also competed in cricket, running, swimming, life-saving, rowing, gymnastics and indeed almost every sport, and the teams and results were read out in assembly. Whenever possible I supported and cheered the teams, and parents always attended in large numbers.

Prizes and certificates were given for 100 per cent attendance over a year while housemasters chased up the non-attenders. Boys were always splendidly turned out. The sixth-formers regularly asked for more duties and more involvement in the school; nor were concessions made to them on uniform or smoking. It was a tight, cheerful ship.

Discipline was enforced by the heads of department and the housemasters. Parents were involved in all serious cases, corporal punishment was given and about once a year a boy was suspended.

What did we give the boys? We gave them self-confidence which came from growing up in a secure structure where the rules were known and kept and yet where a boy could go for help when he needed it.

We prepared boys for life as it is: competitive and cheerful and sometimes cruel.

DR RHODES BOYSON

Xreighton School

The School
Creighton was a mixed Comprehensive School, also in North London, with 1500 pupils. The essential features were: mixed-ability teaching in the first three years, an open sixth, the year system, the option system of subject choice, no corporal punishment, no prizes, school councils, pastoral care, and emphasis on co-operation rather than competition.

The Theory
At a general meeting, the headmistress was asked about competition "which in many schools was felt socially desirable, but seemed to be frowned on at Creighton".

"We're in the business of avoiding labelling children," said [the Head-mistress], "of avoiding distinctions. We're trying to avoid children saying, 'I'm better than you and I've just proved it.' We want them to be able to say, 'I'm better than I was before and I've just proved it'."

"Competition can't be avoided of course. We all live in a competitive society . . . But while children are at school, we want to minimise the competition. The sixth form at the moment have only one thing in their lives — what grades will I get? There should be another way of making them work hard, of encouraging them to enjoy working hard."

"Competition is all right if you win . . . . In fact, if you win, it's lovely . . . ."

Many of the staff agree that outside exams are a handicap to their teaching. [The Headmistress] herself is of this opinion.

"Every school has to work within the system. The system funds it and parents expect the system to produce the best results their children are capable of. We can and do work out alternative non-examination courses, but while there are 'O' and 'A' levels, there will be few takers."

"The exam system is only a device, a device to let people get on in the race. It's the race itself that's wrong . . . ."

"I personally would be in favour of ending outside exams and having internal assessment instead, if it could be done. It would be harder for the schools and would lead to disagreements with parents and pupils, but the onus would be on us to decide the best form of education. Too much of what we have to do at the moment is conditioned by the universities, who take only a small minority of the pupils. What happens is that we are forced to find a combination of idealism and the possible."

The Practice

Mixed ability teaching, which is possibly the most controversial aspect of comprehensive schooling, is a highly complicated issue . . . .

I noticed great variations at Creighton in the methods of teaching a mixed ability class. Some aim simply for the middle band, hoping those on either side will somehow pick it up. Some divide up their mixed class, giving each section slightly different work. Some, as I saw in History, try to keep them all together by preparing massive work sheets. Different teachers have different prejudices and different theories — and of course different subjects do very often require different methods. Most people admit that Maths and Foreign Languages can't really be taught in the same way as History . . . .

During their third year, all children are presented with sets of options to be taken in the fourth and fifth years. These options are so numerous that a process of natural selection takes place. The slow learners, or whatever euphemism one uses for the patently non-academic kids, are naturally not going to opt for German or French. There are twenty-six options in all, ranging from Child Development, Spanish, Sociology, Drama, Business Studies, Home Economics, to the more normal subjects like History, Geography. Up to now each child has studied twelve subjects. Now he or she studies seven subjects, two of which must be Maths and English (which continue to be in two sets), the other five subjects being chosen from the list of options.

In the option groups, the teachers are beginning to work out the likely 'O' level and CSE groups, though the children are not told . . . . Only at the final fence, when mock exams are taken and school work assessed, does the division take place . . . .

The members of Creighton's sixth form have several privileges which are denied to those in the first five years . . . . The prime facility is their own sixth form house [which] is always crowded at lunch time with people dancing or listening to loud rock music, as well as after and before school. Sixth formers have several free periods a week which lower forms don't have. Perhaps most surprisingly of all, if they have free periods they are allowed to spend them in the common room or leave the school. They can arrive at school and go home when they like, just as long as they fulfil their time-table obligations.

The sixth formers perform no school duties. They neither do dinner duty nor playground duty. There is nothing in fact that they have to do. But . . . the sixth form is forever organising voluntary workers − film shows for old people, parties for the first years, playgroups after school, primary school treats, collections for people in distress and lots of other good works.

The social class and academic attainments of comprehensive students can be measured and compared, even if the experts then argue about what the results mean. But there is one aspect of a comprehensive school that can't be measured − the quality of the young people it is producing. This will be my most impressive memory of Creighton. In their concern for tolerance, freedom, equality, fairness and democracy, they are unrecognisable from the pupils of my generation. They help the less fortunate. They try to do what they say they believe. I have no proof but I am sure they will make better citizens and strive to make the world a better place.

HUNTER DAVIES

Discussion points

In your "ideal school" how would you deal with such issues as these:

the question of streaming, setting or mixed ability classes;

the degree of pupils' control over which subjects they should study;

the relative merits of public examination and continuous assessment courses;

the degree of stress on academic competition, through school exams, prizes, competitive marks for classwork, etc.;

the importance of fostering integration between pupils of different academic ability and home background;

the importance of individual attention in the classroom, and pastoral care outside it;

the role of senior pupils in maintaining discipline;

the use of corporal punishment;

the wearing of school uniform;

the importance of regular school assemblies.

Summerhill

The third school chosen for consideration is an independent school. It is called Summerhill and is the most famous "progressive" school in Britain, founded and run for half a century by A S Neill, who wrote a number of books explaining his theories of education and their practical implementation. Here are some extracts from *Summerhill: A Radical Approach to Education*:

The School

Summerhill was founded in 1921. The school is situated within the village of Leiston, in Suffolk, and is about one hundred miles from London.

Just a word about Summerhill pupils. Some children come to Summerhill at the age of five years, and others as late as fifteen. The children generally remain at the school until they are sixteen years old. We generally have about twenty-five boys and twenty girls.

The Theory

Obviously, a school that makes active children sit at desks studying mostly useless subjects is a bad school. It is a good school only for those who believe in *such* a school, for those uncreative citizens who want docile, uncreative children who will fit into a civilisation whose standard of success is money . . . .

When my wife and I began the school, we had one main idea: *to make the school fit the child* – instead of making the child fit the school . . . .

Well, we set out to make a school in which we should allow children freedom to be themselves. In order to do this, we had to renounce all discipline, all direction, all suggestion, all moral training, all religious instruction. We have been called brave, but it did not require courage. All it required was what we had – a complete belief in the child as a good, not an evil, being. For almost forty years, this belief in the goodness of the child has never wavered; it rather has become a final faith.

My view is that a child is innately wise and realistic. If left to himself without adult suggestion of any kind, he will develop as far as he is capable of developing. Logically, Summerhill is a place in which people who have the innate ability and wish to be scholars will be scholars; while those who are only fit to sweep the streets will sweep the streets. But we have not produced a street cleaner so far. Nor do I write this snobbishly, for I would rather see a school produce a happy street cleaner than a neurotic scholar.

The Practice

What is Summerhill like? Well, for one thing, lessons are optional. Children can go to them or stay away from them – for years if they want to. There *is* a timetable, but only for the teachers.

The children have classes usually according to their age, but sometimes according to their interests. We have no new methods of teaching, because we do not consider that teaching in itself matters very much. Whether a school has or has not a special method for teaching long division is of no significance, for long division is of no importance except to those who *want* to learn it. And the child who *wants* to learn long division *will* learn it no matter how it is taught.

Children who come to Summerhill as kindergarteners attend lessons from the beginning of their stay; but pupils from other schools vow that they will never attend any beastly lessons again at any time. They play and cycle and get in people's way, but they fight shy of lessons. This sometimes goes on for months. The recovery time is proportionate to the hatred their last school gave them. Our record case was a girl from a convent. She loafed for three years. The average period of recovery from lesson aversion is three months . . . .

In Summerhill, everyone has equal rights. No one is allowed to walk on my grand piano, and I am not allowed to borrow a boy's cycle without his permission. At a General School Meeting, the vote of a child of six counts for as much as my vote does.

But, says the knowing one, in practice the voices of grownups count. Doesn't the child of six wait to see how you vote before he raises his hand? I wish he sometimes would, for too many of my proposals are beaten. Free children are not easily influenced; the absence of fear accounts for this phenomenon. Indeed, the absence of fear is the finest thing that can happen to a child . . . .

No pupil is compelled to attend lessons. But if Jimmy comes to English on Monday and does not make an appearance again until Friday of the following week, the others quite rightly object that he is holding back the work, and they may throw him out for impeding progress . . . .

Afternoons are completely free for everyone. What they all do in the afternoon I do not know. I garden, and seldom see youngsters about. I see the juniors playing gangsters. Some of the seniors busy themselves with motors and radios and drawing and painting. In good weather, seniors play games. Some tinker about in the workshop, mending their bicycles or making boats or revolvers.

Tea is served at four. At five various activities begin. The juniors like to be read to. The middle group like work in the Art room — painting, linoleum cuts, leather work, basket making. There is usually a busy group in the pottery; in fact, the pottery seems to be the favourite haunt morning and evening. The oldest group works from five onward. The wood and metal workshop is full every night . . . .

Saturday night is our most important one, for it is General School Meeting night.

Some Objections

Summerhill has always had a bit of struggle to keep going. Few parents have the patience and faith to send their children to a school in which the youngsters can play as an alternative to learning . . . .

Summerhill pupils are mostly children whose parents want them to be brought up without restrictive descipline . . . . But we have never been able to take the children of the very poor. That is a pity, for we have had to confine our study to only the children of the middle class . . . .

An American visitor, a professor of psychology, criticised our school on the grounds that it is an island, that it is not fitting into a community, and that it is not part of a larger social unit. My answer is this: if I were to found a school in a small town, attempting to make it a part of the community, what would happen? Out of a hundred parents, what percentage would approve of free choice in attending lessons? How many would approve of a child's right to masturbate?

From the word go, I should have to compromise with what I believe to be the truth.

A S NEILL

Further discussion

How do you think you would have coped with ten years at Summerhill?

Do you think that the extremes to which A S Neill took his ideas of non-coercion and democracy, and of the innate wisdom of children freed from adult pressure, would be likely to have helped your academic and personal development?

Do you think it is desirable or possible for a state school to concentrate, as Summerhill does, on the individual happiness and creativity of the pupils?

Questionnaire

A questionnaire on education might be an interesting project for a few students to undertake. The questionnaire could be prepared and analysed, and a report on it written and printed for the rest of the class to discuss and evaluate, along the guidelines explained on pages 76 – 77.

Here are a few possible questions for inclusion in a questionnaire:

1. What are the most important purposes of education:
   (*i*)   to develop interests for later life;
   (*ii*) to prepare for public examinations;
   (*iii*) to develop skills which will be useful in later life;
   (*iv*) to develop imagination and creativity?
   (List in order of importance).

2. Which school subject do you find
   (*i*) the most interesting;
   (*ii*) the least interesting? Say why.

3. Do you think that discipline should be more, or less, strict in the school you attend(ed)? Say in what way.

4. Do you think that homework is useful or not?
   Do you think you should get more, the same amount, or less homework than you do?

(Some of the questions on page 72 could also be framed for inclusion in the questionnaire.)

Essay Titles

(a) With the advent of the three or four-day working week, should education be for leisure?

(b) Is educational equality a myth?

(c) What are the most important features of a good education?

(d) What changes would you like to see in the educational system of this country?

(e) What are schools and colleges for?

(f) How far do you think students should have a say in the running of the school or college which they attend?

(g) Do schools try hard enough to develop pupils' creativity?

(h) Bearing in mind current trends, what kind of an education would you plan for a child born today?

(i) How far should education be used in an attempt to change society?

Bibliography

(The topic of education is so broad, and so many books have been written on it, that there seems little point in attempting to make any specific suggestions for further reading. The bibliography, therefore, simply lists the books referred to in this chapter.)

Blishen, Edward. *The School that I'd like*, Penguin, 1969

Boyson, Rhodes. *Oversubscribed: The Story of Highbury Grove School*, Ward Lock, 1974

Cox, C.B. and Dyson, A.E. *The Black Papers on Education*, Davis Poynter, 1971

Davies, Hunter. *The Creighton Report: a year in the life of a comprehensive school*, Hamish Hamilton, 1976

Holt, John. *How Children Fail*, Penguin, 1964

Holt, John. *The Underachieving School*, Penguin, 1971

Macbeath, John E.C. *A Question of Schooling*, Hodder and Stoughton, 1976

Neill, A.S. *Summerhill*, Penguin, 1968

Newsom, John. *The Newsom Report: Half Our Future*, HMSO, 1963

Perry, Leslie R. *Bertrand Russell, A.S. Neill, Homer Lane, W.H. Kilpatrick: Four Progressive Educators*, Collier-McMillan, 1976

Spock, Benjamin. *Baby and Child Care*, Bodley Head, 1979

Advice on Writing: Preparing and Presenting a Questionnaire

For a questionnaire to yield meaningful results a number of factors must be taken into consideration.

Before you begin to prepare the questionnaire you must be absolutely clear about your aims, and be able to explain them clearly both when conducting the interviews and when writing up your report.

You must choose your sample carefully, as this is likely to influence the results of the questionnaire. For instance, you can only draw conclusions about the community in general from your data if the sample represents a cross-section of the community. Alternatively, you may wish to concentrate on particular groups, such as social class groups or year groups in a school, and correlate answers with these groups.

You might include a mixture of open and closed-ended questions. The simplest form of closed-ended question just demands a "yes"/"no"/ "don't know" response. If you are collecting opinions or attitudes the interviewees might be given a statement and asked to respond in one of a number of given ways, the usual format being: "strongly agree"/ "agree"/"undecided"/"disagree"/"strongly disagree". These can be numbered for ease of analysis. In the case of open-ended questions, interviewees are free to answer in any way they want. It is important that the questions are clear and unambiguous, and it is a good idea to show your completed draft questionnaire to someone else, to ensure that there is no ambiguity, and re-draft it if necessary.

When you are conducting your survey, it is important to explain to each interviewee exactly what it is about. A sample of fifty is generally considered to be the minimum required to achieve meaningful results, especially if it is to be subdivided into different groups.

The analysis of your questionnaire and the presentation of your report are likely to take much longer than the collection of your information. When you are analysing the answers to each question, it is simplest to put the questionnaires into separate piles according to the replies.

Your report should start with an explanation of the object and aims of your research, and of your research procedure. You should go on to explain the sample in terms of numbers and groupings. Each question should then be quoted, and the percentage response to the questions given. Significant trends in the answers should be explained, and particularly interesting answers to open-ended questions could perhaps be quoted. You should then draw your conclusions about the data on each question. Finally, you should try to draw some conclusions from the questionnaire as a whole.

6

Crime and Punishment

The theme of crime and punishment is explored in this chapter in several aspects; the viewpoints quoted are those of criminologists, journalists, hooligans, Jesus Christ, prisoners and politicians. This chapter begins with a passage for précis written by a psychologist.

Précis

Write a summary of the following passage in not more than 280 words (the passage contains about 835 words). Your summary, in clear, connected English, should be given a brief title and the number of words used should be indicated at the end. You are advised to spend about one hour on this exercise.

Most people would agree that there is an increase in crime in this country, particularly crimes of violence. Sociologists blame the environment, broken homes, unemployment. As a psychologist I would suggest that at least one cause of the increase in crime is our unwillingness to deal with it when it first arises.

Some thirty years ago, Watson, a famous psychologist, gave a clear outline of how children should be brought up; his view was simply that behaviour could be shaped by punishing what one considered wrong and rewarding what one wanted to encourage. Unfortunately, many schools overdid the punishment and children of a nervous, timid disposition became shy, withdrawn individuals. Then neuroses became popular and the pendulum of change swung violently in the opposite direction.

"Progressive schools" sprang up with philosophers like Bertrand Russell and paediatricians like Dr Spock vehemently arguing against all forms of punishment. They pointed to "repressed" children and neurotic adults, insisting that their upbringing was at fault. Progressive schools experimented with a new system of freedom for the pupils, allowing them to attend classes only if they wished, never punishing them and concerning themselves predominantly with their psychological well-being. Many flourished, but the happy-go-lucky high spirited children took advantage of their new found freedom. A system that had rescued the nervous, timid children had clearly put an undue strain on the boisterous, stable ones in expecting them to resist temptation.

Since then Dr Spock has recanted, claiming that much of the violence of American youngsters may be due to his advice to parents to avoid punishment at all costs. An inevitable concomitant of this laissez-faire educational system has been a very considerable deterioration of discipline. Teachers were afraid to punish and deter in case their pupils suffered some kind of vague psychological damage. Parents were afraid to enforce home rules, with equal regard for their "sensitive" offspring. So children, being healthy, hedonistic organisms, saw their opportunities and stood on their rights; the more they "tested the water" the more they discovered that they could get away with it. Though this form of upbringing may well be feasible for some children, it has proved disastrous for all those others on whom it placed an intolerable burden of responsibility, since it is surely unfair to expect them to be law abiding, kind, thoughtful, unselfish citizens without teaching them what is right and what is wrong.

It seems to me that children have been allowed an excess of freedom to act as they please, which has confused them, and they have reacted by indulging increasingly in petty anti-social acts like swearing, rudeness, truancy and vandalism. Those endowed by nature with a bolder streak follow this up by shoplifting, arson and stealing cars. There is the same permissive attitude to the juvenile delinquent once he is brought to court. Social workers are kind, caring people who are understanding, in the extreme, and go out of their way to help delinquents in every way, usually recommending probation and "another chance" in their social reports to the bench. In some cases this works well. In others, young evil-doers leave the courts with yet another conditional discharge, convinced that crime *does* pay.

My fear is that the escalation of crime, due to our unwillingness to take a firm stand and really enforce our laws, is leading to a far greater danger. This is the new public attitude to the police. For many generations there has been a strong unspoken rule concerning the police; nobody dared argue with them, never mind strike them. This taboo has slowly seeped away and assaults on the police are now not uncommon. Where the sight of a blue uniform once made a would-be criminal run, the new attitude is confrontation. Instead of chasing their suspects the police now reckon to have to put up a fight to restrain them.

There cannot be many people who did not feel truly alarmed by the riots in Bristol recently during which the police left the citizens to their own devices for four hours. If we expect police to protect the public, surely we should give them far more support and rather less criticism for their occasional indiscretions. Indeed, can we wonder at the lack of trust the police must feel towards the likes of soccer hooligans and demonstrators who so freely "put the boot in" whenever they get within striking distance of a policeman? Maybe they have come to resent some members of the public and would return to the "gentle bobby" image as soon as respect was restored for them. Magistrates too could do their bit; with £1,000 and six months imprisonment as their maximum sentence for assaults on the police, why do they mete out a fine of £25 on average for such an offence? Nobody would welcome a "chop off their hands" remedy for crime but I for one would like to see a more determined effort to get to grips with the problem of lawlessness.

DR SYBIL EYSENCK

Juvenile Crime

In this newspaper article the sports journalist Dudley Doust reports an interview with a young Scottish football hooligan:

It all ends with a kick in the face

Scotland's defeat in Czechoslovakia last week was reason enough to get drunk and Bobby McTear didn't rouse himself until noon next day. Gazing idly at the Ulster Volunteer Forces's poster and the King Billy portrait on the bedroom wall he dressed and then drifted down to the local pub near Bridgeton Cross in Glasgow. It was Bobby's first day back since he was jailed and fined £40 for assault and breach of the peace at the Aston Villa – Rangers match in Birmingham.

"Pleasure? No pleasure in throwing a bottle, man. Revenge is the word for it. When you throw the bottle you hope you'll hit some bastard, a polis, or a Catholic, a guy who's given you some shit about the Orange or Rangers or Glasgow." His accent was as thick as porridge. "There's always going to be fighting at Rangers matches. Aye, it's a good feeling to kick some guy in the baws. He's down and he's useless, and so you kick him in the face after that. That ends it."

Bobby McTear is not the lad's real name, but his story is true. He is 17 years old. He looks younger. He has a spray of facial pimples and wears a scab, much like a signet ring, on his left little knuckle. He has also a knife-wound which, in the quiet of a nearby library reading room, he later pulled off his shirt to display; an ugly red welt under the shoulder blade.

"Parkhead," he said. "I didn't know what happened to me until I get home and was changing my shirt. Then I saw all this blood, and I went to the Royal Infirmary and got seven stitches. A week later we played the Celtic bastards again, and 16 of us got two guys on the London Road and we done 'em in. I took an open razor and did a guy's jaw. Seventeen stitches."

In two seasons Bobby has been convicted on 11 charges of assault or breach of the peace following football matches. He has served two short spells in prison. "I had my first football fight when I was 13," he said. "I was standing on the railway station after the Rangers – Aberdeen game, and a guy went like this to my dad, and told him to get out of the road. So my dad starts fighting him and I hit the guy over the head with a bottle. Out cold. Thirteen stitches." Stitch-count is important in the language of violence.

Bobby was born in Bridgeton Cross, one of Glasgow's gloomy Victorian slums. His mother was born a Catholic in Northern Ireland and down the years her husband, who is sometimes a long distance lorry driver, has fought with her Catholic brothers. "We all go to the Orange Order," said Bobby. "I'm a Protestant, and I'll always live up to my religion. I'll live up to it until the day I die."

Rangers hooligans – indeed, even most of their orderly fans – have found comfort in the unblinking bigoted policy of the Rangers Football Club. During its 103-year history the club's proud tradition has been not to sign or play a Catholic in the side. That suits Bobby. Further, it is unlikely that he was shaken later when the club announced it was to drop its sectarian bias.

"A Catholic playing for Rangers?" he laughed. "You gotta be joking. You'll never see a Catholic in the side, and if you do you won't see me supporting Rangers." He sensed the irony of this ultimatum. "Maybe that would be a good thing. May if they brought in a Catholic on the side there'd be a lot less trouble because we guys, the trouble-makers, would be finished with Rangers."

Bobby, however, foresaw a closer surveillance of alcoholic liquor at Ibrox; perhaps identity cards, cages for fans and even a lock-out for himself and his hooligan friends. He would like to see lounges and proper seating he said, and then, in the way of a Glaswegian, he delivered a sudden, soft, piercing throw-away line — " . . . and give us more respect."

Bobby left school abruptly at 15. "If I'd finished school I might have been in some better place than this one," he said with neither self-pity or remorse. "I got expelled. I hit the teacher with a case of books." He trained briefly as a bricklayer but, he says, due to his many criminal convictions he has been unable to get work. He drifts, steals, does a bit of house-breaking and, best of all, fights at football matches.

"I'm doing it because there's nothing else to do. There's not even a cinema or a dance hall down here at the Cross. Things might be a wee bit different if I had a job." He smiled. "But I'd still go to games and have a battle."

The Villa battle followed a familiar pattern. Bobby and his mates, joined by three girls and half-a-dozen Rangers' supporters from Belfast, boarded a chartered coach (£6 return) at Bridgeton Cross, at seven o'clock on Saturday morning. They had their standard battle gear: razors, screw-top-bottles of bear, bottles of sweet Old English wine, blue and white Rangers scarves and scattered across the occasional breast, the badge of the Red Hand of Ulster. "If you don't have your gear ready, they'll be ready before you."

On the coach, Bobby slept much of the way down the M6, and now and then joined in the songs exalting the beautiful Rangers and blaspheming the Pope. He was spoiling for the inevitable fight: "If we get beat, we'll look for trouble. If we don't get beat, somebody else will look for trouble and we'll battle them back."

The coach arrived at Villa Park just before noon. Bobby and his mates sent their girls into a pub with the purpose of enticing young Villa fans to the coach. The waiting Scots ambushed and "mingled" the luckless English. Bobby stole £1.50 from one victim. "You got to be half-drunk when this happens. If we weren't drunk? That's a hard question. I'll tell you, I wouldn't do it alone unless I had a bottle of wine in me."

At the turnstiles, Bobby says, a young Villa fan taunted him: "Go back to Glasgow, you yellow Orange bastards." Bobby swung, missed and hit a brick wall. Trouble later broke out when Rangers went two down. Bobby and his mates swept into the passages under the stands. They smashed open a kiosk, went for the beer when "this big polis started waving a stick at us. Then he dropped his stick and we jumped in and gave him a battering."

Bobby was arrested outside the ground and after appearing in court on Monday, ("fined £3 a week and I'm not paying it"), he wandered the

Birmingham streets that night, stealing £20 from a newsagent and finally jumping on a train back to Glasgow without paying the fare. He slept under the seats to avoid the guard. What did his parents think of all this? "They don't know. They don't know anything. My father just says, 'If you do daft things it's your own fault.'"

Bobby one day may kill somebody. Would he be happy to kill anybody? "No," he said, "I don't want to kill anybody. I want to hurt him bad, really mark the bastard, but I don't want to kill him. He has to go home to his mother and father. Same as me."

Bobby was restless. He wanted to leave the library. But it was past 2.30 in the afternoon and the pub would be closed. So he went to a nearby snooker hall. One look at his face, and the attendant stopped the turnstile. The boy wasn't wanted. Bored and barred, Bobby walked back towards the street, pausing to urinate against the big oak door.

DUDLEY DOUST

Analysis and Discussion

The following questions can be answered in the form of a separate written comprehension and argument, and/or as part of a general class discussion of the theme of the chapter.

1. Read Dr Sybil Eysenck's article again, especially paragraphs 1, 5, 6 and 7, and comment on the "Bobby McTear" story in the light of what she says about the attitudes of sociologists, social workers and magistrates towards soccer hooligans.

2. From the evidence of "Bobby McTear's" account of himself, what do you think are the main factors which have contributed to his becoming a juvenile delinquent?

3. Is there anything that could be done − socially, educationally or punitively − to persuade the "Bobby McTears" of the world to behave with a greater sense of social responsibility?

4. "Bobby McTear" in the article is clearly unaffected by the punishment which has so far been meted out to him. Before reading on, try to suggest a more effective punishment than the fine imposed after his latest act of violence.

The Punishment of Young Offenders

Magistrates' courts have a number of options available when sentencing juvenile delinquents. These are some of the main ones:

(*i*)   Prison sentences

(*ii*) Fines, or restitution to the victims of the crimes

(*iii*) Probation. The offender is assigned a probation officer, to whom he must report at regular intervals − normally a half-hour session once a week − for a specified length of time. During these sessions the probation officer tries to find out why his client committed the offence and whether there is anything that can be corrected, and attempts to minimise the likelihood of the offender getting into trouble again.

(*iv*) Intermediate Treatment (IT). Delinquents are "sentenced" to "treatment" intended to prevent them from reaching a stage where institutionalised care and control is needed. They are removed from their immediate home environment for a brief period or a succession of brief periods, often in company with non-offenders from deprived backgrounds. A 1972 government circular explained the rationale behind IT: "It will be an important aim to secure the child's acceptance of his treatment, so that he does not resent it; and this aim is unlikely to be achieved if it involves activities which appear to set him apart from his contemporaries." In practice this means "treatment" such as compulsory attendance at youth clubs or other centres where social workers organise discussions and leisure activities and/or outdoor activities, not normally available to these delinquents, such as rock climbing, canoeing, art and drama.

(*v*) Residential care at Community Homes with education (CH(E)s). Offenders are "sentenced" to an extended period in a Community Home concerned with counselling, discussion and therapy, a central feature of which is education at anything from remedial to public examination level, and job training.

(*vi*) Community Service Order (CSO). Introduced in the 1972 Criminal Justice Act, the CSO means that courts could "award from 40 to 240 hours of service to the community, normally to be completed over a period of not more than twelve months. This new idea of justice grew out of the voluntary service movement . . . . The offender would be brought into direct contact with a variety of social needs in the community . . . . There was also the hope that some offenders, having the experience of helping others, might want to continue such service to the community after the legal obligation had been fulfilled." (Dennie Briggs: *In Place of Prison*).

(*vii*) Borstal, and "short, sharp shock" treatment. The latter "treatment" was introduced in the late 1970s to provide brief periods of tough punishment, involving rigorous discipline and regular, intense exercise in detention centres, the aim of which is to instil a sense of self-discipline. Borstals, which have been in existence for several decades, are detention centres to which young offenders are sent for longer periods of military-style punishment.

(*viii*) Corporal punishment. "The birch" is used only in the Isle of Man.

To illustrate how one of these options can be made to work, here is an extract from the book already referred to by Dennie Briggs. The speaker is a young man of 22 called Dick Marshall, sentenced to a spell of Community Service.

I've spent time in borstal and in prison. I've had suspended sentences, fines and probation orders − I suppose you could say I've had all the alternatives to prison there are. In early 1973 I was due to go to court for "theft". Then I got into an argument with this full-time student when I was on day release to a college from the pits. I butted him and his teeth went through his tongue. I knew I had had it this time.

The probation officer told me about this new idea of CSO. I wasn't interested in helping people, but I didn't want to go to prison again. So, I said I'd like that, as a con. I just didn't want to go to the nick.

I made the right noises in court. The magistrate said this is my last chance as I had a very bad record. The probation officer said I was a good lad at heart. The magistrate finally gave me 200 hours which he saw roughly as seven months in the nick. He warned me that if I didn't do as I was told and stay out of trouble, he'd breach me and this time I'd go to prison.

The next day I went to see John Harding. He gave me this list of jobs that were available. Things like, you know, soup runs, painting and decorating, digging canals. Then there was a chance of doing youth work. I didn't fancy digging canals or painting. Maybe the youth club would have table tennis; I liked that and I thought I could have a good time. I plumped for the youth club. I thought it would be an easy line. There was only one objection to this and that was that they might not want me because I had a record of violence and the animal description used by the magistrate stuck.

Next day I went to see my youth club leader. We got on straightway. He was a young guy with radical views. He ran an easy club and was dead against prison, wanted to open things up.

So I started at the youth club the following week. I was to go there two to three times a week. The idea of CSO is not to cram the hours up but to spread them out over time. I thought it would be a right doss, but that was soon knocked out of me. This particular youth club had the most under-privileged kids in town in it. There was no disciplining the kids, they didn't have to pay fees. There were a hell of a lot of them, all between twelve and sixteen.

I made the first mistake of giving one kid a piggy back ride. I didn't know what else to do. Then I had to give all of them a ride. I was grabbed by the kids to do things. I was so exhausted and pissed off after the first night, I didn't fancy doing two hundred hours of this.

I liked the leader and got on with him. He had a tough job, but didn't seem to get discouraged. I carried on for a couple of months and got to liking some of the kids.

Then wham! I was called to court. I had been on bail for a previous charge. John Harding and the youth club leader both went to court and spoke up for me. The judge listened but he wouldn't hear of it.

"I fought for you in World War Two," is the way he put it to me. Besides he said, "What would others think if I let you off?"

"Six months," he said. Off I went to the nick again. The youth club leader came to see me while I was in prison. We had some talks and I could see I had come around slightly. I probably could have got out of my CSO seeing I was doing six months. But I decided I'd go back to the club when I got out. I didn't know when I'd get out, as another old offence came up. While I was being arrested, a police officer hit me and broke my nose. I got mad and hit him. So I was called to trial and given another three months. I appealed and luckily won. Altogether I did five months.

When I went back to the youth club things had changed and I decided I needed a more definite role rather than just walking around and being grabbed to do any old thing. The most incredible thing happened, you wouldn't believe this. You see there was another bloke who had got a CSO. While I was in prison the leader got another job. There was no one to run the club so they put this guy in charge. He was there when I got out. So I guess technically I reported to him. How about that — one ex-con in charge of another? We never worried about things like that, just got on with the job.

I organised a table-tennis team and this gave me a role in the kids' eyes. The team started doing well and this gave me a sense of achieving something. After I came back the kids knew I was an offender. When they realised this, we got on even better. I became a regular with them and they were less wary of me. They could identify more with me now as they didn't see me as someone coming in to supervise them. I was the one being supervised you might say.

Most of the kids in that club had been in trouble, or were at the time. So were some of their families. Some of the sixteen-year-olds were in fact on bail. They began to talk to me about it and ask my advice. At first it was legal questions, how to talk in court and how to beat their cases. Then they wanted to know what it was like inside and what to expect if they got locked up. I began to feel more a part of the place, more like a counsellor, and didn't think of it as serving an order or sentence.

You know a funny thing happened. Somewhere along the line, I lost my card that had to be signed each night I went to the club and the number of hours recorded. Never thought about it. Then my year was up and only 177 hours had been recorded. I had done many times that amount but no one had kept track. So John Harding had to go back to court and get the order extended for another twelve months to make up the lost time. I didn't resent this, I was going to go on working there anyway.

I was lucky to get a youth club and that particular one. If I'd ended up digging a canal, I'd have been even more resentful and probably never finished it out. This youth club wasn't regulated. And John Harding said he didn't want me clocking-in like at a Detention Centre, but to get involved and perhaps continue on after my time was up.

Most of all it gave me a chance to prove to myself that I wasn't all what people had said I was: a thief, violent, couldn't stick with a job. "You're a right bastard," was the exact words one judge said to me in court. But just as bad, were the professionals who talk nice to you — you know underneath they really think the same.

From *In Place of Prison*

Discussion

Here is an imaginary situation:

> Three youths are travelling on a bus at night, after an evening at a pub. A girl is also on the bus, alone. When she gets up, they do also; she panics, and they chase her down the stairs. The bus driver intercedes, and the youths turn on him. Another passenger comes to his assistance. Both are injured, and the boys run away. The result of the incident is that the driver, after a brief spell in hospital, is traumatised by the incident, and afraid to return to work; the passenger suffers from an eye injury which requires a series of operations over many months, and which leaves his eyesight permanently impaired, and the boys are arrested and appear at a magistrate's court, having been recognised by witnesses. During their trial it emerges that one of them has several previous convictions for violence, vandalism and theft, the second has a single suspended sentence for theft, and the third has no previous convictions.

What do you think is likely to happen to each of the three youths?

Which of the methods of punishment summarised on pages 82 – 83 would be most suitable for each of them?

Do you know of any incidents of hooliganism in which the culprits were taken to court? What do you think caused the individuals concerned to become hooligans?

To sum up:

What is needed to stem the tide of juvenile delinquency – stricter punishment and stronger "law and order", or more enlightened social policies to prevent delinquency from occurring in the first place?

The Morality of Punishment

The biblical viewpoint

The "lex talionis" concept of retributive punishment ("an eye for an eye") goes back thousands of years. Two thousand years ago this ancient law was repudiated, and a very different view of punishment was expressed. Consider the following extracts from the Old and New Testaments:

> And he that killeth any man shall surely be put to death.
> And he that killeth a beast shall make it good, beast for beast.
> And if a man cause a blemish in his neighbour; as he hath done, so shall it be done to him;
> Breach for breach, eye for eye, tooth for tooth: as he hath caused a blemish in a man, so shall it be done to him again.

(Leviticus 24 v 17 – 20)

Ye have heard that it hath been said, An eye for an eye, and a tooth for a tooth:

But I say unto you, That ye resist not evil: but whosoever shall smite thee on thy right cheek, turn to him the other also.

And if any man will sue thee at the law, and take away thy coat, let him have thy cloak also.

(St Matthew 5 v 38–40)

Jesus went unto the mount of Olives.

And in the early morning he came again into the temple, and all the people came unto him; and he sat down, and taught them.

And the scribes and Pharisees brought unto him a woman taken in adultery; and when they had set her in the midst;

They say unto him, Master, this woman was taken in adultery, in the very act.

Now Moses in the law commanded us, that such should be stoned: but what sayest thou?

This they said, tempting him, that they might have to accuse him. But Jesus stooped down, and with his finger wrote on the ground, as though he heard them not.

So when they continued asking him, he lifted up himself, and said unto them, He that is without sin among you, let him first cast a stone at her.

And again he stooped down, and wrote on the ground.

And they which heard it, being convicted by their own conscience, went out one by one, beginning at the eldest, even unto the last: and Jesus was left alone, and the woman standing in the midst.

When Jesus had lifted up himself, and saw none but the woman, he said unto her, Woman, where are those thine accusers? Hath no man condemned thee?

She said, No man, lord. And Jesus said unto her, Neither do I condemn thee: go, and sin no more.

(St John 8 v 1–11)

No large-scale society has ever adopted the view of punishment here ascribed to Jesus Christ in the gospels of Matthew and John, though some serious writers, like Leo Tolstoy, in his late work *What I believe*, have argued, on the basis of such New Testament passages, that society has no right to stand in judgement on individuals.

Discussion points

Do you think that Christ really meant his words to be taken as a disavowal of all forms of punishment, as Tolstoy understood them?

What do you think would happen if they were treated that way, and societies acted upon them?

The Prison System

Imprisonment has for centuries been the main means by which society deals with adult criminals. For at least the past two hundred years, however, questions have been raised as to the purpose of prisons, and suggestions for prison reform have been offered. In this section we will consider these issues.

First, some facts, figures and opinions about the prison situation in Britain, taken from an article in *The Times*:

In spite of a slowdown in the number of people in prison in the early 1980s, the prison population jumped by 3,070 last year to more than 47,303, although there is provision only for 39,804 inmates . . . .

Overcrowding has reached crisis proportions in most prisons throughout the country and in at least three, Leeds, Oxford, and Leicester, the number of inmates exceeds official capacity by 100 per cent . . . .

Mr Cavadino[1] said: "Overcrowding means that in many cases prisoners are held two or three in a cell built for one person in Victorian times. They have no access to proper sanitary facilities while locked up, only a bucket in the cell. It is degrading."

The lack of adequate numbers of prison officials has led to more than 70 prison workshops and educational centres being closed, leaving prisoners up to 23 hours a day behind bars, according to Mr Colin Steel, national chairman for the Prison Officer's Association.

"The more we get people out of their cells, the easier it is to control them," Mr Steel said. "Lock a guy up for 23 hours a day, he is going to get a bit frustrated."

He said: "Signals are being picked up by all our members all over the prison system. The prisoners and the staff working overtime have had enough. If I hear those signals, I listen. If I am stupid, I ignore them."

Although all sides agree that there is a problem, there is little agreement about how to tackle it.

"We are desperately short of staff," Mr Steel said.

"We need at least 5,000 more prison officials and you cannot get them and train them overnight."

"The answer is not in non-custodial service or in probation, because that merely delays the inevitable prison sentence," he said.

But Mr Cavadino argues that more prisons will not solve the problem. "Trying to cope with such an increase by opening new prisons is like running up an escalator which is moving ever so rapidly downwards. Rather than open new prisons, the government must take the lead in calling for a reduction in the use of prisons," he said.

1. Paul Cavadino, a spokesman for the National Association for the Care and Resettlement of Offenders (NACRO).

Prison population at June 30, 1985 (England and Wales)	
Males	**Pop.**
Remand centres	3,748
Local prisons	17,207
Closed training prison	13,159
Open prisons	3,404
Total	37,518
Females	
Open prisons	349
Closed prisons	1,019
Total	1,368
Closed youth custody centres	
Males	5,458
Females	120
Open youth custody centres	
Males	1,390
Females	89
Senior detention centres	1,016
Other detention centres	1,560
Total population:	47,503
Total capacity:	39,804

Nacro statistics

A Nacro briefing paper, "The Costs of Penal Measures", reports that the average weekly cost of keeping a person in prison in the financial year 1983–1984 was £234, ranging from £144 at open prisons to £478 in maximum security jails.

In contrast, the annual cost of a probation order in 1982–1983 was £580 and the average cost of community service orders was £310.

"With the prison population at a record level and widespread concern about acute overcrowding, a much greater use of non-custodial sentences makes practical sense," the paper says.

Mr Paul Cavadino, of Nacro, said: "At least two-thirds of those in prison could be given non-custodial sentences without danger to the public and with at least as good and perhaps a better chance of not being reconvicted for a crime."

from *The Times* (1985)

In their book *The Growth of Crime*, published in 1977, Sir Leon Radzinovicz and Joan King explore the purpose and nature of imprisonment. Here are some extracts:

A time of disillusion

Today it is scarcely possible to mention prisons without bringing in the word "crisis". Recidivism, overcrowding, protest, have contributed to an atmosphere of mounting disillusion, even despair, about penal institutions.

This is in sharp contrast with the optimism that prevailed just before and after the Second World War . . . . After the war [as a result of the Criminal Justice Act of 1948] administrative changes forged ahead. There were open borstals and open prisons. Prison welfare and after-care were reviewed and re-viewed and eventually put into the hands of probation officers, trained as social workers. There were various experiments designed to involve prison officers more fully in rehabilitation as well as custody. Prison hostels, or arrangements for employment outside, were introduced to pave the way for release for long-term prisoners. None of this, however, availed to stem the tide of recidivism.

Now virtually all the features that favoured prison reform and experiment in the thirties have been reversed; few prisons have any longer the elbow-room for improvement. They are crowded beyond belief, with nearly four times as many to hold as they had then.

Why do we still send people to prison?

Every other year the Institute of Criminology at Cambridge holds a Senior Course for people engaged in the practical tasks of dealing with criminals: judges, magistrates and their clerks, administrators, prison governors, senior officers of the police, probation and social services. One participant was recently heard to remark that, by the time they had finished discussing research about prisons, he had wondered why anyone was still being sent there at all. Yet, just afterwards, they had held a "sentencing exercise", and had each been asked to say what sentence should be imposed upon certain offenders. And they had all found themselves deciding upon imprisonment as the only solution where the facts seemed to indicate that the convicted man was especially dangerous or had committed a deliberate and serious breach of trust.

People are not sent to prison primarily for their own good, or even in the hope that they will be cured of crime. Confinement is used as a measure of retribution, a symbol of condemnation, a vindication of law. It is used as a warning and deterrent to others. It is used, above all, to protect other people, for a longer or shorter period, from an offender's depredations. Yet there is a widespread idea that the trouble with prisons nowadays is that they are too soft, that "rehabilitation" has been allowed to take over at the expense of both deterrence and security. No wonder prisoners get out of hand, goes the argument, no wonder they do not fear to go back, if they are allowed to associate with their cronies, have good meals, books, magazines, radio, television, little work, no responsibilities, even home leave before they go out. If prisons were a good deal grimmer, and the regime a good deal stiffer, it is contended, there would be fewer prisoners and less trouble with those there are.

Ironically, the very fact of rising crime and rising committals to penal institutions ensures that for most prisoners conditions remain quite sufficiently grim. More than half of all those sent to prison in England pass the whole of their sentence in the old general "locals", where they are liable to spend eighteen hours a day locked up in their cells – longer at weekends or if officers are too busy with other duties to supervise them outside.

RADZINOVICZ and KING

So what actually *does* it feel like to be in prison? Here are some extracts from a book of selected interviews with prisoners and warders in traditional British "closed" prisons, compiled by Tony Parker, and published in 1973, entitled *The Man Inside*:

If you take the majority of the prison population basically it's made up of only two kinds of prisoner − those who've got no skills whatsoever and are virtually unemployable, and those who could work if they wanted to, but prefer to live by crime. They've no intention of going straight when they get out, and all they think about while they're in is how to get away with it next time.

Principal Prison Officer (50)
20 years service

You can't be a person who works in a prison for long without realising what a terrible waste of time it all is, how men with brains and feelings and hearts are being ruined simply by the struggle to stay alive in the face of the stupid restrictions and regulations they're surrounded with. If only half the energy they had to devote to battling in their minds against that sort of thing could be put to some constructive use I'd say you might even get something worthwhile out of prisons. But under the present system there's not a hope: the important things are ignored and the petty things are all-important.

Prison Welfare Officer (32)
Seconded from Probation Service

No one learns anything that will be any help to them when they go out. I'm not aware, for instance, that there's an insatiable demand at good rates of pay for men who can scrub and clean and polish, or make roughly-fitting shoes or brushes, or boil hundredweights of cabbage and potatoes. Really it's beyond me why they don't do things like buying-up old motor-cars and teaching men the rudiments of being garage mechanics, show them how to rewire a house, repair television sets, or make tables and chairs − anything that's got at least some connection with some sort of job they might get outside. Or it could be clerical work, book-keeping, filing, indexing, storekeeping. The ridiculous thing is it'd hardly cost them anything; there are plenty of men serving sentences themselves who could be put to teaching things like that, which they already know about, to others. So as well as passing on their knowledge they'd be usefully employed themselves while they were in, instead of being kept pointlessly occupied at the tax-payers' expense.

Walter C (54)
Offence: embezzlement
Sentence: 6 years

You're allowed to write one letter a week, but what the hell is there to write about? "We scrubbed the corridor yesterday, it looks terrific. We had a great time in the tailoring shop last Tuesday, we made our one-millionth pair of prison-uniform trousers. I was walking round the yard on exercise today and I completed seventeen circuits before it started to rain and we were brought inside." You couldn't say it was exactly compulsive reading for someone who got it, could you? If you were honest all you'd write would be, "Dear Blank, I hope you are well. I'm dead. Yours sincerely". They could have a printed form to save you writing it, then everyone'd be saved a lot of time.

Ron G (26)
Offence: Possession of drugs
Sentence: 4 years

I can't help it, I hate visits. I can't tell her not to come, I suppose she wants to, but I get choked. I mean I've got another eight years still to do, I don't want to hear about what's going on outside, what she said, what someone else said, how so-and-so is. It doesn't concern me, how can it possibly concern me? When she came today what she was talking about was the present, and that means nothing at all. She was saying things about what happened last week, what's going to happen next week: to her, and to people she knows. But nothing happened to me last week and nothing's going to happen next week, so what else could it be but a completely ridiculous one-sided conversation? The most I wanted was just to look at her, remind myself what she looked like, not to talk or to listen. Now it's what, three hours later, I haven't the remotest idea of a single word she said.

Danny A (35)
Offence: armed robbery
Sentence: 14 years

The incredible way time seems to stop moving altogether, that was the thing I was least prepared for and haven't got used to even now. I'll be in the workshop and my mind'll be far away, thinking of the end of my sentence next year and all the things I'm going to do and the places I'm going to go, and then I suddenly come back with a jerk to where I am. I say to myself, "Oh well, all that helped to pass a bit of time". Then I look up at the clock, and I see the hand's moved on exactly one minute since I looked at it before.

Stuart H (24)
Offence: arson
Sentence: 4 years

All these places do for me is make me determined to hit back harder than ever when I get out. I've a chip on my shoulder, yes, but I don't think I had it so much when I first started being sent to prison. In those days I used to feel I probably deserved it. That's all gone long-since now though. All I've got is this big hatred for what's called straight society, and it's been going into prison such a lot that has turned me like that.

Les M (34)
Offence: housebreaking
Sentence: 6 years

The only sort of way I could tell you about myself, how I am doing this length of time, I suppose it would be to get a cup of water and float a burnt-out match on it and say sit and watch it, see how it got water-logged and gradually got lower and lower sinking under the surface, that'd be about it, how it is, that'd be me.

Len B (45)
Offence: manslaughter
Sentence: life

Over the past few decades there have been attempts to make prison regimes reformative rather than merely deterrent. The rationale behind these attempts is suggested in *The Growth of Crime*:

Since a prisoner has to do time, cannot that time be used constructively to get him to face and change the attitudes that lead him to commit crime? Why should not the various aspects of his life in prison – work, leisure, education, contacts with prison staff, contacts with family or friends outside, contacts with other prisoners, the social environment of the institution itself, be deliberately directed towards his reformation? Surely so much control over every aspect of life should be turned to good account?

Here are a few of the major "reformative" ideas:

Vocational and industrial training
Prisoners are given instruction in work and life skills, in the form, for example, of factory units, where they are paid wages while in prison and where they learn trades which they could use to earn an honest living on release.

Individual welfare and "treatment"
Psychologists, psychiatrists and social workers concentrate on the individual needs of prisoners, as a means of reform and rehabilitation, offering psycho-therapy, or counselling to individuals, or group therapy, or regular contacts with prisoners' families.

Conjugal visits
Prisoners are allowed regular visits from wives or girlfriends in privacy, or periodic "home leaves".

While most prisons in Britain continue to be "closed", with prisoners locked up and closely guarded, there are a number of "open prisons", where there is a strong emphasis on "reformative" measures. The aim of such prisons is to increase informality and opportunities for responsibility and self-determination. Typical features of such prisons are as follows:

Minimal security, in the traditional sense. Roll calls are reduced to a minimum and prisoners are often allowed to go for long unsupervised walks in the prison estates, where they may be engaged in market gardening.

Fury over five-star luxury for Moors murderer

BRADY'S XMAS FEAST

Salmon, turkey scampi and a Christmas pud

MOORS murderer Ian Brady will be eating better this Christmas than thousands of decent Britons.

On his menu over Christmas and the New Year will be scampi, roast turkey, gamekeeper's pie, fresh salmon, sherry trifle, Christmas pudding and gateau.

He may even have his first glass of beer since he was jailed 19 years ago.

But the staff who serve him will only have sandwiches.

Brady is in Liverpool's maximum security Park Lane

EXCLUSIVE

By FRANK CORLESS

Hospital—the Broadmoor of the North—which has been criticised before for its five-star luxury.

Brady was transferred to the hospital from Leicester's Gartree jail three weeks ago.

Staff at Park Lane have been forbidden from speaking to the Press. But there was a storm of protest outside. Mrs Ann West, 56, the mother of Moors victim

Lesley Ann Downey, 12, who was murdered on a Boxing Day said:

"This makes me sick. Christmas is always a bad time for me—but this news will make it worse."

Mrs Winifred Johnson, 52, whose son Keith Bennett is believed to have been a victim of Brady, said: "I've got to work for my Christmas and he gets it all for nothing.

"I don't even know what scampi tastes like because I've never had the money to pay for it."

Accommodation is likely to be in single rooms, or dormitories divided into cubicles, with unbarred windows. Prisoners may be allowed to decorate their rooms, or to have pictures, ornaments and radios.

Recreation is much more varied than the traditional exercise round the prison yard. There may be television rooms, snooker and table-tennis tables, a large, unsupervised common room, music rooms, a gymnasium, with squash and badminton courts and weight-training facilities.

Education programmes are provided, encouraging prisoners to develop hobbies and skills.

Resettlement programmes may be provided with prisoners allowed out to do voluntary work in the community prior to release.

Opposite is a newspaper report about the prison conditions of a particularly notorious murderer.

Studies of the actual results of such regimes in terms of the likelihood of prisoners "going straight" after release from "open prisons" have tended to be disappointing. Studies undertaken in Holland and Finland, where such prisons have been in operation over a long period, are summarised in *Open Prisons* by Howard Jones and Paul Cornes, published in 1977: "treatment in an open institution hardly matters as regards later recidivism".

Themes for Discussion

Do you think that more prisons should be built to deal with the over-crowding in Britain's prisons, or do you think that more use should be made of non-custodial sentences for convicted criminals?

If the recidivism rate is the same amongst prisoners released from both "closed" and "open" prisons, can you see any value in spending extra public money on building more of the latter?

Do you think that the experimental American scheme, whereby first offenders, on probation, are taken into prisons to be lectured by "lifers" about the reality of prison life, should be adopted in Britain?

Do you think first offenders should be kept separate from more experienced prisoners?

What are your thoughts about the *Daily Mirror* report on Ian Brady?

Which, if any, of the reformative measures outlined above, do you consider valuable? What difficulties are likely to arise in the implementation of each?

Why do you think vocational training and work experience schemes in prison have had comparatively little effect on recidivism and employment prospects amongst prisoners?

Why, do you think, do most prisoners return to crime after being released from prison?

Research topics

1. Find out about conditions in 2 or 3 large prisons in Britain. Write a report to present to the group.

2. Find out about and write reports on countries where prison conditions are:
   (a) more pleasant
   (b) more unpleasant
   (c) simply different
   in comparison with the normal conditions in British prisons.

The Capital Punishment Debate

Capital punishment was abolished in Great Britain by Act of Parliament in 1964. Arguments about the morality of capital punishment and its value as a deterrent to murder have continued ever since, culminating in a parliamentary debate and a free vote, in 1983, on amendments to the law which would enable judges to sentence people found guilty of certain categories of murder, to death. The amendments were defeated, and the law stood. The debate in society goes on.

Here are extracts from speeches by MPs, made in the House of Commons on 13 July, 1983, presenting opposing viewpoints on the issue:

. . . I want the House to understand my position clearly, that even were there evidence to demonstrate that capital punishment was a deterrent − such evidence does not exist − I shall still believe hanging to be wrong. I know that some people will argue . . . that hanging as retribution is right in itself and that in our society one can justify, shall I say as a matter of principle, the taking of the life of a man or woman who has himself or herself taken a life. . . . . There is no moral or philosophical justification for that view. It is a cry for vengeance, and nothing except vengeance . . .

Even if the deterrent claim can be justified, its effect on the murder rate in Britain will be negligible . . . . Time after time the hanging lobby repeats the old remedies and the venerable prejudices that capital punishment deters. I tell the hanging lobby what every informed person knows − that there is absolutely no evidence to support the view that capital punishment is in itself a deterrent.

If we compare abolitionist and retentionist countries and countries before and after abolition, we find that there is no evidence to prove that execution reduces the murder rate or reduces crimes of violence . . .

If the deterrent case is to be accepted, if we are to vote for capital punishment as a deterrent, we ought at least to be sure that it deters. If we are to hang men and women by the neck until they are dead, we ought to do it on more than a hunch, a superstition, a vague impression . . . . Unless there is some positive proof that hanging deters, the case for hanging cannot be made even by its most sophisticated proponents.

They cannot provide that case. I must provide for them the other statistic, of which we are certain. Had hanging not been abolished in 1964, at least five innocent men would be dead today. That seems to me . . . the only statistic about which we can be sure in this entire debate . . . .

I conclude as I began. Were all the practical or pragmatic arguments against capital punishment not to apply, I should still resist its introduction. Supporters of capital punishment insist on comparing crime rates before and after abolition, as though abolition itself had created a more violent society. The truth is something different. Violence has grown within our society during the past 25 years for many reasons. To legalise violence in the way proposed would make Britain not a more peaceful nation, but one in which violence had become accepted and institutionalised . . . . By killing murderers we become like the murderers themselves. The whole community is lowered to their standards. For that reason I shall vote against the motion.

ROY HATTERSLEY
(MP for Birmingham, Sparkbrook)

The first duty of this House is not simply to debate what punishment we can place upon criminals. It is also to protect the lives of our people and to safeguard the innocent . . . .

I was in the House when we abolished the capital sentence. We did so largely in the belief that life imprisonment would be an effective deterrent in its place. It has not worked out that way. On the contrary, violence and murder have increased rapidly . . . .

When the capital sentence was abolished the Police Federation warned the House that it would lead to a dramatic increase in the carrying and using of firearms. That is exactly what has happened. In the year before abolition the number of guns used in crimes in London was 43; last year the number was close to 2,000. That is a 25-fold increase. Before abolition, when a professional gang planned a job the elder members frisked the younger members to ensure that they were not carrying guns. They did so because they knew, to put it in the vernacular, "If you kill a cop we all get topped". It is no longer that way. Today, it is the norm and not the exception for criminals to carry guns when they commit robberies. They do so for the simple reason that they know that their lives are not at risk.

There is also a new balance of risk for the police officer. When a policeman confronts a criminal with a gun, the odds are tilted against him. In that split second when the armed robber must decide whether to pull the trigger and shoot the policeman, the robber knows that if he surrenders he will go to prison for, perhaps, five to seven years for armed robbery. But if he shoots the policeman, he eliminates the witness and greatly improves his chances of getting away with the loot. And even if he is caught and convicted of murder the worst that can happen to him is life imprisonment. With remission that can mean little more than ten and a half years . . . . I do not accept, and I doubt if the House would accept, that the difference between five to seven years for armed robbery and only ten years for murder is worth the life of a police officer . . . .

There is a further consequence. Whereas, before abolition, unarmed police officers would not hesitate to tackle armed criminals because they knew or they believed that they were protected by the invisible bullet-proof waistcoat of the capital sentence, today even the bravest of policemen hesitates. He often sends for a gun.

What the Police Federation and I predicted when the House abolished the capital sentence has come to pass. We have put an end to the once-proud tradition of our unarmed police force. We therefore face the risk . . . that we have not succeeded in abolishing the capital sentence. On the contrary, it will be administered more and more not by due process of law and by courts, but by armed criminals and, on occasion, by armed police officers defending themselves and the public.

ELDON GRIFFITHS
(MP for Bury St Edmunds)

Questions for Research and Discussion

1. Both MPs, in the selected extracts from their speeches, concentrate on the question of whether or not capital punishment is a deterrent to murder and violent crime, both claim to draw upon the available statistical evidence, and yet they reach opposite conclusions. Who do you think is right? (To answer the question, of course, research will be necessary, possibly undertaken by a small group of students, who report back to the rest. You will need to work out exactly *what* evidence each MP is drawing on, find the relevant evidence and statistics, and present them to the class, before judgements about the viability of the opposing claims can be made.)

2. On what grounds does Roy Hattersley argue that capital punishment is morally indefensible? Do you consider that he is right when he argues that, "even were there evidence to demonstrate that [it] was a deterrent, capital punishment would be wrong"?

3. What do you think Eldon Griffiths meant when he said, "we have not succeeded in abolishing the capital sentence"? Do you think that there is any fundamental difference between the kinds of "death sentence" he is talking about in the last quoted paragraph of his speech, and capital punishment carried out by legal process?

4. According to one of the speakers in the debate, Albert McQuarrie (MP for Banff and Buchan), "an estimated 87 per cent of the total adult population have called for capital punishment to be made available to the courts again". Yet the House of Commons voted against the restoration of capital punishment. Is this democratic?

Essay Titles

(a) Vandalism – inevitable social evil?

(b) The European Court decided that birching is an offence against human rights. What is your opinion?

(c) Punishment should fit the crime.

(d) "All punishment in itself is evil."

(e) In defence of discipline and order.

Bibliography

Non-fiction

Briggs, Dennie. *In Place of Prison*, Temple Smith, 1975
Evans, Peter. *Prison Crisis*, Allen and Unwin, 1980
Fitzgerald, Mike, and Sim, Joe. *British Prisons*, Blackwell, 1981
Gowers, Sir Ernest. *A Life For A Life: The Problem of Capital Punishment*, Chatto and Windus, 1956
Jones, Howard and Cornes, Paul. *Open Prisons*, Routledge and Kegan Paul, 1977
Parker, Tony. *The Courage of his Convictions*, Hutchinson, 1962
Parker, Tony. *The Man Inside*, Michael Joseph, 1973
Radzinovicz, Sir Leon, and King, Joan. *The Growth of Crime: the International Experience*, Hamilton, 1977

Fiction

Koestler, Arthur. *Darkness at Noon*, Penguin, 1969
Malamud, Bernard. *The Fixer*, Penguin, 1966
Orwell, George. "A Hanging" in *The Collected Essays, Journalism and Letters*, Vol I, Penguin, 1970
Sartre, Jean-Paul. "The Wall" in *Intimacy*, Panther, 1960
Sillitoe, Alan. *The Loneliness of the Long Distance Runner*, Granada, 1985

Advice on Writing: Note-making Technique

Whether you are making notes in lessons, or from books, or as an exam exercise, there are various methods which you can use to simplify and clarify your note-making.

The advice which follows, as you can see, is set out in note-form. This is the form you should follow when asked to rewrite given information in note-form as an exercise; it may also be a useful method to use for note-taking from books and lessons; you can modify it as you wish, of course, for your own purposes.

I Making notes in lessons/lectures.
A Don't try to write down everything.
B Concentrate on main points.
C If possible, try to make sure you understand an idea before writing it down.
D Use a system of abbreviations:
  (*i*) miss out unimportant words like "a", "the".

    (*ii*) use abbreviations for as many words as possible:

        a) common abbreviations, e.g.:

           1. ∵ − because

           2. ∴ − therefore

           3. + − and

           4. c.f. − compare, remember in this context

           5. i.e. − that is

           6. N.B. − note well

                    etc.

        b) personal abbreviations: work out as many as possible, e.g.:

           1. sim. − similar (to)

           2. diffic. − difficult

           3. diff. − different

           4. poss. − possibly

           5. prob. − probably

           6. char. − character

                    etc.

        c) use initial letters for name of characters and titles, e.g.:

           1. O − *Othello*

           2. "P.I." − *A Passage to India*

    (*iii*) N.B.: never use abbreviations in writing intended to be read by someone else.

II Making notes from books

A Decide first whether book is suitable:

    (*i*)   skim over chapter(s).

    (*ii*) concentrate on headings + 1st + last paragraphs of sections.

B Make notes by one of the following methods:

    (*i*)   using a pencil:

        a) read through a section

        b) re-read, underlining or marking in margin relevant points in pencil

        c) write out marked sections, trying to use own words

    (*ii*) relying on memory:

        a) read through a section

        b) re-read, pausing over each key point

        c) make notes from memory, as far as possible

        d) check back to book whenever necessary in making notes

C Use format illustrated here in setting out notes:

    (*i*)   use indentations for major and subsidiary points

    (*ii*) mark points with letters and figures, if it makes notes clearer

    (*iii*) use colour, underlinings, etc. to emphasise key points

    (*iv*) use new page for each new set of notes

III Note-making as an exam. exercise

A Read through passage as many times as is necessary to understand main argument.

B Underline each main point.

C Write each main point as a heading, underlined, + write notes under each heading, with sub-headings and subsidiary points, using format illustrated here.

IV Making revision notes

A Don't just keep re-reading your notes.

B Organise your revision:
  (*i*) Take a theme or a character in literature.
  (*ii*) Read through your notes, jotting down in *brief summary form*, with page references if relevant, each important detail relating to theme or character.
  (*iii*) Re-order your summary notes into a logical pattern.
  (*iv*) Learn your summarised points, looking back to original notes and/or book for amplification when necessary.

C Write out a realistic revision schedule for each day up to the exams.

D Answer exam questions in note-form, as part of revision.

V Conditions for note-making

A Try to make notes in a quiet, well-lit and comfortable place.

B Don't start if you have something on your mind which will distract your concentration.

C Have regular breaks (but avoid watching television during them!).

D Always have a clear end in view for each work session.

7

Women

The question of women's role and identity in the modern world has become, over the past two decades, an issue which few people of either sex in the western would are able to ignore, and it is the theme of this chapter.

The chapter begins with a comprehension passage from the most influential feminist book of the early 1970s, *The Female Eunuch*, by the Australian writer and journalist Germaine Greer, and the chapter is then divided into sub-themes, each of which is followed by discussion questions. The themes are explored largely through extracts from books written in the 1980s by women.

There is no particular reason to tackle the sections and questions in order; in fact, the questions themselves could well be ignored altogether, and a free-ranging discussion conducted after the chapter has been read as a whole. Alternatively, the sections can be discussed separately, without specific reference to the questions, or particular issues suggested by some of the questions can be discussed. The questions provide plenty of scope for research by students of other disciplines, ranging from history and sociology to music and art, but the only essential requirement is to read and consider the extracts themselves.

Comprehension

Read the following passage and answer the questions which follow it. You are advised to spend about one hour on this exercise.

Energy is the power that drives every human being. It is not lost by exertion but maintained by it, for it is a faculty of the psyche. It is driven to perverted manifestations by curbs and checks. Like the motive force that drives the car along the highway, when it meets with an obstacle it turns to destructive force and shakes its source to pieces. It is not too hard to point out to the averagely perceptive human being that women have plenty of the destructive kind of energy, but far fewer people can see that women's destructiveness is creativity turned in upon itself by constant frustration. Nervous diseases, painful menstruation, unwanted pregnancies, accidents of all kinds, are all
10 evidence of women's energy destroying them. It extends beyond them, wreaking havoc with the personalities and achievements of others, especially their husbands and their children. That is not to say that women must hate all their relatives, but that if children are presented to women as a duty and marriage as an inescapable yoke, then the more energy they have the more

they will fret and chafe, tearing themselves and their dependants to pieces. When children are falsely presented to women as their only significant contribution, the proper expression of their creativity and their lives' work, the children and their mothers suffer for it.

The adult woman has already established a pattern of perversity in the expression of her desires and motives which ought to fit her for the distorted version of motherhood: it will not disappear if she is allowed alternatives. Any substituted aim is likely to be followed in a "feminine" way, that is, servilely, dishonestly, inefficiently, inconsistently. In most cases women are not offered a genuine alternative to repressive duties and responsibilities: most would happily give up unskilled labour in a factory or the tedium of office work for the more "natural" tedium of a modern household, because their energies are so thwarted by the usual kinds of female work that they imagine even housework would be a preferable alternative. Women who are offered education are offered a genuine alternative, insofar as they are offered genuine education, a rare commodity in these days of universal induction. And yet, when they were offered education at first the result was not the creation of an instant race of superwomen. This is one contemporary's account of the first female undergraduates, and university teachers will recognise a familiar phenomenon:

> "At lectures women students are models of attention and industry; perhaps they even apply themselves too much to carrying home in black and white what they have heard. They generally occupy the front seats because they enter their names early and then because they arrive early, well before the beginning of the lectures. Only this fact is noticeable, that often they merely give a superficial glance at the preparations that the professor passes round; sometimes they even pass them on to their neighbours without even looking at them; a longer examination would hinder their taking notes."

What this rather prejudiced observer noticed is real enough: the girls were diligent, even too diligent, but their efforts were expended on mistaken goals. They were anxious to please, to pick up everything that they were told, but the preparations handed around by the lecturer were the real subject of the lecture, and in that they were not interested at all. Their energy is all expended on conforming with disciplinary and other requirements, not in gratifying their own curiosity about the subject that they are studying, and so most of it is misdirected into meaningless assiduity. This phenomenon is still very common among female students, who are forming a large proportion of the arts intake at universities. It is not surprising then that women seldom make the scientific advances, but rather serve men as laboratory assistants, working under direction: it is merely a continuation of the same phenomenon that we observed in their undergraduate days.

By the time they have come to apply for entrance to a university the pattern of their useless deflection of energy is already set. In the very great majority of cases they have not retained enough drive to desire to qualify themselves any further; the minority who go to university do so too often as a response to guidance and pressure from their mistresses at school, still not knowing what the real point is, still not interested in developing their own potential: we are not surprised to find that many of them think of even their professional life either as a stop-gap or an indirect qualification for marriage.

All the blanket objections to women in professions may be understood as ways of stating this basic situation. They may appear to be the judgements of prejudice and, insofar as they adduce no other cause than sex, we must admit that they are. However, unless feminists admit that the phenomena
70 described by critics of women's performance in industry, offices, school-rooms, trade unions and in the arts and sciences are real, they must fail to identify the problem, and therefore to solve it. It is true that opportunities have been made available to women far beyond their desires to use them. It is also true that the women who avail themselves of opportunities too often do so in a feminine, filial, servile fashion. It must be understood that it will not suffice to encourage women to use an initiative that they have not got, just as it is useless to revile them for not having it. We must endeavour to understand how it is that women's energy is systematically deflected from birth to puberty, so that when they come to maturity they have only fitful resource
80 and creativity.

GERMAINE GREER

Note: Your answers should be *in your own words* as far as possible.

(a) Explain the point of the simile of the car (lines 1–5).   (3 *marks*)

(b) Explain the writer's theory of the causes and effects of "women's destructiveness".   (5 *marks*)

(c) Why is the word "feminine" in inverted commas (line 22)?   (3 *marks*)

(d) What is the writer's purpose in quoting the "account of the first female undergraduates"?   (4 *marks*)

(e) Why is it "not surprising that women seldom make the scientific advances" according to the writer?   (4 *marks*)

(f) Explain the writer's attitude to "the blanket objections to women in professions".   (4 *marks*)

(g) Discuss the implications of the final sentence.   (4 *marks*)

(h) Give the meaning of three of the following phrases as they appear in the passage:
   i)   a faculty of the psyche (line 2);
   ii) a pattern of perversity (line 19);
   iii) meaningless assiduity (line 51);
   iv) filial, servile fashion (line 75).   (6 *marks*)

(i) Comment on the overall view of women expressed in the passage.   (7 *marks*)

(*Total:* 40 *marks*)

Introduction

The modern "feminist" or "women's liberation" movement has its
origins in nineteenth century women's rights organisations. First sketched
out by Mary Wollstonecraft in her book *Vindication of the Rights of
Women*, published in 1792, the feminist cause was taken up more
concretely in Europe and America in the late 1840s and early 1850s, as
British sociologist Ann Oakley explains in *Subject Women*:

The "Declaration of Sentiments" and "Resolutions" adopted by the first
American women's suffrage convention in 1848 summarised the outlines of
women's position in many countries of the world at that time. It stated the
feminist grievance in no uncertain terms:

> The history of mankind is a history of repeated injuries and usurpations
> on the part of man toward woman, having in direct object the establish-
> ment of an absolute tyranny over her . . . .
> He has never permitted her to exercise her inalienable right to the elective
> franchise . . . .
> He has made her, if married, in the eyes of the law, civilly dead.
> He has taken from her all right in property, even to the wages she
> earns . . . .
> He has so framed the laws of divorce, as to what shall be the proper causes
> and in cases of separation, to whom the guardianship of the children shall
> be given, as to be wholly regardless of the happiness of women − the law,
> in all cases, going upon false supposition of the supremacy of man, and
> giving all power into his hands . . . .
> He has monopolised nearly all the profitable employments, and from
> those she is permitted to follow, she receives but a scanty remuneration.
> He closes against her all the avenues to wealth and distinction which he
> considers most honourable to himself. As a teacher of theology,
> medicine, or law she is not known.
> He has denied her the facilities for obtaining a thorough education, all
> colleges being closed against her . . . .
> He has endeavoured, in every way that he could, to destroy her con-
> fidence in her own powers, to lessen her self-respect, and to make her
> willing to lead a dependent and abject life . . . .

The first women's suffrage society in Britain was formed in 1865, and by
the end of the century the suffragette movement was intensely active,
under the forceful leadership of such women as Emmeline Pankhurst,
becoming organised in 1903 in the Women's Social and Political Union.
During the First World War women were encouraged to undertake a
whole range of jobs and skills for which they had previously been
considered incapable or unsuitable, and, as a result of this as well as the
fierce and persistent suffragette activity, women were at last given limited
access to the franchise in Britain in 1918.

   After that, for over forty years, the feminist movement fell into
abeyance, to be revived in the early 1960s by women's liberation

organisations in Britain and America, coming to the forefront of public consciousness once more in 1968.

The significance of the arrangements for men and women in Western society before their recent modifications is suggested by the British philosopher Janet Radcliffe Richards in *The Sceptical Feminist*:

The facts are stark, but beyond any question. All social arrangements, institutions and customs which defined the relative position of the sexes were designed *to ensure that women should be in the power and service of men*.

This no doubt sounds like pure feminist rant, but it is not. It is proved by many quite incontrovertible facts about the formal devices which for most of history were employed by men to make sure that women were kept in their power, and involves no recourse to extravagant assertions about the general moral turpitude of men . . . .

To see the position of women in this way is to see clearly what femininity traditionally was. Feminine characteristics were the ones needed for making a success of the position into which women were forced, and roughly, therefore, to be feminine was to be pleasing to men. The whole essence of femininity is, or at least traditionally was, the limiting of all endeavour and activity to a confined end. Ideal femininity has never consisted in weakness and incompetence (contrary to much popular opinion, which seems to confuse descriptive and prescriptive femininity at this point as at many others); no man ever wanted a total loss of a woman. The idea was only to direct all abilities to being useful to men and their offspring, using a great deal of skill (the more the better) but always carefully directing it so that it presented no threat to men's position. It was unfeminine of women to want to study at universities or have the vote because in doing so they were showing that they had ideas about stepping beyond their allotted sphere: higher education and political power were not among the requirements for being a devoted wife and mother, and to seek them was to want to compete with men and become independent of them, rather than to remain in service to them.

RADCLIFFE RICHARDS

The advances made by women in the twentieth century away from this enforced domesticity and subservience owe much to advances in contraception, offering a control over reproduction which was never previously possible. As the French philosopher and novelist Simone de Beauvoir points out in her classic study of women, *The Second Sex*:

One of the basic problems of woman . . . is the reconciliation of her reproductive role and her part in productive labour. The fundamental fact that from the beginning of history doomed woman to domestic work and prevented her taking part in the shaping of the world was her enslavement to the generative function. In female animals there is a physiological and seasonal rhythm that assures the economising of their strength; in women, on the contrary, between puberty and menopause nature sets no limits to the number of her pregnancies . . . . Contraceptives have been in existence since antiquity, . . . but [they] were practically unknown to the Middle Ages in Europe; scarcely a trace of them is to be found up to the eighteenth century. For many women in those times life was an uninterrupted succession of pregnancies . . . .

[Birth control and abortion] are of tremendous importance for women in particular; she can reduce the number of her pregnancies and make them a rationally integral part of her life, instead of being their slave.

DE BEAUVOIR

Discussion Points

Why do you think the situation of women in Europe and America summarised in the 1848 American women's suffrage convention was as it was?

What were the original conditions for female suffrage in the 1918 act? Why do you think these restrictions were imposed? When were they removed?

What happened to most of the women who were employed in "men's" jobs at the end of the First World War? Why?

Why do you think the women's movement died down after 1918? Why did it revive in the 1960s?

Women's Inferiority in the Arts and Sciences

Compared with men there have been very few women of recognised genius. Many people feel that this is because women as a sex are generally intrinsically less capable of inspiration and more narrow in their range of feeling and thinking than men.

Simone de Beauvoir takes up this point:

The anti-feminists obtain from the study of history two contradictory arguments:
1. women have never created anything great; and
2. the situation of women has never prevented the flowering of great feminine personalities . . . .
The women who have accomplished works comparable to those of men are those exalted by the power of social institutions above all sexual differentiation. Queen Isabella, Queen Elizabeth, Catherine the Great were neither male nor female − they were sovereigns. It is remarkable that their femininity, when socially abolished, should have no longer meant inferiority: the proportion of queens who had great reigns is infinitely above that of great kings. Religion works the same transformation: Catherine of Siena, St Theresa, quite beyond any physiological consideration, were sainted souls; the life they led, secular and mystic, their acts, and their writings rose to heights that few men have ever reached.

It is quite conceivable that if other women fail to make a deep impression upon the world, it is because they are tied down in their situation. They can hardly take a hand in affairs in other than a negative and oblique manner.

DE BEAUVOIR

Themes for Discussion

How were musicians and painters generally financed in Europe, up to the nineteenth century? Does this have any bearing on the lack of notable women musicians and painters in the earlier times?

Why was George Eliot so called? What does this show about the problems of aspiring women writers in the nineteenth century?

How many great nineteenth-century British writers were women? How many of them were married, with children?

In what fields have women generally achieved fame and distinction in the twentieth century? Why these, rather than others?

Does the comprehension passage from Germaine Greer's book help to shed any light on the reasons why women continue to be outshone by men in the arts and sciences? What other reasons are there to explain this phenomenon?

Biology or conditioning?

The most intense controversy between feminists and anti-feminists concerns *the nature of women*. Most men, and many women, tend still to argue that the sexes are by nature psychologically different because of their biological make-up. Post-war feminist writers, on the other hand, have generally contended that these differences are simply or largely the result of conditioning and that there are no fundamental differences between the sexes, beyond the obvious physical ones. Girls, it is argued, are conditioned to think of their future preeminently in terms of wife and motherhood, by being given dolls to play with and being expected to stay in the home to help with household chores, and by being taught such subjects in school as cookery and needlework, whilst boys are prepared for their future role as breadwinners and decision-makers by being given toys like guns, being encouraged to be aggressive and independent, and being taught technical subjects from an early age.

Janet Radcliffe Richards attempts to shed some light on this endlessly contentious issue:

Common beliefs about the differences between the sexes are still usually based only on differences between men and women as they appear. Men are seen to be interested in politics or business while women tend to talk about homes and men and babies; men are seen to have mechanical or business abilities while women are baffled when confronted with the engine of a car and don't know what to make of bank statements, and so on. But even to the extent that propositions such as these stem from impartial observation (which is true of by no means all of them) they are still not enough to show that women and men really are different by nature. You cannot tell the nature of anything just by looking in a casual and unsystematic way at how it appears, because whenever something is observed it is in some environment or other, and the total phenomenon results not only from the nature of the thing under observation, but also from the environment it is in. If, therefore, two things appear different, they may not be different in nature at all: they may simply be in different environments. And this, of course, is what most feminists claim about many of the alleged differences in nature between men and women . . . .

The feminist argument is that there are all kinds of systematic differences in the environments of men and women which are so subtle, or so universally taken for granted, that they have gone completely unnoticed or are underestimated. It is only relatively recently, for instance, that we have noticed that boy and girl children are treated differently almost from birth, or understood how radically people's performances are influenced by what is expected of them . . . .

Recent discoveries of the extent and significance of systematic differences in environment between men and women are indeed enough to prove that most of the evidence people thought they had about the natures of men and women is totally inadequate to support the usual conclusions. However, it is important to realise that that is all they do. We may know that traditional views are almost certainly wrong, but it does not follow that we know which views are right.

When we find the environmental differences between two things are probably enough to account for their appearing to be different from each other, it certainly follows that they may be intrinsically alike in nature, but not that they certainly are. For instance, the difference in social expectations of the behaviour of men and women is enough to account for the fact that women show emotion far more readily than men do; even if they were precisely the same by nature this would account for different behaviour. It does not, however, prove that they are the same by nature. Perhaps women really are by nature more inclined to show emotion, as well as being socially encouraged to do so. Or again, the fact that women have, during most of history, been forced by their biology (and men) to spend nearly all their time in the care of small children is a perfectly sufficient condition of their having made relatively little impact on the history of the world; if men had had to do the same they would not have had time for other things either. However, it does not follow that men and women have the same inherent capacities.

Perhaps women are inherently different; perhaps nature made them less interested in other things to ensure that they would be sufficiently inclined to care for their children.

Of course our ignorance is lessening. In several areas we have made a great deal of progress, and have certainly shown that women are capable of acquiring skills traditionally thought beyond them, as soon as they are given the opportunity. In the most complicated areas, however, dealing with innate desires, temperament and so on, it is very difficult to find out how different men and women are. In the first place, social customs are so deeply entrenched that there are relatively few natural variations in environment we can watch, and manipulating society for the purpose of experiment is difficult . . . .

The reason why it is important for feminists to study history and anthropology is that knowing how women acted in different times and under different circumstances gives us a greater understanding of their natures than seeing them only here and now.

This is a kind of work which must be carried forward with care and perseverance if we are to find out about the raw material we have to work with in planning our ideal society. And in the meantime we can certainly argue strenuously that traditional ideas about women and their differences from men are founded on totally inadequate evidence, and ought to be abandoned forthwith.

RADCLIFFE RICHARDS

Themes for Discussion

Do you think that there are any differences between men and women which we can be *fairly certain* are biological differences in the nature of the sexes?

Is the possibility that most of the apparently natural differences between the sexes may be produced by conditioning sufficient reason to treat the sexes equally, since differences *do* still exist, whatever the cause?

What areas of employment have recently ceased to be exclusively male preserves? Is there any good reason why any of them should have always been reserved for men before?

Should positive discrimination in favour of women be introduced, to help women to overcome their traditional disadvantages? If so, in what areas?

What anthropological evidence has come to light about "primitive" societies in which men and women do not behave according to their traditional sex roles? Is it of any significance?

Should parents try to avoid guiding their children into conventional sex roles? Would social and peer group influence have the effect of conventional gender differentiation anyway?

Should schools treat boys and girls equally in the choice of school subjects?

Men's Attitudes to Women

There can be little real doubt that throughout history men have treated women as their inferiors, and regarded feminine traits with contempt. In the late 1960s the phrase "male chauvinist pig" was coined to describe men who allowed their prejudice to show, and masculine assumptions of superiority led some of the more radical women's groups to advocate avoidance of all dealings with men. This attitude can be seen, for instance, in the women's peace camp at Greenham Common, from which men are discouraged on the grounds that as soon as men take part in activities with women they attempt to take over.

Let us look at what some modern women writers have to say about sexual attitudes and their implications. First, another extract from *The Sceptical Feminist*:

It must be said on behalf of feminists who are inclined to resist any differences in function, convention and expectation between the sexes that they have one very strong argument on their side in men's quite astonishing record of downgrading whatever is associated with women. Margaret Mead commented that in every known society, men's activities were regarded as more important than women's, quite irrespective of what those activities were. "Men may cook or weave or dress dolls or hunt humming birds, but if such activities are appropriate occupations of men, then the whole society, men and women alike, vote them as important. When the same occupations are performed by women, they are regarded as less important."

That is very striking, but even without any special knowledge of all known societies we have a pretty good idea of what an uphill struggle we should have even within our own if we tried to establish respect for what has traditionally been associated with women. The average woman is very pleased if she has any understanding of any such male terrain as the engine of a car, but there are still a good many men around whose claim not to know where to find anything in the kitchen is really a boast about their never demeaning themselves with women's work. Women on the tube are happy to be seen reading city newspapers, but no man would dream of knitting in public as some women do. It is quite unthinkable that the general relaxation of conventions of dress which has led to women's wearing trousers might have resulted in men's taking to skirts, for reasons having nothing at all to do with the relative comfort of the two. Girls in schools are doing more science and metal work, but most people are still slightly shocked at the thought that boys might learn to sew. And as Michael Korda in his book on male chauvinism quotes Jules Feiffer as saying, "Whatever ground women manages to establish for herself man abandons, denying its importance." It is not at all difficult to understand the point of view of feminists who see that in any difference there lies potential inequality, and who suspect that wherever there is potential inequality men will contrive to make it actual.

However, not all women are willing to give up the struggle just because they are not very optimistic about the moral improvement of men. There are feminists who think that to abandon feminine things just because men are determined to downgrade them is to give in altogether, and what we should be doing is demanding respect for whatever deserves respect, feminine or not.

RADCLIFFE RICHARDS

The alternative to ignoring male prejudice for women with ambitions in male-dominated areas of work − aping men − is discussed by the

American writer Betty Friedan in a magazine interview from *The Sunday Times*, with Rosemary Wittman Lamb:

> "I had lunch with a group of women executives, and I was horrified," she told me. "They were so grim, so dressed-for-success. And they told me: 'We have to be hard-headed, like the men, and get rid of all vestiges of femininity'."

In the area of love and marriage, many feminists argue that only a genuine feeling of equality between the partners can engender mutual respect which is necessary if love is to last. Here is a fairly radical view of love and marriage by the British journalist and writer, Jill Tweedie, from her book *In the Name of Love*:

It is a bitter irony for men that their insistence on women's inferiority, their refusal to grant her a place in the sun, has robbed them of the only chance they have to be loved properly. They cannot love women because they have made women unequal and forced them into all the unloving patterns of inequality. And women cannot love them because the inferior do not properly love their masters, they only prostrate themselves or live vicariously through them. Contrary to the old wives' tales, the real joy of love lies in the knowledge that your lover could manage without you, that he or she has no *need* of you but simply feels a great deal happier that you are there.

With unequals you must always lie a little, if only to save them pain. Equals know that pain is part of growing and believe each other strong enough to stand what is necessary for growth. This applies as much to the minefield of outside sexual encounters as anything else. True love accepts that one person cannot provide everything for another — indeed there is a kind of obscenity in the very notion. Besides, what have you gained if you force anything, even faithfulness, on another person? Their presence, perhaps, but who wants a body with a mind elsewhere? What is the point of trying to coerce what cannot be coerced? Love does not "allow", "permit", or "forbid" or it is not love.

TWEEDIE

Discussion points

Why do you think that women have tended to accept the idea that their activities, whatever they may be, are less important than those of men?

Should women try to develop the kind of toughness and aggressiveness normally associated with men in order to compete with them in the job market? What is the alternative?

Do you agree that a feeling of equality between partners is the strongest basis for marriage? How possible is it to achieve?

Do you think it is right for married partners to separate if they no longer feel in love?

A Woman's Place: at home, at work, or both?

Arguments have raged, since the renaissance of the feminist movement in the 1960s, about the extent to which home and family should dominate a woman's life. At the one extreme is the traditional view that a woman fulfils her biological destiny as a mother and housewife, and that no other role can fulfil her *as* a woman. At the other extreme is the radical feminist rejection of the family, which is seen as a means of repressing women and keeping them in subjection, and preventing them from achieving their fulfilment as *people*, which can only come through the pursuit of an independent career. Housework, according to this view, is seen as a dreary and endless routine, as was colourfully expressed by Simone de Beauvoir in 1949: "Washing, ironing, sweeping, ferreting out fluff from under wardrobes – all this halting of decay is also the denial of life; for time simultaneously creates and destroys, and only its negative aspect concerns the housekeeper".

Writers in the 1940s and 1950s developed the image of the happy housewife, competent in a wide range of domestic skills, providing sympathy and support for her breadwinner husband, and creatively bringing up her children in a loving home environment.

The first English-speaking writer to emphasise the discontent felt by many women with this role, evidenced by the large number of housewives dependent on tranquillisers, was Betty Friedan, in her book *The Feminine Mystique*, published in 1963. She called it "the problem without a name", and characterised it thus:

> It was a strange stirring, a sense of dissatisfaction, a yearning that women suffered in the middle of the twentieth century in the United States. Each suburban housewife struggled with it alone. As she made the beds, shopped for groceries, matched slip cover material, ate peanut butter sandwiches, chauffeured Cub Scouts and Brownies, lay beside her husband at night, she was afraid to ask even of herself the silent question: "Is this all?"

Many feminists in the late 1970s and 1980s, Betty Friedan included, have arrived at a kind of synthesis, arguing that most women need both work and family in order to be fulfilled. In *The Second Stage*, published in 1982, Betty Friedan takes this viewpoint:

Personal choices and political strategies of women today are distorted when they deny the reality of both sets of needs: woman's need for power, identity, status and security through her own work or action in society, which the reactionary enemies of feminism deny; and the need for love and identity, status, security and generation through marriage, children, home, the family, which those feminists still locked in their own extreme reaction deny. Both sets of needs are essential to women, and to the evolving human condition . . . .

The enemies of feminism insist that woman's move to equality, self-realisation and her own power in society is destroying the family, which they feel is woman's real focus of power. Many feminists insist that the family was, and is, the enemy, the prime obstacle to woman's self-realisation. There are pieces of the truth in these interlocking fears, shadows of conflicts that were insoluble in the past. I believe that the first stage, woman's movement to equality and her own personhood, was, in fact, necessary for the survival and economic/emotional health of the family, and that the second stage can, and must, transcend these conflicts. For I believe, from all we know of human psychology and history, that neither woman nor man lives by work, or love, alone: the absolutely powerless, the denigrated, the self-abnegating ones are too hungry for power, too lacking in self, to love, and nurture; the loveless crave power because they lack both love and self. The human self defines itself and grows through love and work.

Why are some women so afraid, on either side of this conflict, to put to the test of personal reality our own needs for power in the world and for love and family?

FRIEDAN

Such a choice can of course cause immense practical problems, especially when childcare facilities are lacking and husbands are not supportive in the home. Betty Friedan interviewed many working mothers before writing *The Second Stage*. Here are two typical "cris de coeur":

A young woman in her third year of Harvard Medical School tells me, "I'm going to be a surgeon. I'll never be a trapped housewife like my mother. But I would like to get married and have children, I think. They say we can have it all. But how? I work thirty-six hours in the hospital, twelve off. How am I going to have a relationship, much less kids, with hours like that? I'm not sure I can be a superwoman. I'm frightened that I may be kidding myself. Maybe I can't have it all. Either I won't be able to have the kind of marriage I dream of or the kind of medical career I want."

"The worst problem for women today is trying to juggle it all," said a thirty-eight-year-old lawyer in Chicago, mother of two. "Wanting to get ahead in your career, wanting to have a perfect marriage and really be with your husband, wanting to do all the right things about your kids, and not giving up any of it. The guilt, because you can't really do all these things and do each one perfectly."

FRIEDAN

For many women, of course, there is no dilemma. In this letter to the *Guardian*, Anne P Heaton expresses her feeling of fulfilment in having adopted the traditional role of homemaker and mother:

I like being a housewife. It is 30 years since I left university, but I hope my mind has not been completely atrophied by staying at home to look after my family. Bringing up my family has been a joyous occupation for the most part, and far more satisfying and entertaining than any of the jobs I held before. I have always had time for them and for my husband, and have not missed any of their childhood. Now that I am older I have time for myself and the freedom to do what I choose. I certainly don't feel like a dodo, or a parasite for that matter.

Similarly, for many women who *do* seek outlets for their creativity beyond their traditional role, the experience of bringing up children remains their greatest source of satisfaction and achievement. The Nigerian novelist, poet and television playwright, Buchi Emecheta, expressed this view in an article in *New Internationalist*, in 1985:

I had my photograph taken once in my "office" where I do my writing. The photo-journalist was a staunch feminist, and was so angry that my "office" was my kitchen and that packets of breakfast cereals were in the background. I was letting the women's movement down by allowing such a photograph to be taken.

But that was where I worked, because it was warmer, because it was convenient for me to be able to see my family when I put my typewriter to one side. I tried in vain to tell her that, in my kitchen, I felt I was doing more for the peace of the world than the nuclear scientist: in our kitchens we raise all the future Reagans, or the future Jesuses. In our kitchens we wash for them and cook for them. In our kitchens they learn to love and to hate. And we send them out from our kitchens to be grown men and women.

What greater work is there than that? I do not think it low. A mother with a family is an economist, a nurse, a painter, a diplomat, and more. Those who wish to control and influence the future generation by giving birth and nurturing the young should not be looked down upon. If I had my way it would be the highest-paid job in the world.

BUCHI EMECHETA

Despite two decades of women's liberation, many people continue to take the stereotyped sex roles for granted. Here are some instances:

A son to carry on the family name, and share in all the excitement of cheering on his dad's favourite football team, or a daughter who will dress in pretty frocks, borrow mum's make-up and raise the next generation? That's what every parent wonders about when a baby's on the way. And it's the biggest mystery in the world.

from *Sunday* magazine (1985)

He's earned the sort of millions that could provide a life of super luxury. Yet Paul McCartney has not forgotten his working-class roots, insisting that his wife Linda does the laundry, washes the dishes and rises at seven to cook the family breakfast.

from *Woman* magazine (1984)

If the good Lord had intended us to have equal rights to go out to work, he would not have created man and woman.

PATRICK JENKIN, MP

Discussion points

Do you think it is better if women stay at home while their children are young?

Do you think that most women with children who work do so mainly in the interest of personal fulfilment or financial security?

How realistic do you think it is for a woman to attempt to pursue a demanding full-time career while bringing up young children?

Do you think that employers should be compelled by law to provide crêche facilities for the children of female employees?

Women at Work

In the 1970s in Britain two acts were passed — the Equal Pay Act of 1970 and the Sex Discrimination Act of 1975 — aimed at ending discrimination against women in employment.

Many fields of employment opened up for British women in the 1970s, but in terms of pay the results of these acts have not been as dramatic as might have been expected, as the following extracts from the 1983 *Low Pay Reviews* reveal:

Women, young workers and the ethnic minorities are the main groups within Britain's low paid workforce.

Women represent 39.5 per cent of Britain's total workforce (*Equal Opportunities Commission Annual Report*, 1981) but three-quarters of all the low paid. Half of all full-time women workers earn less than the LPU's target of £90 per week in April 1982 . . . with many jobs paying wages very much below this target . . . .

In a quarter of all occupations in which women work they outnumber men 9 to 1. This is one reason why the Equal Pay Act has had limited effect in raising women's wages. Women's position relative to men's since the introduction of the Equal Pay Act has changed very little, and has slipped one per cent in the year to April 1982.

Even where men and women are employed in the same occupation women are likely to earn much less. Compare the gross average weekly earnings . . . of a male bar worker (£81.90) with that of a female barmaid (£61.60). The differential between the sexes is still wide. (Figures taken from the *New Earnings Survey*, 1982) . . . .

The argument that women's low wages are of little real importance is without justification. The pin money myth should be laid to rest. Between three and four times as many families would be in poverty were it not for the contribution of a second wage to the household budget. One tenth of women under retirement age are heads of households in England, and many are heads of single parent families, which, with 1 in 4 marriages ending in divorce, will inevitably increase.

(*Low Pay Review*, 12 February 1983)

The problem of the undervaluation of women's domestic responsibilities can result in them viewing paid work as a peripheral activity, and, of course, the very low pay which such work offers reinforces this. The result is that very often women themselves undervalue the work that they do.

Clearly a major requirement in overcoming these problems is the adoption of trade union and government policies which make it easier both for men to take an equal role in child care and other domestic work and, at the same time, which allow women to exercise more choice in terms of their participation in economic activity. Trade Unions are beginning to recognise the need for policies which would help achieve these aims such as better maternity/paternity arrangements and shorter working hours designed to erode the distinction between full-time and part-time work. In the long term there is a need for work and school hours to be tailored to fit in with each other rather than conflict as they do now.

(*Low Pay Review*, 14 June 1983)

The country which has gone furthest in legislating for equality between men and women in employment is Sweden. Here is a report by Anuradha Vittachi on the Swedish system and its effects at the beginning of the 80s:

Officially, women in Sweden are more liberated than anywhere else in the world. "It's socially unacceptable in Sweden today to think women are anything less than the equal of men," I was told by a young male teacher in one of Stockholm's suburbs. "Male chauvinists here have to retreat to the frozen North."

In every country, rich and poor, the biggest barrier to equality for a woman is her burden of "bearing and caring" for children. That is why you cannot travel in Stockholm now by bus or train without being confronted by government-sponsored posters promoting the idea that men should share fully in the task of bringing up their children. "Father's freedom to be with children" reads the caption, "it's natural. Make the most of your rights".

Now under Swedish law men can take as much as six months "paternity leave" when a child is born, without loss of pay or job security. Or men and women can decide to share "parenthood leave".

Men and women can also take up to three months leave at any time before the child's eighth birthday if they feel they need to spend time with a son or daughter – for example during the settling-in period at the start of school.

Men as well as women can take up to twelve days a year leave when their children are sick – and they do. On several occasions in Stockholm I found my appointments postponed because the men concerned had to go home to look after an ailing child.

Swedish law also gives couples the right to share one job so they can be free to look after their children equally. Nor can a father of a young child be legally refused his right to work a six-hour day. And there is mounting pressure to pay him for the two hours he spends at home. All these changes mean men have more time for sharing family duties.

To back up these changes there have been other reforms to help equalise the sexes. The retirement age is the same for men as for women. Free abortions are available up to the eighteenth week of pregnancy. Free contraception counselling services are available to all. Husbands and wives are taxed separately. Wives are no longer classified as "dependents". Marriage is seen now as just one form of "voluntary cohabitation between individuals". Custody of children following a divorce may be shared between parents and is not automatically awarded to the mother.

"There's a big crisis in Sweden now and it's a crisis for the men," I was told by Lars Nilsson, a young journalist. "The men have to face the problem of changing their traditional role to keep up with changes in society and the demands of women. The man who can't change loses all the time. He is stuck, like Superman where there is Kryptonite about."

Even men with traditional views of the submissive and domesticated wife can find their expectations shattered by the matter-of-fact acceptance of equality of women.

"My parents had pretty conservative ideas about men and women," said the owner of a small business in his late thirties. "But not so my wife. So when I got married I had a problem. It forced me to change. Now my wife and I take care of the business and the children, and the cleaning. At first it was unusual for me − especially the laundry. But now at home we share fifty-fifty, and I'm happy my 14-year-old son takes sharing for granted. He's been cooking dinners all week" . . . .

So the foundations seem to have been laid for achieving equality between the sexes in Sweden. But there is still a long way to go. Cooking and childcare classes for boys and metal-work for girls may be compulsory at school but 86 per cent of students in technical courses are still boys and girls still flock to nursing and pre-school training colleges. And although men have been entitled to parenthood leave since 1974, less than 10 per cent of fathers have been taking advantage of their rights.

Women may earn equal pay but their access to equal work is only theoretical. The labour market is split between "men's jobs" in heavy industry and "women's jobs" in the service sector. Three quarters of "all gainfully employed women work at only twenty-five different jobs" − and it can be no coincidence that these jobs are badly paid. Even in female-dominated professions the top jobs usually go to men. For instance, teachers tend to be women, but head teachers tend to be men. The management of the hotel I stayed in was almost exclusively male but invariably my bed was made and my room cleaned by women.

Sweden's radical ideal whereby the "time-cake" of men and women would be carved into four equal portions − one for paid work, one for family, one for community service, and the last for leisure − is still a dream. But things are on the move. Where else in the world could a woman feel within her rights to complain that her husband "only" took two months leave to look after the baby?

from *New Internationalist* (1980)

Discussion points

Why do you think the Equal Pay and Sex Discrimination Acts have not had a greater impact on removing the discrepancies in pay between men and women?

What do you think of the various methods outlined above for promoting equality of employment prospects between the sexes?

Do you think the traditional division between men's jobs and women's jobs should or could eventually be broken down?

Some Final Thoughts

In a magazine interview in *The Sunday Times* (November 1981), the American journalist Nora Ephron looked back on the women's liberation movement in the USA in the 1970s:

"My point is, we started out in the Sixties with this great burst of energy, and then degenerated into *massive* divorce. In 1973, 1974, 1975 the basic feminist act was to get divorced. In 1973 it seemed to me that five million women turned around and said: 'I divorce you! I divorce you! I divorce you!'

"The one thing that happened in 1972 was that all these men cleared the table. That was what everyone got their husbands to do. They all screamed and yelled about household chores and made lists about who did what and the men said: 'Okay, I'll clear the table'; and then looked round as though they deserved a medal. And they hoped it would all go away. And it did. It all went away. Their wives went away, everything went away. And they found someone else and they went back to being princes.

"So many of us in that period were trying to sort of smash feminism into our marriages. We ended up absolutely drained."

A magazine article in *The Sunday Times* (November 1978), written by Anna Coote, ended thus:

Will men's liberation be the movement of the 1980s, a natural successor to women's liberation? I doubt it. I am sure men are ultimately oppressed by their own machismo; but that is the price of power and most men are willing to pay it. Rarely, if ever, has any power group willingly surrendered power.

Discussion points

Has the women's liberation movement been essentially beneficial or damaging in its effects on the lives of men, women and children?

Do you think that a "men's liberation movement" is needed? What might its goals be? Are there any signs in the 1980s of men's attitudes to their position in the world radically changing?

Women in the Third World

The whole of this chapter so far has been concerned with the situation of women in the developed world. In large parts of the developing world the very idea of women's liberation is meaningless, as women continue to cope in the same ways as they have for centuries with the effects of male assumptions of women's inferiority and subservience.

In many areas of the Third World women are forced to play a major role in agriculture as well as child-rearing and home-making, and often gain little or no recognition for their contribution to the economic and domestic life of the family. The situation of women in developing countries is, however, far too varied for brief analysis. Instead, we will take a glimpse into the life of just one woman in Latin America, whose story has been repeated across the world countless millions of times over numberless centuries. She comes from the state of Rio Grande do Norte, in north-east Brazil, where rural mothers have an average of more than seven living children. She was met by Paul Harrison while he was researching for his book *Inside the Third World*, from which the extract is taken:

You often meet women like Luisa Gomez, a slight, small thirty-nine-year-old. She married at fourteen. Since then she has been pregnant sixteen times, once every eighteen months. For half of her adult life she has been pregnant, and for the other half breast-feeding the most recent addition. Only six of those sixteen are still alive. There were three stillbirths and seven died in their first year. Ten wasted pregnancies. Seven and a half years of drain on an already weak organism, for nothing. Worse than nothing, for all the anxiety, all the care, all the concern, and then the grief.

Life goes on like that. Before the first one is even on its feet, the next is on the way. Housework becomes a crushing burden with no labour-saving devices to help out. Feeding the family is like cooking for a works canteen. And with each successive birth the figure collapses a little further, the breasts sag and a paunch develops, making the women look pregnant even when they are not. Privacy, time to yourself, time to rest even, is an unheard-of, undreamed-of luxury. Bearing and rearing children, every girl is told, is a woman's only function. And because to believe otherwise would be to condemn herself to utter despair, the woman accepts the idea: and teaches it to her daughters.

HARRISON

Discussion points

Research and discuss some of the religious and cultural traditions which affect women in different countries and areas of the world.

Is it possible to envisage a time in the future when men and women all over the world will treat one-another as equals at home and at work?

Essay Titles

(a) ". . . most women nowadays expect to marry, have children and work."

(b) "Room at the top, but not for women!"

(c) "Women's liberation has resulted in men's enslavement."

(d) Is the status of women in our society still unsatisfactory?

(e) "Marriage is still a woman's best investment!" Discuss.

(f) Do you think it desirable or undesirable that men and women should maintain separate and clearly differentiated roles at home and at work?

(g) To what extent can male supremacy in commerce and industry be justified?

(h) How far have we got in equalising opportunities for the sexes, and how much further should we go?

(i) "Literature is the only art form in which women have excelled." How far do you agree?

Bibliography

de Beauvoir, Simone. *The Second Sex*, Penguin, 1983
Friedan, Betty. *The Feminine Mystique*, Gollancz, 1971
Friedan, Betty. *The Second Stage*, Michael Joseph, 1982
Greer, Germaine. *The Female Eunuch*, Paladin, 1971
Greer, Germaine. *Sex and Destiny: The Politics of Human Fertility* Picador, 1985
Oakley, Ann. *Subject Women*, Robertson, 1981
Millett, Kate. *Sexual Politics*, Virago, 1977
Radcliffe Richards, Janet. *The Sceptical Feminist*, Routledge and Kegan Paul, 1980
Spender, Dale, (ed). *Feminist Theorists*, The Women's Press, 1983
Tweedie, Jill. *In the Name of Love*, Jonathan Cape, 1979
Wollstonecraft, Mary, and Mill, John Stuart. *Vindication of the Rights of Women, Subjection of Women*, Everyman, 1982

Advice on Writing: Using Facts, Figures and Sources in Essays

It is perfectly possible to write a satisfactory argumentative essay with very little precise factual content, as was illustrated in Chapter 1. Facts and figures, however, give substance and conviction to an argument and it is sensible to learn a good deal of "hard" information in preparation for an examination language essay. The degree to which this information needs to be detailed and exact is largely a matter of common sense. It may be helpful, nevertheless, to give some examples of the kinds of factual information which do and do not need to be exact.

Quoting sources of information is sometimes important, but it's obviously not necessary to give the source of every piece of information you include in an essay. If you are offering general information which is common knowlege, or is the kind of information which could be checked from a number of sources, such as details of the paternity leave system and parenthood reforms in Sweden, there is no need to quote your source.

If you are giving precise figures, on the other hand, such as the percentage of the world's resources consumed by the USA, or the drop in the price of a commodity on the world market over a specified period, you ought to quote the source of the figures. The date when figures were issued also needs to be given sometimes, as when quoting the projected world population in the year 2000, since such projections are likely to change. Equally, if you quote an opinion, rather than presenting it as your own, you should be precise about the source of the opinion. For example, if you quote the opinion of Paul Cavadino, given on page 89, about the suitability of non-custodial sentences for two-thirds of the people now in prison, the point would gain much more bite and conviction if you quoted his name and official position, instead of saying "as has been suggested recently" or some similarly vague phrase. Sometimes it may be necessary to be *very* explicit in giving your source, for instance, in the case of information about the living conditions of Bolivian tin miners' families mentioned on page 25. If you merely quote the source as Domitila Barrios de Chungara, without mentioning who she is, and the title of her book, it will simply seem obscure. In this case you also need to quote the year of publication of the book, since the conditions referred to may have entirely altered since it was written. Generally speaking, however, there's no need to mention the actual book from which information or ideas are drawn, as long as the author is reasonably well known.

Exact figures and details should be given if doing so will clarify the point being made. In the case of historical background, for instance, precision is important. If you are mentioning acts of parliament, such as the Equal Pay Act, you should learn the date. If you mention the capital punishment debates in parliament, it is useful to know the years in which they took place. A proper historical perspective on events can only be given if you can quote dates; the year in which women achieved the vote, for instance, or the year when Mary Wollstonecraft achieved publication of the first feminist book.

Drawing comparisons between different groups of people in some particular respect is another case where precise back-up information is helpful. For instance, if you are arguing that women often earn less than men for similar work, despite the Equal Pay Act, you need at least to specify in which areas of work this is so, even if you can't quote figures. Similarly, if you are making the case that one of the reasons for women's wages being lower than men's on average is that many jobs are still heavily female-dominated, the statistic that women outnumber men 9 to 1 in a quarter of all occupations in which women work will add considerable strength to your argument. In this case, since the figures are not particularly well known or recognised, it would be useful to quote your source.

In general, exact facts and figures can often make an otherwise vague point precise and persuasive. A statement about Britain's prisons being seriously overcrowded is a case of point. If you could refer to the fact that prisoners are often held two or three to a cell built for one in Victorian times, you would establish the point convincingly. Greater detail than this, such as *how* often and in which prisons these conditions exist, is unnecessary. Here the source is less important, since the information is generally known and admitted. If you are mentioning famous people and places, you should try to make sure that you can give their names; instead, for instance, of referring to ''the headmaster of a progressive independent school'' when discussing the idealogy of Summerhill, you should be able to mention A S Neill and Summerhill by name.

Very often, of course, points can be made perfectly convincingly without precise facts and figures; you can, for instance, make the point that, despite anti-sexist legislation in Sweden, the great majority of students on technical courses there are boys, without needing to quote an exact figure. Common sense is ultimately the only guide in this matter.

8

Race

Ready, steady, Go! (handwritten annotation)

The riots which occurred in some inner city areas of England in the summer of 1981 shocked the whole of Europe and the English-speaking world. Though the riots stemmed from deprivation in general in those areas, and were by no means entirely "race riots", they starkly illustrated the tensions which exist between the "races" in Britain. This chapter will concentrate, on the racial situation in modern Britain. It begins with a passage for précis, taken from Mary Grigg's book *The White Question*.

Précis

Write a summary of the following passage in not more than 240 words (the passage contains about 710 words). Your summary should be in clear, connected English and the number of words used should be indicated at the end. You are advised to spend about one hour on this exercise.

Talking to a cultured Indian or Pakistani, who can make the profoundest comparisons between his own religion and Christianity, whose knowledge of English history surpasses the average Englishman's knowledge, whose political theory is derived from a deep insight into a hundred years of British political development, one ceases to understand those well-meaning Englishmen and women who want to "absorb the immigrant into our culture". This phrase is being used increasingly without any definition of culture or what aspects of life are being considered when it is used so haphazardly. Does preference for one culture exclude appreciation of another? Can national cultures not exist within an international, multi-racial culture to which all nations may subscribe? Cultural activities, says Senghor, are "living in communion, by and within the community of other men. Culture is inside and outside, above and beneath all human activities: it is the spirit that animates them, that gives a civilisation its unique style". And in the same breath he adds: "We are now living in the final stage of world unification through interdependence". Senegal's poet-statesman is, of course, black.

I do not meet any white people who have this kind of world vision when they talk of culture, nor any who show signs of excitement at the meeting of cultures. "Can't you see," said an education expert in one town, "what tremendous opportunities there are for human relationships?" But he, too, was black. The white reaction varies from a stolid refusal to accept the need for coloured immigrants and a weary confrontation with the problems

(handwritten margin notes: "The author poses question")

arising, to a dutiful attitude of accepting them now that they are here and trying to treat them fairly. There is a general understanding that the immigrants must adapt to the British way of life if they wish to live harmoniously with their British neighbours; and an unquestioning assumption that the British way of life is something fixed and unalterable. The fact that the British way of life includes a hostility to foreigners and to all foreign ways is also accepted as both necessary and right.

Foreign cultures are regarded as not only queer but rather a nuisance. In towns where there is a sudden and apparently unreasonable request for a Sikh temple, or where Pakistanis inexplicably stop work to pray, the difficulties are treated as being much greater than the cultural enrichment of the town. The contempt for foreign cultures co-exists with an ignorance of the fact that many of the immigrants are steeped in the British intellectual tradition. Students and professional workers from India, Pakistan, Africa and the West Indies come with a background of English law and constitution, English educational methods and democratic theory. These cultured men and women are thought, however, to lower the tone of a lounge in an English public house and are met by cold-faced landladies who feel they will be degrading their households if they "take in blacks".

The colour problem has already grown out of all proportion to any of the efforts being made to solve it. It is not merely a question of helping a number of immigrants to adapt themselves to British society, not merely a matter of extending friendship to people from overseas. It is a matter of an entire nation adapting itself to a multi-racial culture.

The rigid division of cultures is as much the responsibility of the immigrants as that of the English community and they cannot retain the "purity" of their cultures without causing immense harm and unhappiness. Some young people who are growing up in Britain now are suffering not only the hostility of a society which regards them as foreigners but the coercion of parents and other relatives who believe they should uphold Indian, Pakistani or West Indian traditions. These youngsters are not "being absorbed" into the British culture so much as absorbing it, and can be caught in the conflict between values and customs they absorb at school and those which they obtain in their parents' homes. Whether or not Britain can absorb them is another matter and if they are not accepted as equal citizens they may learn much later that the painful process that appears to be adaptation is merely a process of being robbed of a culture.

MARY GRIGG

What is "Race"?

Before we can talk sensibly about "race", it is necessary to establish what we mean by the term. This definition of "race" is taken from *A Dictionary of Race and Ethnic Relations* edited by E Ellis Cashmore:

Physical anthropologists used to speak of human "races" in the sense of sub-species, the most common scheme being the great tripartite division of mankind into Negroid, Mongoloid, and Caucasoid. Over the last forty to fifty years, however, it became increasingly clear that no meaningful taxonomy of human races was possible. Not only were numerous groups not classifiable as belonging to any of the three main groups, but physical anthropologists could not agree with each other as to where the genetic boundaries between human groups were to be drawn, or even on how many such groups there were. Humans have migrated over large distances and interbred extensively for thousands of years. Especially with the maritime expansion of Europe starting five centuries ago, this process of interbreeding has greatly accelerated, thereby blurring "racial" boundaries, and contributing more than ever to the genetic homogenization of our species.

A "race" can also mean a group of people who are socially defined in a given society as belonging together because of physical markers such as skin pigmentation, hair texture, facial features, stature, and the like. To avoid the confusion, some people specify "social race" when they use "race" in this meaning. Nearly all social scientists only use "race" in this sense of a social group defined by somatic visibility. It is important to stress here that any resemblance with the first usage is little more than coincidental. For example, "blacks" in South Africa and in Australia, although they occupy somewhat similar social positions in their respective societies, are no more closely related genetically to each other than each of them is to the "whites".

So, when we talk about "races" in this chapter, we will simply be talking about groups of people of different skin colour. For the sake of simplicity, the term "black" is used to cover all dark-skinned people of Asian, African and West Indian origin.

It should be borne in mind, of course, that tensions between groups within societies arise from factors other than simply "race", and in some societies different factors are paramount. Antagonism between Protestants and Catholics in Northern Ireland, or Sikhs and Hindus in India, stem from cultural and religious, rather than "racial" distinctions, while in many nations of Africa conflict arises principally from tribal divisions.

Immigration: some facts

There have been black people in Britain for centuries. It was only after World War II, however, that immigration from black Commonwealth countries became at all significant. The background to the influx of black Commonwealth immigrants which began in the late 1940s, and which was originally mostly from the West Indies, is explained by Peter Fryer:

Ten years after the "Empire Windrush"[1] there were in Britain about 25,000 West Indians who had come since the end of the war.

British industry gladly absorbed them. In some industries the demand for

---

1. The ship on which the first Commonwealth immigrants from the West Indies sailed to Britain in 1945.

labour was so great that members of the reserve army of black workers were actively recruited in their home countries. In April 1956 London Transport began recruiting staff in Barbados, and within 12 years a total of 3,787 Barbadians had been taken on. They were lent their fares to Britain, and the loans were repaid gradually from their wages. Even this number was not enough and in 1966 London Transport would begin to recruit in Trinidad and Jamaica too. The British Hotels and Restaurants Association recruited skilled workers in Barbados. And a Tory health minister by the name of Enoch Powell welcomed West Indian nurses to Britain. Willing black hands drove tube trains, collected bus fares, emptied hospital patients' bed-pans.

From the early 1950s, Britain's other black community − the hitherto tiny community from the Indian sub-continent − also began to grow as rural workers from India and Pakistan came to work in Britain, again with official encouragement. By the end of 1958 there were in this country about 55,000 Indians and Pakistanis.

All these West Indians and Asians were British citizens. The 1948 Nationality Act had granted United Kingdom citizenship to citizens of Britain's colonies and former colonies. Their British passports gave them the right to come to Britain and stay here for the rest of their lives.

In their own countries there were strong incentives to take advantage of their right to settle in Britain. In the Indian sub-continent, millions had found themselves adrift from homes and jobs when Pakistan and India went their separate ways after independence. Emigration to Britain offered the prospect of a new life unthreatened by flood, famine, or the miserable poverty that was their countries' chief legacy from imperial rule. In the British West Indies, the cost of living had almost doubled during the war. There was large-scale unemployment, and those without work were desperate. There was no relief of any kind: no dole; no children's allowances; no social security at all. "No one knows exactly how the jobless live", wrote Joyce Egginton in 1957. She added: "It is not surprising that thousands have left the West Indies. The surprising thing is that so many have stayed."

FRYER (1984)

This "open door" immigration policy for Commonwealth citizens lasted for a decade and a half, but by the early 1970s it had been entirely reversed. The following passage from *Racial Disadvantage in Britain* by David J Smith explains how and why:

Government policy in the early stages of the immigration has been described as laissez-faire; that is, there was no policy. Bowing to increasing pressure, given further weight by racial disturbances in 1958 and 1960, the government introduced immigration control through the Commonwealth Immigrants Act of 1962. By this time about half the present minority population had already entered the country. One of the effects of control was to stimulate an enormous increase in immigration over the 18 months before the Act became operative. Another was to help switch the balance of immigration from the

Caribbean to India and Pakistan, though it was not entirely clear how this came about.

Controls were tightened in 1965 within the framework of the existing legislation. The previous controls were superseded by the Immigration Act of 1971, which gives the "right of abode" to people it defines as patrial. The definition of this term is complex, but essentially it means people who, as well as being Commonwealth citizens, or citizens of the United Kingdom and colonies, have some substantial connection with the UK; for example, they were born in the UK, or acquired UK citizenship by naturalization or registration, or one of their parents or grandparents acquired UK citizenship in one of these ways. Those who are patrial have the right of free entry. Those who are not may enter only if they are granted a special voucher. Thus in three stages from 1962 onwards the right of entry to Britain has been withdrawn from most of the population of the New Commonwealth countries, and a strict control of immigration has been imposed. Since 1971 most of those granted entry under the voucher scheme have been the dependants of people already living in Britain.

It is worth noting that over the whole period, immigration policy has been taken to mean finding a way of limiting the flow of immigration.

SMITH (1977)

The following diagrams, which appeared in *Society Today* in 1979, offer some perspective on trends of immigration to and emigration from Britain over an extended period.

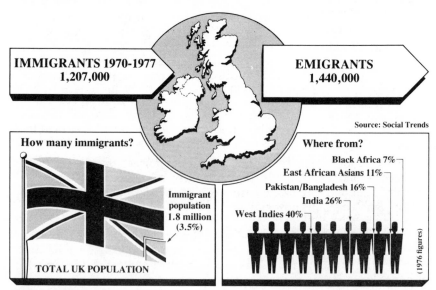

Discussion points

What factors do you think influenced various British governments to abandon the original post-war "open door" immigration policy, and to tighten immigration controls?

Why do you think the distinction between Commonwealth and non-Commonwealth citizens was effectively withdrawn in the 1971 Immigration Act? Do you agree with the Act?

Do you consider the current immigration controls too severe, about right, or insufficiently severe?

Black People in Britain

An ever-increasing proportion of black Britains have spent all their lives in this country. But their experience of life in Britain depends to a large extent on their country of origin; their cultural background has an enormous bearing on their attitudes and aspirations.

In the extract which follows, from a book edited by E Ellis Cashmore and Barry Troyna, the term "black" is used to mean people of West Indian origin, as distinct from "Asian", which refers to people of Indian, Pakistani and Bangladeshi origin.

As the 1970's drew to a close, apprehension mounted in regard to black youth in England. Maybe they were expected to exhibit docility, indifference to what was going on about them, resign themselves to social circumstances. If there was optimism about their ability, or inclination, to integrate fully into the society that had played host to their parents, it faded as the years passed by . . . . The futility of technical measures directed at avoiding the type of furores caused by blacks in the USA in the 1960s became apparent as unemployment grew disproportionately amongst this group, street offence and theft convictions spiralled ominously, feelings of disengagement intensified . . . .

Perspectives on the problematic nature of young blacks were provided by simple comparison with another major ethnic group – Asians. Studies suggested that the first wave of Asians to England were materially in the same position as West Indians; further, they housed similar expectations as to what they might get out of the new society: a relatively smooth reception, better living conditions, possibly an accumulation of wealth followed by a return to the homeland. Objectively, the position of Asians was in alignment with that of West Indians; both groups crystallised in the less salubrious regions of urban centres where housing was most available but least desirable.

Discernibly, the Asians made most inroads in the commercial sphere, establishing small businesses, retail outlets, wholesale and manufacturing services, and many grew to prosperity. West Indians, on the other hand, seemed anchored. Young Asians, highly motivated by their parents to work steadfastly at school and maximise the benefits they might receive from formal education, improved quite dramatically. The emphasis on education in Asian culture had its effect on them and, by the late 1970s, they were comfortably in range of white school-children in terms of actual achievements.

The picture was very different for black youth, very, very different. Study after study led to the depressing conclusion that young blacks were making little or no impression. Continually, they achieved less than both whites and

Asians and there were utterly no grounds for expecting a change. If any-thing, black youths seemed to be reinforcing their own lack of achievements by consciously promoting an attitude of rejection of education. Whether the lack of achievement bred the loss of affiliation or vice versa is a chicken-and-egg conundrum; for the moment, however, we rest with the observations that young blacks did not do well at school and their orientations to educa-tion were such that they gave no cause for believing they would do better in the future. In brief, they did not want to know.

Depicted is a scene where Asian youths, supported by their parents, entertained positive orientations towards education and improved steadily in terms of actual achievements. The importance of formal education as a route to social mobility and material gain was not lost on Asians as it seemingly was on blacks. Their collective attitudes towards education was captured nicely by a black youth whom one of us encountered whilst engaged in research in the late 1970s: "Education. What good is that to the black man? Qualifications? Them mean nothing so long as you're black."

from *Black Youth in Crisis*

Generalisations about human beings always distort to some extent. But some experiences and personal conflicts are extremely common to black people living in Britain.

In the extracts which follow, which appear in a book called *"Race" in Britain*, edited by Charles Husband, two young men, one of West Indian and the other of Indian origin, talk about their lives in this country:

A West Indian/British male

Ever since I can remember, and this is going way back, early sixties, from being very small I was always aware of being dark − black − and for a 6-year-old it wasn't very pleasnt being called "darkie" and "monkey". Because if you're dark then you're stupid − a fool − and I wasn't stupid, I wasn't a fool, but I was quiet and different. I remember wanting to be white when I grew up because being black was something bad and awful and in all my dreams I was white and I'd go round in space from planet to planet in my spaceship doing good deeds and rescuing people. Then we moved to Leeds and Leeds was a big frightening place . . . .

I remember the first day I went to school in Leeds. I don't know why − perhaps it was because I spoke differently or looked different but this white kid came up and started to pick on me. All the resentment, all the fear and frustration of coming to Leeds just came out and I found myself attacking him. I'd never done anything before like that in my life and I haven't since, but I had to be dragged away. Since then nobody ever picked on me, which was surprising because there were kids who were stronger than me who got picked on and cowed. I still wanted to be white and most of my friends were white, I suppose, and then we moved to junior school which was just across the playground. There I had to be much more aware of black kids because we all seemed to be lumped together in the same class and I suppose because we were all black we just got on − it wasn't a question of making friendships but I still went around with my white friends. I felt I didn't belong to either group − white or black. I was in a sort of limbo of my own . . . .

The weird thing was, that although I had this attitude in me that I wasn't going to be a "blackie" no matter what, the people I used to go round with used to come out with "nigger" jokes. It was okay because I was supposed not to mind, "It's all right he doesn't take offence", I was part of their group so I had to accept it. I did mind, but I didn't say, because it was something apart from me, I wasn't what they were talking about − I was almost like them. It was a really strange attitude when I look back on it now − I don't understand it − but at the same time I wasn't going to conform to what other people wanted me to be. I wasn't going to be a "happy nigger" or an athlete, or a footballer, I wanted to be something that everyone else was − everyone white that is. As far as I could see there were no black guys doing 'A' levels and writing essays, they were all playing football − and I wanted to be somebody . . . .

Racism doesn't exactly help you feel secure as a person. I've been followed by the police and I don't look your sort of heavy dread guy. I've had the police follow me in a car all the way up Roundhay Road at ten o'clock at night, just cruising by the side of me not saying a word. It was really eerie and I just carried on walking, because I knew that if I stopped or jumped over a wall or something they'd have got me and there'd have been no witnesses. And I've had people in the middle of town trying to run me over and other people don't believe it. Patti and I have suffered abuse from people − it happens all the time and when we tell people they're so amazed. Drivers have made U-turns to come back at me, shouting "you wog, you bastard, you nigger' and peole just walk on − I just v.alk on, I mean I'm so hardened to it now. I've been attacked in Safeways in Headingley and nobody did a thing − and that was when I was out with one of the children from the home where I work. You can't go into a shop without being the focus of attention because people expect you to steal something. If you go into a restaurant for a meal then you are shunted off into a corner where you won't offend the other all-white clientele.

Being a mixed couple we tend to move in racially mixed circles when we can, except where we have to move in all-white ones because of work or colour reasons. This means that for a lot of the time we are with a lot of white people and we stand out. We have to fight continuously against people's stereotyped ideas about us as a racially mixed couple. When you are out you are always aware of people because they are always aware of you. They are always staring and making comments and you learn to sum people up in one go, because you have to for your own survival otherwise you could be walking straight into trouble. You learn to read body language − you immediately know if someone is being friendly or not, then you have to decide how to deal with it . . . .

Younger generation blacks who don't know us would feel that it was a promotion of the sexual stereotype − perhaps some of those who do know us as well − but most of them accept us for what we are. The same with our white friends, but for the majority of white people who see us in the streets, we just fulfil their idea of the sexual stereotype − white girls who go with black men must be of "loose morals", just looking for sexual excitement.

I'm a lot more secure now in my black identity than I have ever been, but it took a long time getting there, through a lot of stages. I didn't go through what some would term the "ethnic road" of, say, youth cult groups. For white kids there's always been teds, skins, mods, rockers, punks, but for black kids there's never been anything they could really identify with, that was really culturally theirs, until Rasta came along. Like, it was embarassing to be black − for me anyway − I didn't even speak patois, I didn't want to sound like an ignorant "wog". It was easier to get along without any hassle by conforming to a stereotype because you were being what people expected of you, whereas it was harder and more threatening if you were something that was close to them. If you acted like the jolly buffoon or the thicko who was good at sports you were then conforming to all the stereotyped attitudes that are around, of black people being musical, good dancers etc., but not very intelligent. If you wear a woolly hat and spend your time building a sound system then you also conform to the stereotype, but if you aspire to be something else, a substitute white, an imitation white as they see it, wanting to study and do well, then you are threatening because you have the ability to take people's jobs away and be in a position of telling other people − especially white people − what to do. But in doing that you don't feel comfortable on either side of the fence because you're not black and you're not white . . . .

Black people tend to be more accepting than white people and Patti often feels a lot easier in all-black gatherings than I do in all-white ones. White people often forget that black people have to face this every day of their lives, yet if the situation was reversed they would feel a lot less confident. A white friend of mine is a good example of this − he says he feels uncomfortable if there are a lot of black people and he is the only white, yet he never expects me to mind being in all-white situations . . . .

Most of the things I've been talking about are psychological − how people see themselves and how they see other people. Black people in Britain in my opinion are still slaves, but the chains are not on their bodies but on their minds, and black kids especially need someone to help them break out of these chains, because otherwise they've got no future, they've got nothing. They've got to learn, but more important, white people have got to learn to accept them for themselves, then perhaps we can learn to accept each other.

A young Gujerati/British male

Being about five years old when I came to England, I had few memories of India − I had not formed by Indian identity. Having emigrated to England, I was to form two identities alongside each other: that which my family and community socialised me into, and that which the white society wanted.

My first 'real encounters of racial violence were when I moved into secondary school. Gangs of white youths used to go around "Paki-bashing". Only when this persisted did Indians form gangs and retaliated. However, by now I had some idea of the British class structure and knew that these "troublemakers" were from the lowest rungs. I was convinced and knew that the "others" were not like them. Though objectively I was from the same class as they were, I differentiated myself from them and identified myself with those above me. I aspired to their good, commonsense way of life, values, attitudes, etc.

By now I was about 15 years old and I was becoming well integrated into the white culture. It was about at this age that I realised that I was leading two lives, that of an Indian at home, and the black man with a white mask outside. I realised that I was experiencing culture conflict and had difficulty in identifying with either and coming to a compromise. I now realise that in the few years before the age of 15, when I thought that I was going through the normal phase of being a rebellious teenager, that they were really acts which really manifested the internal cultural and identity crises that I was going through.

Difficulties arose when for example the norm in the white society was in the belief of "individualism". Youths were expected to drink, smoke, have girlfriends etc. This was not the case in the Indian culture. The family was a tightly knit and integrated unit with the Indian community. The belief was that of "collectivism": life was with the people.

This presented real problems to me because on the one hand, I was expected to conform with my white friends and their culture, and on the other hand, with my family and the Indian community culture . . . .

There were frequent periods of confrontation with my family when it became apparent to them, from my behaviour, that I was slipping away from them, rejecting the Indian culture and becoming totally immersed in the white culture. These confrontations often served to bring me into a state of equilibrium. From there, I would again try the futile pursuit of trying to find a compromise between the two cultures, for this seemed the only logical way ahead. It seemed to me that my parents wanted me to succeed in the white society, yet retain my identity as an Indian; and the white society was making demands upon me to fully incorporate myself into their culture and only then would I be accepted. In a sense, they were ready and waiting with their arms to embrace me.

It was when I started to date white girls and generally go out with them that I realised that this was not so. The malicious and contemptuous looks and abuse that were received made me realise that though I wanted to be fully integrated into the white society, the white society would only let me at a superficial level. Thus, underneath the surface the divisions were to be maintained and reinforced. The purity of the Indian culture and race was insisted upon by my parents. Whereas before I felt that this was not the case for the white man, (for he could "understand" the culture conflict and be more "liberal" minded), I was to change my mind. Any notion that I had of being fully integrated, finding a compromise, or marrying a white girl in society, had to be rejected. I was in a situation where, should I marry a white girl, I would be excommunicated from my Indian community and be virtually in the same situation with the white society. Thus, the cost outweights the benefits . . . .

So I set out positively to form a white identity. This resulted in a conflict and a period where I was in search for a compromise. This leaves one in a precarious and difficult situation. This leaves the vast majority of Indians, (including myself), being forced to go back and identify with their Indian culture. For I am in a situation where I cannot integrate fully into the white society, and, not wanting to be rejected by both, opt for the safest and surest way of identifying with my Indian culture more.

Perhaps the majority of my generation will take this route, because to some extent we are still able to identify with the poor social and economic conditions with which they started when arriving as immigrants. So, we also suffer from a guilt complex in that we feel our parents have given their lives and suffered so that we would be better off, and yet here we are repaying them by denouncing everything they believe in and have worked for. Their blood, sweat and tears have been worthless.

However, the children of my generation will hopefully not suffer too much from the cultural and identity crises. At least my generation will have a better understanding of the acculturation processes that their children will be going through and the crises that will confront them. Thus I hope the assimilation processes will be a little easier for them, for the pressure from Indian parents will ease a little. But I doubt very much if the same will happen with regards to the white man's view on integration.

Themes for Discussion

What factors do you think might have influenced the differing general responses of people of West Indian and Asian origin to life in Britain?

What do you think of the idea of "positive discrimination" in employment, such as legislation demanding that a certain proportion of vacancies in factories must be filled by people of ethnic minority background?

Do you think that more should be done in schools in Britain to make education genuinely multi-cultural, so that children of different ethnic backgrounds can be helped to understand and appreciate one-another's cultures better? Alternatively, do you think special schools should be set up for children of ethnic minority ancestry, paying more attention to their cultural and linguistic background?

What is your attitude to "mixed marriages" between people of different racial origins?

Do you think that black and white people will ever "learn to accept each other"?

Racial Prejudice

Racial prejudice is born largely of ignorance and insecurity. In his book, *Black Testimony: The Voices of Britain's West Indians*, Thomas J Cottle explains some of the most widespread misconceptions concerning black people in Britain:

During the last few years, I have spoken with people in Great Britain who, never having met families from the West Indies, were in doubt of the language spoken by West Indians . . . . I have heard estimates of the number of blacks in Great Britain reach as high as 25% of the population. It was not uncommon for people to believe that fewer than 5% of England's black citizens were English born.

In point of fact, some 2,000,000 blacks live in England, 40% of whom were born in this country.

COTTLE (1978)

Here are some of the most commonly-heard complaints of white Britons against blacks and vice-versa, taken from *Learning to be Prejudiced* by Alfred Davey:

"They don't fit in."
"They take the houses needed by the whites."
"They won't learn the language."
"They don't like us, they just tolerate us because they have to live here; they should ship them back."
"They don't mix; they pretend to be tolerant but they're not."
"There's too many of them."
"They do their toilet in the street; they take houses and turn them into slums."

"Blacks seems to be synonymous with barbarians."
"Too many black kids are relegated to ESN schools; they see us as inferior."
"Parliament pays lip-service to equality; we are dominated by whites; they treat us like second-class people."
"They say we take their jobs; they think only of themselves."
"We're picked on by the police."

DAVEY

Prejudice can take horrifying forms, as was illustrated in a BBC radio *File on 4* programme, in which Janet Cohen interviewed residents of the East End of London:

Cohen: Teachers too complain of growing racial hostility in the classrooms. J., a teacher, who is considering joining a vigilante group, says he faces a daily tide of abuse from his pupils.

J: Oh, it affects me all the time.

Cohen: How?

J: Because they call me, you know, "Paki" and "Paki out", and they scrawl on the door of my teaching room. I mean, I've been in the school for seven years but now things are deteriorating. They may say, well, we're doing it for a laugh or something like that, but then they are influenced by the older people, you see, because in that area where I live there are, you know, lots of demonstrations organized by the British Movement.

Cohen:	You know it's the British Movement, do you?
J:	They write on my blackboard, they write BM, and then they have these Nazi signs you know under their lapel and they show it to me and they ask me to read their leaflets, they carry them around. Oh yes, I know – the leaflets from these various movements, the New National Front, the National Front, the British Movement, kids now start saying to me, oh, you have taken our job; suddenly they have found that I have taken their job, so why don't I go back, you Paki, you see, they shout.
Cohen:	Many black families don't even feel safe at home; in the heart of the East End one family claims their house has been attacked 35 times. White gangs, they say, have aimed bricks, bottles and air-gun pellets through their front windows. The glass is now protected by two layers of metal grilles, sheets of plywood, and then shutters. The police have advised the three adults and ten children to move into the two back rooms of the house. But the attacks continue and they aren't limited to the home. This man, who's too frightened to broadcast his name, fears for his and his brother's children; all of them have been threatened and assaulted on the streets . . . .
	Today's violence takes place against a background of rising unemployment. In some boroughs, one person in seven is out of a job. A report published today claims that blacks are more likely than whites to lose their jobs in the economic recession, but skinheads on the streets don't see it this way. Their heads shaved, their trousers cropped six inches above their ankle, their faces pinched in the cold, they feel the blacks are stealing their jobs. As for violence against the ethnic communities:
1st skinhead:	Do I condone it? Yes. They've got no right to be here.
Cohen:	That families should have bricks thrown through the window, airgun pellets, that kind of thing?
1st skinhead:	Well, only blacks like, and Jews, yeh. White European race, right, is the superior race and always will be.
Cohen:	Is it really fair that families should be intimidated; after all, they are people?
2nd skinhead:	Yes, course it is. They're not people, they're parasites, they're just poncing off us . . . .
3rd skinhead:	The fact is, right, ordinary people don't like 'em moving in round the East London environment round there, right, and they want 'em out.
Cohen:	But is it fair to attack these families?
All skinheads:	Yes, it is.
3rd skinhead:	It's the only way isn't it, I mean the Government ain't doing nothing are they, nobody's doing anything, are they?
1st skinhead:	It takes 10 years for a bill to get through Parliament, right,

and nothing happens, right, so if you give them like a good dig and all that like, it might just send a couple of them home; you know what I mean. They might think, oh, you know like, we've had enough like, we're going to get home. So we're doing our little bit.

4th skinhead: We believe that the blacks are taking over our country, the Yids are taking over our country.

Cohen: So how much violence do you think there is around here, then, towards . . . .

All skinheads: There's a lot more, there's a lot more, there should be a lot anyway. There is, there's a lot going around.

Cohen: It's gangs of youths like those who are blamed for the growing number of racial assaults, but where in some boroughs immigrants make up 14% of the population, members of the older generation too say they understand the powerful feelings of the young, even if they don't support violence.

1st man: Well, it's out of order, isn't it? Everyone's entitled to live, you know, you know, there's a little bit of racial in everyone, but there you go. Especially if we're sort of, we're inundated with them, ain't we, it's getting overcrowded. I mean you've got to admit, even though the housing problem's enough, isn't it?

2nd man: I think, quite honestly, the economic situation today forces them into this: you get kids who are left on the streets, they haven't got any work or anything like that; they've got to take their anger out on somebody, so they take it out on the unknown. It'll certainly take years before we sort the problem out, we'll probably have to go through the sort of problems that America has suffered before we can really sort it out.

The experience of encountering prejudice is captured in this poem by Wole Soyinka:

Telephone Conservation

The price seemed reasonable, location
Indifferent. The landlady swore she lived
Off premises. Nothing remained
But self-confession. "Madam," I warned,
"I hate a wasted journey − I am African."
Silence. Silenced transmission of
Pressurized good-breeding. Voice, when it came,
Lipstick coated, long gold-rolled
Cigararette-holder pipped. Caught I was, foully.
"HOW DARK?" . . . I had not misheard . . . "ARE YOU
   LIGHT?

OR VERY DARK?'' Button B. Button A. Stench
Of rancid breath of public hide-and-speak.
Red booth. Red pillar-box. Red double-tiered
Omnibus squelching tar. It was real! Shamed
By ill-mannered silence, surrender
Pushed dumbfounded to beg simplification.
Considerate she was, varying the emphasis –
"ARE YOU DARK? OR VERY LIGHT?'' Revelation came.
"You mean – like plain or milk chocolate?''
Her assent was clinical, crushing in its light
Impersonality. Rapidly, wave-length adjusted,
I chose. "West African sepia'' – and as afterthought,
"Down in my passport.'' Silence for spectroscopic
Flight of fancy, till truthfulness clanged her accent
Hard on the mouthpiece. "WHAT'S THAT?'' conceding
"DON'T KNOW WHAT THAT IS.'' "Like brunette.''
"THAT'S DARK, ISN'T IT?'' Not altogether.
Facially, I am brunette, but madam, you should see
The rest of me. Palm of my hand, soles of my feet
Are a peroxide blonde. Friction, caused –
Foolishly madam – by sitting down, has turned
My bottom raven black – One moment madam.'' – sensing
Her receiver resting on the thunderclap
About my ears – "Madam,'' I pleaded, "wouldn't you
    rather
See for yourself?''

Themes for Discussion

Why do you think that white people have stereotyped views of what black people are like? Do you think other minority groups are stereotyped in a similar way?

Consider the list of complaints by whites against blacks and blacks against whites, and discuss the reasons for them.

How do you explain the degree of hatred of black people expressed by the skinheads in the "File on 4'' interviews?

How do you think you would feel if you encountered the kind of racial prejudice described in the poem?

Do you think that racial tension in Britain is increasing or decreasing? Do you think that the government could or should do more to promote racial harmony?

Research suggestion

Write a brief report on British government legislation to combat racial discrimination, and its effectiveness.

Racial Tension in America

In his novel *Go Tell it on the Mountain*, the black American writer,
James Baldwin, explores the feelings of black people in the 1960s living in
a society in which racial prejudice is deep-rooted and often intense. Here
is an extract from the novel, which forms, in effect, a short story:

Go Tell it on the Mountain

She lived quite a long way from Richard – four underground stops; and
when it was time for her to go home, he always took the underground
uptown with her and walked her to her door. On a Saturday when they had
forgotten the time and stayed together later than usual, he left her at her
door at two o'clock in the morning. They said goodnight hurriedly for she
was afraid of trouble when she got upstairs – though, in fact, Madame
Williams seemed astonishingly indifferent to the hours Elizabeth kept – and
he wanted to hurry back home and go to bed. Yet, as he hurried off down the
dark, murmuring street, she had a sudden impulse to call him back, to ask
him to take her with him and never let him go again. She hurried up the steps,
smiling a little at this fancy: it was because he looked so young and defenceless as he walked away, and yet so jaunty and strong.

He was to come the next evening at supper-time, to make at last, at Elizabeth's urging, the acquaintance of Madame Williams. But he did not come.
She drove Madame Williams wild with her sudden sensitivity to footsteps on
the stairs. Having told Madame Williams that a gentleman was coming to
visit her, she did not dare, of course, to leave the house and go out looking
for him, thus giving Madame Williams the impression that she dragged men
in off the streets. At ten o'clock, having eaten no supper, a detail unnoticed
by her hostess, she went to bed, her head aching and her heart sick with fear;
fear over what had happened to Richard, who had never kept her waiting
before; and fear involving all that was beginning to happen in her body.

And on Monday morning he was not at work. She left during the lunch
hour to go to his room. He was not there. His landlady said that he had not
been there all weekend. While Elizabeth stood trembling and indecisive in
the hall, two white policemen entered.

She knew the moment she saw them, and before they mentioned his name,
that something terrible had happened to Richard. Her heart, as on that
bright summer day when he had first spoken to her, gave a terrible bound
and then was still, with an awful, wounded stillness. She put out one hand to
touch the wall in order to keep standing.

"This here young lady was just looking for him," she heard the landlady
say. They all looked at her.

"You his girl?" one of the policemen asked. She looked up at his sweating
face, on which a lascivious smile had immediately appeared, and
straightened, trying to control her trembling.

"Yes," she said. "Where is he?"

"He's in jail, honey," the other policeman said.

"What for?"

"For robbing a white man's store, black girl. That's what for."

She found, and thanked Heaven for it, that a cold stony rage had entered her. She would, otherwise, certainly have fallen down, or begun to weep. She looked at the smiling policeman.

"Richard ain't robbed no store," she said. "Tell me where he is."

"And I tell you," he said, not smiling, "that your boyfriend robbed a store and he's in jail for it. He's going to stay there too − now, what you got to say to that?"

"And he probably did it for you, too," the other policeman said. "You look like a girl a man could rob a store for."

She said nothing; she was thinking how to get to see him, how to get him out. One of them, the smiler, turned now to the landlady and said: "Let's have the key to his room. How long's he been living here?"

"About a year," the landlady said. She looked unhappily at Elizabeth. "He seemed like a real nice boy."

"Ah yes," he said, mounting the steps, "they all seem like real nice boys when they pay their rent."

"You going to take me to see him?" she asked of the remaining policeman. She found herself fascinated by the gun in his holster, the club at his round, red face; to take that club and strike with all her strength against the base of his skull where his cap ended, until the ugly, silky, white man's hair was matted with blood and brains.

"Sure, girl," he said, "you're coming right along with us. The man at the station-house wants to ask you some questions."

The smiling policeman came down again. "Ain't nothing up there," he said. "Let's go."

She moved between them out into the sun. She knew that there was nothing to be gained by talking to them any more. She was entirely in their power; she would have to think faster than they could think; she would have to contain her fear and her hating, and find out what could be done. Not for anything short of Richard's life, and not, possibly, even for that, would she have wept before them, or asked of them a kindness.

A small crowd, children and curious passers-by, followed them as they walked the long, dusty, sunlit street. She hoped only that they would not pass anyone she knew; she kept her head high, looking straight ahead, and felt the skin settle over her bones as though she were wearing a mask.

And at the station she somehow got past their brutal laughter. (What was he doing with you, girl, until two o'clock in the morning? Next time you feel like that girl, you come by here and talk to me). She felt that she was about to burst, or vomit, or die. Though the sweat stood out, cruelly, like needles on her brow, and she felt herself, from every side, being covered with a stink and filth, she found out, in their own good time, what she wanted to know. He was being held in a prison downtown called the Tombs (the name made her heart turn over), and she could see him tomorrow. The state, or the prison, or someone, had already assigned him a lawyer; he would be brought to trial next week.

But the next day, when she saw him, she wept. He had been beaten, he whispered to her, and he could hardly walk. His body, she later discovered, bore almost no bruises, but was full of strange, painful swellings, and there was a welt above one eye. He had not, of course, robbed the store, but, when he left her that Saturday night, had gone down into the underground station to wait for his train. It was late, and the trains were slow; he was all alone on the platform, only half awake, thinking, he said, of her.

Then, from the far end of the platform, he heard a sound of running; and, looking up, he saw two coloured boys come running down the steps. Their clothes were torn, and they were frightened; they came up the platform and stood near him, breathing hard. He was about to ask them what the trouble was when, running across the tracks towards them, and followed by a white man, he saw another coloured boy; and at the same instant another white man came running down the underground steps.

Then he became full awake, in panic; he knew that whatever the trouble was, it was now his trouble also; for these white men would make no distinction between him and the three boys they were after. They were all coloured, they were about the same age, and here they stood together on the underground platform. And they were all, with no questions asked, herded upstairs, and into the station wagon and to the station house.

At the station Richard gave his name and address and age and occupation. Then for the first time he stated that he was not involved, and asked one of the other boys to corroborate his testimony. This they rather despairingly did. They might, Elizabeth felt, have done it sooner, but they probably also felt that it would be useless to speak. And they were not believed; the owner of the store was being brought there to make the identification. And Richard tried to relax: the man could not say that he had been there if he had never seen him before.

But when the owner came, a short man with a bloody shirt − for they had knifed him − in the company of yet another policeman, he looked at the four boys before him and said: "Yeah, that's them, all right".

Then Richard shouted: "But I wasn't there! Look at me, godammit − I wasn't there!"

"You black bastards," the man said, looking at him, "you're all the same."

Then there was a silence in the station, the eyes of the white men all watching. And Richard said, but quietly, knowing he was lost: "But all the same mister, I wasn't there." And he looked at the white man's bloody shirt and thought, he told Elizabeth, at the bottom of his heart: "I wish to God they'd killed you."

Then the questioning began. The three boys signed a confession at once, but Richard would not sign. He said at last that he would die before he signed a confession to something he hadn't done.

"Well, then," said one of them, hitting him suddenly across the head, "maybe you will die, you black son-of-a bitch." And the beating began. He would not, then, talk to her about it; she found that, before the dread and the hatred that filled her mind, her imagination faltered and held its peace.

"What are we going to do?" she asked at last. He smiled a vicious smile − she had never seen such a smile on his face before.

"Maybe you ought to pray to that Jesus of yours and get Him to come down and tell these white men something." He looked at her a long dying moment. "Because I don't know nothing else to do," he said.

She suggested, "Richard, what about another lawyer?"

And he smiled again. "I declare," he said, "Little-bit's been holding out on me. She got a fortune tied up in a sock, and she ain't never told me nothing about it."

She had been trying to save money for a whole year, but she had only 30 dollars. She sat before him, going over in her mind all the things she might do to raise money, even to going on the streets. Then, for very helplessness, she began to shake with sobbing. At this his face became Richard's again. He said in a shaking voice: "Now look here, Little-bit, don't you be like that. We going to work this out all right." But she could not stop sobbing. "Elizabeth," he whispered. "Elizabeth, Elizabeth." Then the man came and said it was time for her to go. And she rose. She had brought two packets of cigarettes for him, and they were still in her bag. Wholly ignorant of prison regulations, she did not dare to give them to him under the man's eyes. And, somehow, her failure to remember to give him the cigarettes, when she knew how much he smoked, made her weep the harder. She tried − and failed − to smile at him, and she was slowly led to the door. The sun nearly blinded her, and she heard him whisper behind: "So long, baby. Be good."

In the streets she did not know what to do. She stood awhile before the dreadful gates, and then she walked and walked until she came to a coffee shop where taxi drivers and the people who worked in nearby offices hurried in and out all day. Usually she was afraid to go into downtown establishments, where only white people were, but today she did not care. She felt that if anyone said anything to her she would turn and curse him like the lowest bitch on the streets. If anyone touched her, she would do her best to send his soul to Hell.

But no one touched her, no one spoke. She drank her coffee, sitting in the strong sun that fell through the window. Now it came to her how alone, how frightened she was; she had never been so frightened in her life before. She knew that she was pregnant − knew it, as the old folks said, in her bones; and if Richard should be sent away what, under Heaven, could she do? Two years, three years − she had no idea how long he might be sent away for − what would she do? And how could she keep her aunt from knowing? And if her aunt should find out, then her father would know too. The tears welled up, and she drank her cold, tasteless coffee. And what would they do with Richard?

And if they sent him away, what would he be like, then, when he returned? She looked into the quiet, sunny streets, and for the first time in her life, she hated it all − the white city, the white world. She could not, that day, think of one decent white person in the whole world. She sat there, and she hoped that one day God, with tortures inconceivable, would grind them utterly into humility, and make them know that black boys and black girls, whom they treated with such condescension, such disdain, and such good humour, had hearts like human beings, too, more human hearts then theirs.

But Richard was not sent away. Against the testimony of the three robbers, and her own testimony, and, under oath, the storekeeper's indecision, there was no evidence on which to convict him. The courtroom seemed to feel, with some complacency and disappointment, that it was his great good luck to be let off so easily. They went immediately to his room. And there − she was never all her life to forget it − he threw himself, face downward, on his bed and wept.

She had only seen one other man weep − her father − and it had not been like this. She touched him but he did not stop. Her own tears fell on his dirty, uncombed hair. She tried to hold him, but for a long time he would not be held. His body was like iron; she could find no softness in it. She sat curled like a frightened child on the edge of the bed, her hand on his back, waiting for the storm to pass over. It was then that she decided not to tell him yet about the child.

By and by he called her name. And then he turned, and she held him against her breast, while he sighed and shook. He fell asleep at last, clinging to her as though he were going down into the water for the last time.

And it was the last time. That night he cut his wrists with his razor and he was found in the morning by his landlady, his eyes staring upward with no light, dead among the scarlet sheets.

JAMES BALDWIN

Discussion points

Why do you think Richard committed suicide in the story?

Do you think that Elizabeth in the story is exhibiting racial prejudice in her attitude to white people?

Suggestions for writing

Write two newspaper articles about the arrest, acquittal and suicide of Richard. In the first one, think out what you would imagine to be the point of view of the policeman and the shopkeeper to the events of the story, and slant your article accordingly. In the second, make your report and comments those of a reporter in sympathy with Richard and Elizabeth. The articles should include reports of the details of the court case, interviews with characters in the story, conclusions to be drawn from the events, and, possibly, recommendations for action.

Research suggestions

Write a brief report to present to the class on the history of relations between American Indians, whites and blacks in the U.S.A.

Write a brief general report on relations between American Indian, "mestizo" (people of mixed racial origin) and white people in Latin America.

Essay Titles

(a) Colour.

(b) "Race relations have little to do with race itself."

(c) Problems and opportunities in a multi-racial society.

Bibliography

Audio-visual materials and pamphlets

Divide and Rule − Never (Film and support materials)
Racism the Fourth R (VHS cassette made for BBC2 *Open Door*
    programme)
(both issued by ALTARF − All London Teachers Against Racism and
    Fascism, Room 216, Panther House, 38 Mount Pleasant, London
    WC1X 0AP)

Roots of Racism
Patterns of Racism
(both issued by the Institute of Race Relations)

Non-fiction

Cashmore, E. Ellis (ed). *A Dictionary of Race and Ethnic Relations*,
    Routledge and Kegan Paul, 1984
Cashmore, E. Ellis, and Troyna Barry (eds). *Black Youth in Crisis*, Allen
    and Unwin, 1982
Cottle, Thomas J. *Black People in Britain: The Voices of Britain's West
    Indians*, Wildwood House, 1978
Davey, Alfred. *Learning to be Prejudiced: Growing up in Multi-Ethnic
    Britain*, Edward Arnold, 1983
Fanon, Frantz. *Black Skins, White Masks*, McGibbon and Kee, 1968
Fryer, Peter. *Staying Power: The History of Black People in Britain,*
    Pluto Press, 1984
Grigg, Mary. *The White Question*, Secker and Warburg, 1967
Husband, Charles (ed). *"Race" in Britain: Continuity and Change*,
    Hutchinson, 1982
Segal, Ronald. *The Race War: The World-Wide Conflict of Races*,
    Penguin, 1966
Smith, David J. *Racial Disadvantage in Britain*, Penguin, 1977
Wilson, Amrit. *Finding a Voice: Asian Women in Britain*, Virago, 1978

Fiction

Baldwin, James. *Go Tell it on the Mountain*, Corgi, 1984
Ellison, Ralph. *The Invisible Man*, Penguin, 1965
Icaza, Jorge. *Huasipungo*, Dennis Dobson, 1962
Wright, Richard. *Uncle Tom's Children*, Harper and Row, 1965
Wright, Richard. *Native Son*, Penguin 1972

Advice on Writing: Illogical Argument in Essays

Logicality of argument is obviously one of the absolute essentials of language essay writing. A basic logical flaw can invalidate a whole line of argument, with disastrous results. The purpose of this section is to help students to recognise varieties of false reasoning.

One of the most damaging errors of logic in essay writing is to stray from the point at issue into a discussion of something which has no direct relevance to the essay title. An absolutely cardinal rule of essay writing is to keep the point at issue constantly in mind, and the simplest way to do that is to glance back at the title frequently, and check whether the argument which is being developed is relevant to it. All manner of irrelevancies can creep into essay writing. Here are a couple of typical examples. You are writing an essay on crime and punishment, the title of which reads: "The only way to reduce the crime rate is to make punishment more severe." If you have strong feelings about capital punishment, it would be easy, if you were not careful, to enter into a discussion of the morality of capital punishment, making a case for its restoration on the "eye for an eye" principle. This is a different issue altogether from the question of whether or not the restoration of capital punishment would reduce the crime rate, which would be the only valid reason for mentioning it. Similarly, if you were writing an essay on education, with the title: "What changes would you like to see in the educational system of this country?" it would be irrelevant to discuss the relative merits of the comprehensive and selective school systems, unless you concluded the discussion by relating it precisely to the question; by arguing for instance, that you would like to see comprehensive or selective schools abolished entirely.

Failure to define terms used in an essay is another error which can have a damaging effect on the validity of an argument. This is particularly the case when you are dealing with abstractions such as "freedom", or "democracy", or "communism", or "equality", which can have different meanings for different people or in different contexts. Many words are simply ambiguous, and it is impossible to argue sensibly about them without defining what you understand by them. When a term about which you are writing has a straightforward, generally recognised meaning, on the other hand, there is no point in wasting time and effort on defining it.

A further problem can arise when you *do* attempt to define the terms you are using. If you define a term or an issue too *narrowly*, then the subject becomes oversimplified. For example, if you are answering the question: "Is educational equality a myth?" you should consider a variety of possible ramifications of the term "equality". If you see the issue simply in terms of the debate over comprehensive and selective school systems, and/or over the abolition of private education, and concentrate exclusively on inequality of access to a "good" education, higher education and top jobs, you are limiting the range of the question unduly. Aspects of "equality" such as natural aptitudes for and parental attitudes towards education, ethnic factors, and so on, should also be considered.

Oversimplification is a particular danger when discussing politics, especially since political propaganda relies on gross oversimplification. If politicians sometimes use terms like "totalitarian" to mean states which are ruled by a "communist" system, and "the free world" to mean all the states which are not, you should avoid falling into the same error.

Generalisation is another pitfall to be wary of in essay writing. However common a particular phenomenon may be in a particular human group, there are virtually always exceptions which invalidate a sweeping generalisation. Some quite frequently repeated generalisations, such as the assertion that "women are illogical" are patently illogical. Generalisations about foreigners are particularly common. Many West Indians, for instance, are good dancers, but it would be absurd to state baldly "West Indians are good dancers". Generalisations are often introduced by phrases such as "It is a known fact that . . . ." and "History proves that . . .". Such expressions do not make dubious statements any more convincing, and should always be avoided. A particularly common and dangerous variety of false generalisation is the error of arguing from the particular to the general. This commonly takes the form of drawing general conclusions from personal experience. An example of this would be to argue that your own education was lacking in creativity, and to draw from this the spurious conclusion that British education generally is insufficiently creative. Newspaper "scandal" stories frequently give rise to unwarranted generalisations. A report of a prison where the inmates are allowed to watch colour television and wander in the extensive grounds for instance, might lead the unwary to the conclusion that prisons in Britain generally resemble "holiday camps".

A similar error of logic is that of drawing conclusions from selected evidence, and ignoring the evidence which tends to point in the opposite direction. A classic illustration of this is in the popularity of newspaper horoscopes, which depend to some extent on people's willingness to ignore predictions which are *not* fulfilled and take notice only of the ones which *are*. Literary criticism, at its worst, is prone to this error, when critics select quotations from a text to support their theses, and conveniently ignore quotations which tend to refute them.

False analogy is a further common flaw in logical reasoning. Its most popular form is in drawing irrelevant conclusions about human behaviour based on observation of other species. Darwin's theory of "the survival of the fittest", for example, is used as "proof" that human affairs are most effectively conducted on a competitive, "dog eat dog" principle, taking no account of the complexity of human social evolution.

Essays which specifically ask for arguments for and against some premise can easily lead to another error. Students sometimes argue an apparently personal case for the proposition, and then present the opposite case in such a way as to suggest that they agree also with the arguments *against* it. Care must be taken to avoid appearing to agree with incompatible viewpoints.

Care must also be taken to distinguish between opinions and facts. The former should never be presented as the latter. You should never make statements, for example, like this: "The fact that the government has allowed in too many coloured immigrants is one of the major causes of racial tension in this country". This is a value judgement, not a fact.

Finally, care should be taken over the use of statistics. It has became an axiom that statistics can be used to prove anything, and assessing the validity or otherwise of published statistics requires some understanding of the complexities of statistical method. Probably the best advice that can be offered with regard to statistics is that they should be used with caution, and should never be offered as proof of any contention. Statistics showing that crimes of violence have increased dramatically since capital punishment was abolished, for instance, should not be treated as a proof that abolition was a mistake, since the increase could equally be attributed to other factors. Likewise, statistics showing that world population and deaths from starvation have both increased alarmingly over the past thirty years do not prove that the population explosion is the cause of starvation. Other factors may in fact be more significant.

Many other types of false reasoning could be mentioned, but if you can succeed in avoiding all of the ones discussed here, you're unlikely to lose marks in an essay because of invalid argument.

9

The New Technologies and the Future

Computers provoke extreme reactions. For many the very word "computer" provokes scorn or fear; to many others they are objects of veneration. There can be no doubt that the microtechnological revolution will have profound effects on the lives of everyone living in the developed world in the last decade of the twentieth century, as dramatic an impact as the agricultural and industrial revolutions of the past, according to some analysts. The purpose of this chapter is to explore the implications of this new branch of science, through a series of extracts from recent books on the subject.

The chapter begins with a passage for comprehension from Christopher Evans' book *The Mighty Micro*.

Comprehension

Read the following passage, and answer the questions which follow it. You are advised to spend about one hour on this exercise.

1   What if computers tell us something we do not like or do not want to know about the universe? If we create super-intelligent computers to probe the mysteries of the universe, then we should be prepared for the possibility that what they have to tell us may be intellectually shocking or emotionally
5   unacceptable. It is true that even through routine, non-computerised science we always risk finding out horrific or alien facts, and it might be argued that we have already survived quite a few of these shocks. The realisation that the earth was not the centre of the universe rocked quite a few people at the time, as did the discovery of our planet's stupendous age, the fossil record of pre-
10   historic life and Darwin's insight into the origin of Man. But momentous though these discoveries have been, they have unfolded at a discreet and manageable pace. Assuming that the universe contains further shocks, doubtless of a far more unsettling kind, are we not in danger of having them thrust quite brutally upon us?
15   It could be argued that the true nature of any apocalyptic facts will only be obvious to the super-intelligences of the computers, in the way that some of the paradoxes of space and time are comprehensible to us but would be quite meaningless to a chimpanzee. There may be some comfort in this view, that the computers, as we have frequently pointed out, will turn out to be
20   excellent tutors, capable of teaching us everything that we want, or even that we don't want, to know. Equally the reverse may hold, and the more we find out about the universe the more benevolent it will turn out to be, in which

148

case the computers will be doing us a favour by hustling the news along. Somehow I doubt it. The best we can hope for from the universe, I fear, will be supreme indifference. But whatever happens, we will soon be in danger of finding out.

Since the foundations of social life Man has been aware of his special role on earth, and until the significance of the Darwinian thesis began to sink home, he considered himself to be unique in the universe, second only in status to God. But even when identifying himself with the animals, he has still been able to convince himself − justly − of his uniqueness. The evidence has been that he is the possessor of intellectual powers vastly superior to those of his closest rivals within the animal kingdom. There is no doubting the importance that we all assign to this sense of intellectual dominance, and of our pride in human endeavour and success. Most creative art is committed to glorifying or dramatising those aspects of humanity which emphasise this special place in nature and our implicit claim to divinity. Furthermore, ingrained in our unconscious minds is a psychologically potent self-image which helps us to accept our role in a frightening and mysterious universe. This self-image has been tarnished − the Inquisition, Passchendaele and Belsen did little to keep it polished − but never seriously doubted. The coming of the computer may be the event that first calls it into question, by casting doubt on the assumption that problem-solving, thinking, even creativity are exclusively human. If these talents can be shown to be within the domain of computers, then this self-image may be shaken or destroyed. The problem will be compounded if we find ourselves not just equalled, but surpassed in these areas.

The situation will be roughly analogous to that arising if, after the fashion of the movie *Close Encounters of the Third Kind*, the earth was suddenly visited by extraterrestrial life forms who possessed a science and technology of overwhelming, almost incomprehensible power. In the movie, incidentally, far too little was made of the culture shock which would ensue, and humans trotted amiably in and out of the alien spaceship as if all that was necessary to ensure instant and complete détente was a linguaphone course. But the appearance of intelligences greatly superior to our own, whether they come from outer space or from within computers of our own creation, would pose some tremendous problems.

How will we, as a species, feel if all our endeavours, all our scientific knowledge and expertise, all our philosophical deliberations, all our artistic and cultural strivings are suddenly revealed as shallow and inconsequential? And how will we feel at the realisation that the gap between ourselves and the Ultra-Intelligent Machines is unbridgeable, and that any advances we make will be easily outdistanced by their superlative endeavours? This may explain why, if the universe is teeming with intelligent life, we have not, despite all the testimony of Ufologists, been contacted by aliens. The culture-shock, as the highly advanced aliens must know, would be too much for us to handle. As long as the UIMs are solidly under our control, we ought to be able to prevent them from flinging us into a terminal case of culture-shock. Even so, we shall have to re-appraise our role, our goals, our future and, so far as this is possible, our purpose in the universe.

CHRISTOPHER EVANS

Note: Your answers should be *in your own words* as far as possible.

(*a*) What link is established in the first paragraph between non-computerised scientific discoveries and those which "super-intelligent computers" might make? What is the difference between them?

(*6 marks*)

(*b*) Explain the parallel between men and chimpanzees, in paragraph 2.

(*4 marks*)

(*c*) How might the computers "be doing us a favour"? (*2 marks*)

(*d*) What is the author's "fear" (line 24)? (*2 marks*)

(*e*) Explain the meaning of the statement "This self-image has been tarnished . . . but never seriously doubted" (line 40). (*4 marks*)

(*f*) What point is the author making by his reference to *Close Encounters of the Third Kind*? For what does he criticise the film? (*6 marks*)

(*g*) Explain why, according to the writer, "if the universe is teeming with intelligent life, we have not been contacted by aliens". (*4 marks*)

(*h*) Give briefly the meaning of the following as they appear in the passage:
   (i)   alien (line 6);
   (ii)   apocalyptic (line 15);
   (iii) deliberations (line 59);
   (iv)   inconsequential (line 60);
   (v)   terminal (line 68). (*5 marks*)

(*i*) Comment on the idea that computers might force unwanted discoveries upon us, and give three examples of your own of the kinds of discovery which the author is talking about. (*7 marks*)

(*Total:* 40 *marks*)

Introduction

The effects of the microcomputer are already being felt by everyone living in the Western world. Yet in the mid-twentieth century, when the earliest computers were being developed, no one, not even the experts, had the slightest conception of how, within another quarter of a century, computers would be all-pervasive. The development of the silicon chip means that hundreds of thousands of circuits can be concentrated on a single finger-nail-sized piece of silicon, and the microtechnological revolution is upon us.

These developments are explained by Alan Burkitt and Elaine Williams in their book *The Silicon Civilisation*:

When it was invented, the computer – often nicknamed an electronic brain – was so totally a tool of the mathematician that only a brave or foolhardy person dared suggest there might ever be other uses. Alan Turing, the Englishman who developed the idea of controlling computers with stored instructions or programs, and who worked on the wartime decoding machines, thought that Britain would never need more than three computers. There were not enough mathematicians to operate more, he reasoned. A similar prediction was made in America . . . ''not only because of a shortage of mathematicians, but also because machines would be so expensive to build and operate that they could only be justified economically in a few applications . . . . As we know, computers have not been so limited. Today they are found in the factory, running machine tools and complete production lines. Small firms keep their accounts on them. Linked to a typewriter, a computer can write letters. It can operate trains, control oil refineries; fly aircraft. A computer records sales in a supermarket and orders replacement stocks; a miniature computer can monitor the pollution in a car's exhaust and regulate the engine to bring it within the law; an even tinier computer can control a washing machine. Giant installations can store, and supply to anyone, more information than the Encyclopaedia Britannica.

The reason can be expressed in two words: silicon chip. When computers were built of valves they were expensive, large, greedy in terms of energy, and, by our standards, not very intelligent creatures. The transistor brought down the cost and size, reduced their energy consumption, and provided enough computing power to make computers easily programmable. No longer did they have to be tended by mathematical geniuses. In the 1970s the integrated circuit completed the revolution. The microcomputer arrived, and each was more powerful than one of the earliest giant valve models.

. . . . And price is what makes modern computers so attractive and so ubiquitous. A machine tool fitted with a microcomputer costing a few thousand pounds can make parts so quickly and so accurately that the extra cost is soon recouped.

A microcomputer can pay for itself within months when it saves energy running a building's heating and air conditioning. Some applications would not be possible for valve computers − such as in washing machines, car engines or automatic typewriters − but no one would have considered using electronics if the cost was still that of the valve era. The cheapness of silicon integrated circuits means such previously outlandish proposals are now completely practicable.

BURKITT and WILLIAMS

Exercise and discussion suggestion

List all the things affecting your life which use microcomputers. Compare your list with other people's.

On the basis of the facts which emerge from this comparison, discuss the importance of microcomputers in the lives of ordinary people in Britain at the moment.

The Social Effects of the New Technologies: Optimistic and Pessimistic View

In his book *The Microchip: Appropriate or Inappropriate Technology?* Alan Burns devotes a chapter to "Two Views of the Future". In it he presents the views of both an imagined optimist and pessimist about the social effects of microtechnology. Here are some extracts:

The optimist

No element of traditional home life will be spared the helping hand of the micro; . . . Some homes in the USA are already heavily computerised, and systems such as central heating or cooking which can be activated via the telephone, from outside, are on sale now in the UK. The optimist's home will be a completely controlled but personalised environment where every need (well, almost) will be anticipated and fulfilled in a totally relaxed atmosphere which is just as well as considerable amounts of time will be spent there.

Work

"Once computers infiltrate a society, their virtues override any intrinsic objections to their use, and their continued infiltration and ultimate domination is from that point inevitable. They achieve their subtle take-over by demonstrating first their usefulness and, when that has been established, their indispensability. The laws of survival in the modern world apply and those companies that employ computers to their maximum effectiveness will achieve a monumental economic advantage. Those that reject or ignore them will sooner or later find themselves in ruins." (Evans)[1]

That computers will take over work is irrefutable, and this must be to our eventual benefit even though, at first, large-scale redundancies, short-time working and early retirement will bring a host of social problems. Boring work, by definition, is repetitive, and repetitive work is just what robots are good at; therefore the unattractive jobs in our society will become the forte of the machine. Similarly, dangerous work will become increasingly unacceptable, and automated systems in the mines and chemical plants will become the norm.

No area of work will remain unaffected by the micro; manufacture will be undertaken by robots, and data handling by automated information systems; even the professions will eventually be superseded by intelligent machines that will organise education, diagnose illness, and adjudicate in legal disputes. Whether this means the end of work as we know it or just a radical restructuring with other jobs being created to replace the redundant ones is still not clear, but obviously the role of work will never be the same

---

1. See bibliography, page 165.

again. It will no longer dominate our lives, in terms of hours spent or significance given . . . .

Education and health

These two pillars of society, which in Britain have formed the basis of our welfare state, will change out of all recognition by the turn of the century. Teaching machines ranging from hand-held dictionaries to complete class-room systems will, to a great extent, replace the human teacher. Schools themselves may decline in importance when the home information system supplements, or even supersedes, traditional methods of education. It is not, however, only the children that will need or require education; all ages in a rapidly changing society will be demanding retraining and refresher courses. This demand will be impossible to satisfy if the potential of automated computer-aided teaching is not fully utilised.

In health care changes will be even more significant. When a patient arrives at the local GP surgery, she or he will not be met by a nurse or a recep-tionist but by a computer terminal linked to a national data processing network. This computer will contain complete records of the patient, and built into it will be routines for undertaking the preliminary diagnosis. Having done this it will produce a report and recommendations to the doctor who will then decide on the course of treatment. Few GPs can have a work-ing knowledge of the complete range of drugs currently available for prescription; the computer system will have such knowledge and will be able to advise the doctor on the most apposite medication for each patient.

Possible side-effects of drugs can be monitored by the national network; if a new specialised drug is brought into use today, perhaps only one or two patients per doctor would be prescribed it. This sample is too small for all but the most obvious and consistent side-effects to be noticed. With an over-all medical monitor, detrimental effects could quickly be highlighted and the drug taken out of use. When everything else is equal the cheapest form of the tablet or medicine would be recommended, and with computerised dis-pensing equipment the exact quantity of drug could be given. These two facts alone would probably pay for a national computer in only two or three years.

Doctors and surgeons of the future will be trained by computers that have learnt from previous experts in the field. This ability of intelligent machines to learn from interacting with humans may even be put to good use in psychoanalysis:

"Current experiments with computer-interviewing . . . suggest that patients can strike up a surprising rapport with the computer, particularly in sensitive areas such as those involving psychosexual or emotional problems. Might not the very much more powerful machine intelligence of the late 1990s, trained to respond to every nuance of a patient's voice, patterns of speech, hesitancies, even his facial expressions and eye movement provide exceptional relief and perhaps, therapy?" (Evans)

One area in which the micro is already providing considerable help is in the development of aids for the handicapped. The automated home will be a boon to people who have limited mobility, and "intelligent" wheelchairs with many robotic features will have a similar role outside. In addition, individuals who suffer from visual and hearing disabilities will find an increasing number of electronic aids on the market, particularly voice-controlled equipment. Some injuries, such as a severed nerve, may even be bypassed by some appropriate microelectronic appliance.

In the long term the micro may well find more of a role in preventive medicine. External apparatus will continually monitor the somatic functions and broadcast alarm at any irregular or inadvisable behaviour. Internal probes equipped to sense malignant cells may be implanted in patients at risk so that the earliest warning of possible cancer growth can be given. There is really no limit to the number of uses that the micro can be put to in health care.

The government

International organisations and governments will become more dependent on computers to fulfil their administrative and political objectives. Economic planning will be almost entirely taken over by sophisticated computer controlled analysis which will finally make economics an exact science. Democratic control will be maintained by "instant elections" and referenda in which the people are asked, via their viewdata communication network, to give their opinions on whatever is the subject of the moment.

As computers become more intelligent – the generic term for future computers is UIM, Ultra Intelligent Machines – they will systematically gain control over functions and roles currently considered exclusively human. For instance, Professor J McCarthy of the Artificial Intelligence Laboratory at Stanford University has remarked: "What do judges possess that we cannot tell a computer?" A UIM would contain detailed knowledge of the defendant's previous convictions, if any, and would have access to a vast store of case history upon which to base its decision. New laws would be instantly accommodated and might even be initiated by a UIM suggestion. The important thing to remember is that judgements would be correct . . . . As a further aid to crime-fighting, personal identifiers based upon a single communication chip will enable the police to check the whereabouts of all citizens at all times.

The basis of this optimistic view is that if change is inevitable, as appears to be the case, then there is no reason why it should not be for the better. As people in an information society gain more knowledge they will have greater control over their own lives and more freedom from the state. But to get the most from this technical revolution, attitudes must change and quickly; society must be sufficiently adaptable so that this image of a golden future will be realised. In particular, the wealth created through the widespread use of efficient microelectronic based machinery and services must pass to the population at large; who will then buy the goods and use the services necessary to sustain the economy. A truly brave new world is ahead.

The pessimist

The pessimistic view is based upon a resignation to the inevitability of a continuing exponential growth in the electronics industry, and a fear that the social changes needed to meet the resulting cultural upheavals will not happen at anywhere near the rate necessary. Technology growth will continue because the primary users and the technology manufacturers have a vested interest in it doing so; the remaining population have no say in how the machinery should be controlled and gains little direct benefit from its deployment . . . .

Two issues which provoke great concern, and form the foundation of the pessimistic outlook, are the future of work and the fear of the Big Brother State.

Work

"The people who develop and control technology are not interested in the quality of our lives; they are only interested in increasing profits. So instead of building a new world of freedom and leisure, new technology is bringing the fear of mass unemployment to the hearts of millions." (CIS Report 1980)

From car manufacture to chocolate packing, the most labour intensive element of production is the assembly of the final product, and that is therefore where most effort will be focused in the introduction of new systems. Manufacturers find themselves caught in a Catch 22 position; to employ the same number of workers they must retain their share of the market by remaining competitive, but if other firms are increasing their efficiency by the use of new technology, then the only way to remain competitive is to make similar rationalisations by laying off staff. Companies are forced to either cut their labour costs or to go out of business altogether.

Though factory workers are quite familiar with the pressing demand for greater productivity and have accommodated new skills in order to achieve it, office personnel have been working in an industry that has changed very little over the past fifty years. The situation will not continue, for electronic equipment is already revolutionising the office. Copy typing will disappear, filing will be done automatically as will data processing, and all communications will be carried out by electronic mail. A vastly diminished flow of business letters will lead to refinements in the telephone system resulting in increased reliability and automation. The impact of this upon employment will be devastating; clerical work (traditionally female) will virtually vanish and the Post Office, being the largest employer in Britain, must suffer considerably from this "progress". Another alarming aspect of the communications revolution is that office work can easily be transferred around the world. This will lead not only to manufacturing taking place in the third world, for cheaper labour, but also data processing and document preparation. This would exacerbate unemployment in the developed world whilst being of little real benefit to the emergent nations.

The net result of all these effects will be gross and permanent unemployment on a scale as yet unknown. It may be that in the long term attitudes to work will alter, but the protestant work ethic is deeply rooted in our society and will not be removed overnight. In the interim we face the prospect of having many millions of "second class citizens" who may not be happy just to sit back and accept this role.

Big Brother is watching!

Unemployment, however bad, is not a new phenomenon in our society, even if in the future it will be of unparalleled severity. By comparison, the use of sophisticated electronics to monitor an individual's every move is a new and sinister development which will have far greater effect on our way of life in the so-called post-industrial society.

In the future it will be possible for security forces to record each person's movements, wherever they may be, by making it compulsory for everyone to wear a communication beacon. This development would be considered by most people as an infringement of civil liberties, and it is unlikely that this situation could actually arise in a democratic society. There are, however, examples of company systems that come close to these ideas. Computerised factories are currently in operation where all personnel must carry an identification card to gain access to each area of the factory through electronic locks. This card does not just unlock the door, it also records the event, therefore a worker's progress around the buildings can be followed, and such activities as clocking on and off are done automatically at the main gate.

Computerised cash registers are becoming a familiar feature of the modern supermarket; they work efficiently and have a number of special functions not available on the standard till. One of these enables the operations of the person working the register to be timed . . . . New technology word-processors are also capable of automatically measuring the work efficiency of typists in a manner not known or understood by the typists themselves.

The office and supermarket are only two examples of what could be a general application of microprocessor equipped tools. If one's job has anything to do with a microcomputer then it is possible, and in many instances likely, that your ability to work with the machine will be continually recorded for your employer. It is rare for any job to consist entirely of interacting with a computer, therefore to take just one measurement as an evaluation of overall performance and, moreover, to do so without the knowledge of the employee is a gross misuse of an employer's power.

In an information society all data, including personal records, is kept in computerised data bases. These computers will be linked together to form networks and give the effect of there being just one enormous file containing information on every member of society. This file will be open to local and national government officials, tax officers, the police and security forces. Additionally, unlawful and unsanctioned access to the file will make a mockery of any concept of privacy in tomorrow's society, for no matter how modern the equipment, there are always means of "getting into" the data bases, especially if you have the backing of expertise and equipment.

The pessimistic consequences of computerising personal information are high-lighted by the following questions: Is it reasonable for your employer to have access to your medical and possible criminal records? Should a credit firm be able to check all your bank accounts? Is it right for tax inspectors to automatically have knowledge of every financial transaction you make? Would you be happy for commercial organisations to know that you have not bought a television for five years nor taken a holiday abroad for three, and to be send unsolicited advertising because of that knowledge? Should the police know where you spend your money, how much you have and how much you earn? Should government officers have access to all your personal records?

There is at least one more disquieting feature of this technology that should be related; the libraries of the future will not be collections of printed books but visual display units where all reading material can be obtained, from a novel to a government report. It is not unheard of for books to be banned and the mere possession of sensitive material to be an offence. Even with technology currently available it would be possible to restrict access to material and monitor the reading habits of the nation. In the name of national security, will such data be used to draw political conclusions about individuals? Freedom of information has a somewhat hollow ring to it when its consequences are fully appreciated.

The ownership of technology

The electronics business is one of the world's fastest growing industries, and this will presumably continue to the end of this century and beyond. IBM, the gigantic computer manufacturer, can amass over \$5 billion[2] gross profit per year and spend \$1 billion of that on research and development. The rewards from this area may be high, but so too is the cost of taking part. Small firms cannot compete in the production of "new technology", and the faster this technology changes the more likely it is that manufacture will be concentrated in just a few large multinationals, based either in the USA or Japan . . . .

If a government cannot control the use and distribution of computer technology and microelectronics, what chance does an individual have? Information technology will rationalise most aspects of everyday life and make it virtually impossible for anyone to contemplate any alternative lifestyle. In a cashless society you must have a direct-debit card and an "open" bank account or you will not even be able to use the local shop. If all information comes from a VDU linked to a central system, then failure to have this equipment will prohibit one's access to books, magazines, newspapers and government data; it may even eliminate one's democratic right to vote in elections. To work, pay taxes or visit the doctor will necessitate computerised data files being kept on you. There is no choice; if you are a member of society you must play the game.

Discussion Suggestions

How do you react to the various predictions in this section? You might consider them one by one:

2. 5 thousand million.

The short-term disappearance of jobs in various areas of employment:
(i)   assembly line work in factories
(ii)   dangerous jobs
(iii) office work

The longer-term possibilities either of new types of jobs being created to replace redundant ones, or of "gross and permanent unemployment".

Teaching machines replacing teachers and "home information systems" superseding schools.

Computers taking over the functions of lawyers and judges.

The use of microtechnology in medicine:
(i)   national computerised monitoring of drugs
(ii)   psychoanalysis by "intelligent machines"
(iii) preventive medicine by micro

The role of computers in politics and economics:
(i)   "instant elections" by "viewdata communication network"
(ii)   economics becoming "an exact science" by computerisation

The use of "personal identifiers" enabling the police to check everyone's whereabouts constantly.

Built-in efficiency records on word-processors.

The availability of personal records on "data bases" available for official scrutiny.

The replacement of printed books by "visual display units".

Overall, do you take an optimistic or pessimistic view of the effects of the increasing computerisation of society?

Leisure and Home Life in Tomorrow's World

For good or evil, there seems little doubt that leisure will become much more important that ever before in the years ahead. In his book *The New Revolution: The Impact of Computers on Society*, Barrie Sherman suggests some of the implications of this:

Many forecasters believe that unemployment will be with us through to the twenty-first century and will be oriented towards the young and more especially those young people with the poorest record of educational attainments. More women will be at home without paid employment. There will be more job sharing, perhaps even permits to work, a school leaving age of at least eighteen (paid for the last two years), less night shift production work but more night-time maintenance work, and twenty-five hours paid employment per week with little or no overtime will not be unusually low. The likelihood is that these hours will be spread over three days rather than five so that the new leisure time will be taken in large blocks. Retirement will be part-time, then full-time and will be taken between 50 and 65. Computers will have some degree of responsibility for these changes as they will for the changes within the home. As the cabling of homes goes ahead so the computer potential of each home increases. There has been a significant drift towards working from home for typists using word-processors, for programmers using home terminals and for managers. Home working has an unenviable reputation in most countries as a method of paying exceptionally low wages for not very skilled jobs, but this is now changing to a marked degree. Another form of homework will be by the self-employed, especially in creative programming and analysis. Most of these prophecies have been discussed by economists, philosophers, sociologists, futurologists, scientists, and ordinary people; it is both sad and instructive that politicians have not joined in.

As an entertainment centre, shopping and banking centre using Prestel (or its equivalent), work station, and centre of social life, the home appears destined to take on new functions. Problems resulting from such changes stare back at an observer from all angles. Nowadays we get most of our social contacts from the workplace. If we spend more time at home how will we meet people, where will friends come from, and will we develop electronic friends, use picture telephones as a substitute for meeting people, or play video telephone bridge as a substitute for kicking one's partner under the table? How will permanent relationships, marriages for example, stand up to the extra strains of partners being in close proximity to each other when one suspects that the reason for their survival has been the relative lack of contact and togetherness. When the diminution of personal stimulation in the new forms of shopping or when using public transport are taken into account too, loneliness or a marked lack of variety in social contacts will become major sources of concern.

At the same time it will be easier, perhaps nicer, to live at home. Domestic robots and controls and systems computers will do both the menial tasks and plan the cheapest uses of energy or food or even travel. Appliances like washing machines, bathroom scales, cookers, do-it-yourself equipment, or even light switches will all become more sophisticated and more reliable – even "intelligent". Whilst many factors will be increasing the hours that people spend within the home so the need to be there diminishes. Free time will emerge, time which could be used for educational or socially aware purposes or, on a less high-minded Victorian vein, to enjoy oneself, to travel the world, and to do and see new things.

SHERMAN

Discussion points

How do you view the prospect of a 25-hour, 3-day working week?

Do you think that a home-based culture would inevitably lead to greater loneliness and marital stress?

How do you feel about the idea of conducting personal relationships via electronic technology, as illustrated in the extract?

Do you feel that society will be able to react quickly enough to the problems resulting from increased leisure?

Try to imagine a typical day in your life in the year 2000. Compare your vision with those of others.

The Use of Robots

Throughout this century science-fiction writers have delighted in picturing a world in which robots take over the functions of human beings. It is now beginning to happen in reality. David Bleakley, in his book *In Place of Work . . . The Sufficient Society*, discusses this phenomenon:

> Hand-made by Robots
> Less room for human error
> More room for humans
> (Strada car advertisement)

Even bigger developments are forecast in the changing balance of power between robots and people. Scientists are now predicting that a future world war would be computer controlled and directed. A disturbing thought. More disturbing – one suspects that if ordered to arrange the final folly, the robots would have the "intelligence" to make sure that neutron bombs were employed so favouring the survival of their own species. A case of, "Robots of the World unite, you have nothing to lose but your humans" . . .

The typical industrial robot, especially when at rest, is indistinguishable from many other pieces of engineering equipment. Where modern robots differ is in their "thinking" capacity – they can be computer programmed to do an infinite variety of tasks and, unlike human beings, they can be instructed to carry on regardless of time, season or any of the many other factors which complicate production, using traditional methods. In fact . . . it is becoming a matter of industrial pride to boast that people are no longer much involved in the productive process. As one delegate remarked to the 1978 Trades Union Congress, "They are saying about one company in California's silicon chip valley that it has done so well it is moving into smaller premises". It is only a small step away to the suggestion that "man-made" is tantamount to a seal of inferiority.

Nor is the computer revolution confined in application to heavy industry. Robots can be "told" to mow the lawn, do household chores, educate our children and control almost any mechanical or electrical system from a toy train to the most complicated of our space machines.

But there is promise as well as threat in this potential. We do not need to create the meaningless leisure of H G Wells' *The Time Machine* which was every bit as soul destroying as the monotonous activity in which many millions must engage in modern industrial society. As one American philosopher once reminded us, we can cheerfully eliminate those types of work "that deform the body, cramp the mind, deaden the spirit". The exploitation of machines becomes the alternative to the exploitation of people — the Robot becomes a friend and ally.

BLEAKLEY

Discussion points

Do you find the Strada car advertisement disturbing?

How widespread do you think the use of computers in industry will become?

Do you think that the robot actually will become "a friend and ally"?

Research suggestion

Anyone interested in modern warfare might undertake research into the various applications of microtechnology to offensive and defensive weapons production.

Ultra Intelligent Machines

For many years experts have talked of the eventual production of computers which will be intellectually superior to human beings. These will be the "Ultra Intelligent Machines" of the twenty-first century.

Christopher Evans, in *The Mighty Micro*, considers the possibilities and implications of their production.

The concept of the Ultra Intelligent Machine (or UIM as it is abbreviated) is a controversial, challenging and, at the same time, slightly frightening one — the more so because it is a logically coherent idea which springs naturally out of our present understanding of computer science. By Good's[3] definition an Ultra Intelligent Machine is a computer programmed to perform any intelligent activity at least marginally better than Man. Intellectual activity, incidentally, excludes such things as enjoying bacon and eggs and admiring good-looking men or women, and includes such things as solving problems, making tactical decisions, exploring logical possibilities and even carrying on interesting conversations. Good points out it might be necessary to teach the computer some of the principles of aesthetics — a task which is already being attempted on an experimental basis at one or two computer centres — for the computer's conversations might be horribly bland and limited without some understanding of aesthetics. But the most interesting question to consider is what will we do with the Ultra Intelligent Machines when they arrive?

Clearly, the first thing would be to put them to work on some of the numerous problems facing society. These could be economic, medical or educational matters, and also, perhaps, strategic modelling to forecast

---

3. Professor Jack Good, originator of the term "Ultra Intelligent Machine".

trends and produce "early warnings" of difficulties or crises. Weather fore-
casting, for example, has already been substantially improved through
computer analysis, and has great economic significance in parts of the world
where the climate is unpredictable and hostile. But as the UIMs improve and
expand their capabilities, other areas of interest will fall to their inspection
with substantial benefits to mankind . . . .

During the 1990s computers will increasingly serve as intellectual and
emotional partners . . . . In the course of this strange partnership computers
will inevitably acquire ways of behaving which allow them to converse with
us, exchange ideas and concepts, stimulate our imagination and so on . . . .
When they do overtake us computers will, in my view, become extremely
interesting entities to have around. Their role as teachers and mentors, for
example, will be unequalled. It will be like having, as private tutors, the
wisest, most knowledgeable and most patient humans on earth: an Albert
Einstein to teach physics, a Bertrand Russell to teach philosophy, a Sigmund
Freud to discuss the principles of psychoanalysis, and all available where and
when they are wanted.

Many people, in particular those who have never had the experience of
fiddling with computers, may fail to believe that any machine, no matter
how intelligent, could engage one's wholehearted attention for more than
the briefest of moments. One can understand the scepticism, and can
respond to it emotionally, but it is dangerously misleading. Even in their
present lowly state, computers are very interesting to interact with – bearing
in mind that I am talking about intellectual interaction and not going on
country walks, sailing a boat or falling in love with them. A glimpse of just
how interesting they can be often comes when you play chess with them –
they are already considered by many skilled players to be more satisfactory
competitors than humans. For those who do not play chess, a spell of playing
some of the other powerful computer games will provide much the same
insight, for they are enormously versatile companions, and pitting wits
against them is fascinating to the point of obsession . . . .

Progress will be slow at first, for the problems are numerous and complex.
Nevertheless, if we so choose, limitless computer effort could be applied,
and sooner or later machine intelligence will be not only above that of
humans, but also above that of the first UIMs. Then the second generation
of UIMs will be available for work and they, too, will be put to general
problem-solving and, because of their enhanced IQ, might advance at a
dramatic pace. Some Mark 2 UIMs could be assigned to produce further
advances in artificial intelligence and a third generation of even smarter
machines would result. And so it will go on: the brighter the machines, the
more capable they will be of enhancing their own intelligence, and they will
begin to leap-frog ahead, each bound being progressively larger than the
previous one.

EVANS

In the following extracts from an article in *The Times*, Andrew Moncur
reports a meeting at which computer experts followed through the
implications of microtechnology to offer their view of the future:

Artificial "super brains" could take over from the family doctor and make other professional people redundant in under 40 years, Sir Clive Sinclair predicted yesterday.

Sir Clive, head of Sinclair Research and a pioneer in electronics, forecast the arrival of mega-computers, costing no more than a family car and so knowledgeable and quick-thinking that they would supplant the professionals by 2020.

He was looking forward 36 years – the same time span that George Orwell bridged in writing his grim portrayal of 1984 – at a Mensa symposium in Cambridge.

Dr Madsen Pirie, president of the Adam Smith Institute, suggested that the age of the helpless individual dwarfed by the giant, bureaucratic state would be over long before 2020.

Dr Pirie described a family as it might be in 2020. The father is a miner, who took his doctorate in bio-chemistry from an electronic university and whose firm extracts coal products with the aid of coal-eating micro-organisms.

The mother works for a special unit organising business conferences, often through audio-visual links. She decided to have two children in her late forties. Her daughter will probably wait until her sixties before she, in turn, conceives. She has already spent a week in China, camping with friends, and has won an award for living under water for 72 hours.

The boy is 14 and has been sexually mature for several years. He is taking a degree in marine biology.

from *The Times* (1984)

Finally, Michael Shallis, in a chapter of his book, *The Silicon Idol: the Micro Revolution and its Social Implications*, entitled "Futures", describes what he terms "the wired society" of the future:

Houses will become places of work and play, eliminating the need for costly transport, because you will be able to talk to your co-workers or friends, by video channel . . . .

Money will become bits of information passed round electronically . . . .

Two-way channels will enable TV terminals to serve as input as well as output devices. The viewer will be able to comment on and criticise the programme he is watching. Instant polls can be taken on issues, with viewers participating by sending their opinion over the lines to a vote-counting computer. Instant democracy could be extended to serious political decision-making . . . .

The new technologies will reduce pollution because the techniques are "cleaner" than the old mechanised industries. Congestion on the roads and even the spread of motorways will ease as people "travel" by sitting at home, "visiting" their friends by electronic communication . . . .

Technologies transform, and in these future worlds what transformations will have happened? A goods-dominated society will have become an information-oriented culture. There will be no cash, no paper, little work as we now know it. To read a newspaper will be to scan a TV screen, pushing buttons to flip the pages. To talk to an acquaintance will be to "see" each other on screens, unable to touch, smell or taste things that otherwise could be shared; the meeting reduced to sight and sound and those not real, but sights and sounds emerging from electronic hardware. Shopping will be done by terminal, goods will be displayed on the customer's screen, selected and paid for automatically and delivered to the door. Exercise can be part of leisure. Factories will be run by robots, offices by computers. Children will be taught by machine; machines will act as doctors, lawyers and consultants. The home will become a new type of place, isolated from nature, defended against the have-nots.

What about those who choose not to participate, who refuse to have an EFT card, who want cash? What about those who want their children taught by people, who want to talk to people face to face, not image to image? What of those who choose not to have a home terminal, will they be able to shop, to discover the news, to vote? Will there be an alternative society parallel to the electronic one, a wired society and a wireless one? Are the futures based on where this technology is leading a form of progress, a cultural growing up, or do they constitute the ingredients of a nightmare? Future outcomes are never what people expect and the two alternatives I have drawn are extremes. The wired society is being advocated strongly, being sought actively; its alternative seems to be neglected. The future will probably consist of ingredients from both possibilities but the concern now should be with the processes of choice.

The technological imperative demands the information society and demands it world-wide. It assumes that developments, such as those outlined here, constitute progress and social evolution to a higher form. Progress, however, implies some purpose, some goals to be achieved; rather than buy "progress" for its own sake people should first decide what goals they seek and then choose how best to achieve those goals. The futures I have sketched in this chapter would all arise from where computing and communications technologies can take us.

SHALLIS

Discussion points

Do you feel enthusiastic or depressed at the prospect of "Ultra Intelligent Machines", as described by Christopher Evans?

How do you react to Sir Clive Sinclair's predictions about medicine, and the professions in 2020, and to Dr Pirie's visions of family life?

Do you think man is capable of controlling the new technologies, and establishing clear cut "goals", rather than allowing technological "progress" to carry us on to wherever it leads?

Essay Titles

(a) "Machines are extensions of man's capability; they cannot replace man himself."

(b) What, in your view, are the positive benefits of a branch of modern science?

(c) "Progress is not an accident, it is a necessity."

(d) Will science abolish work?

(e) Has the age of the inventor passed?

(f) How far do you think the computer an indispensable asset to our way of life, and how far do you consider it disadvantageous?

Bibliography

Bleakley, David. *In Place of Work . . . The Sufficient Society*, SCM Press, 1981

Burkitt, Alan and Williams, Elaine. *The Silicon Civilisation*, W H Allen, 1980

Burns, Alan. *The Microchip: Appropriate or Inappropriate Technology?* Ellis Harwood, 1981

Evans, Christopher. *The Mighty Micro: The Impact of the Computer Revolution*, Gollancz, 1979

Macrae, Norman. *The 2024 Report*, Sidgwick and Jackson, 1984

Renmore, C.D. *Silicon Chips and You*, Sheldon Press, 1979

Shallis, Michael. *The Silicon Idol: The Micro Revolution and its Social Implications*, Oxford University Press, 1984

Sherman, Barrie. *The New Revolution: The Impact of Computers on Society*, John Wiley and Sons, 1985

Simons, Geoff. *Silicon Shock: The Menace of the Computer Invasion*, Blackwell, 1985

Toffler, Alvin. *The Third Wave*, Pan Books, 1980

Advice on Writing: Preparing and Presenting a Report

The biggest problem about preparing a report for presentation to other people may well be encountered at the initial stage: finding the information. Let's imagine you are planning to present a report on the uses of computers in modern weapons production, and have to start from scratch. Where do you look for information? If your teacher cannot help, the obvious person to ask is a librarian; he or she will at least be able to guide you to the relevant sections in the library. In this case, the section on computers may have a subsection of books specifically on their applications to weaponry. If it doesn't, how do you choose what book to consult? The titles may provide clues to the contents, and a flip through some promisingly-titled books, especially at their indexes, should unearth the information you're seeking fairly quickly. You could also ask the librarian if there are any relevant periodicals, and if the library doesn't actually carry suitable titles, it will at least have the addresses of current periodicals, so that you can send off to a suitable one for information or relevant back issues.

Having found a section of a book which looks useful, it will save you time, if the section is fairly long, to skip-read it, concentrating on the first and last paragraphs of subsections. It may be worth consulting two or three books on the subject of your research, to achieve a fully-rounded picture.

In making your report, it is vital to consider the time it will take to read it, and keep the length within reasonable limits. You should never simply copy chunks out of a book or article. You must consider your audience; they probably have no prior knowledge of the subject at all, and it must be offered to them in an easily-comprehended fashion. The best approach is to assimilate a section of information and write it down as straightforwardly as possible from memory, checking it when complete against the published material, to test for accuracy and completeness. You should include no technical detail without adding an explanation in simple terms. Simplicity and clarity are the main qualities to strive for. Dividing it into sub-sections, dealing with different aspects of the subject, may help your audience to follow the development of your report.

When you have finished writing it, you should read your report out aloud, timing yourself to ensure that it doesn't overrun the time-limit. If it does, of course, you will have to prune it.

When presenting your report, it is absolutely essential to read as slowly as possible, pausing frequently to allow your fellow students to assimilate what you are saying, to make notes and perhaps to ask you to clarify or repeat points you have made.

10
The Mass Media

Children in the late twentieth-century have grown up with the mass media. In Britain, over ninety per cent of households own a television set, and it is watched, on average, for twenty-five hours a week. Few homes are without daily or Sunday newspapers, and the most popular British Sunday paper has a circulation which is topped only by *Pravda*. The rise of television since the Second World War has brought about a steady decline in the importance of film and radio: the latter, in fact, has become, for most young people, merely an endless supplier of "rock" music, which is now, in itself, a major mass medium. It is a feature of the media that they feed off one another. Tabloid newspapers constantly report the peccadilloes of "rock", film and television stars, and for many readers such tittle-tattle provides the primary interest in the papers they buy.

This chapter is concerned with exploring and analysing different mass media. It begins with a précis passage dealing with one of the most controversial and frequently discussed aspects of the mass media: the social impact of violence on television.

Précis

Write a summary of the following passage in not more than 260 words (the passage contains about 806 words). Your summary should be in clear, connected English, and the number of words used should be indicated at the end. You are advised to spend about one hour on this exercise.

The question of violence looms large in any discussion of the mass media among educationalists. When the Pilkington Report set out to analyse the causes of public "disquiet about television", it was obliged to begin with violence. Yet this question of violence in the media is more complex than appears at first sight. There may certainly be some point in the complaint that there is too much traffic in violent themes. But this complaint should be seen for what it is: a criticism of the balance of content in the media generally, and not a qualitative judgement on the particular kinds of violence treated, nor an informed opinion on their various effects. We must deal with the general question first. But since violence, death and human suffering have always been the subject matter of at least some great art, we must go on to draw the more complex distinctions between different kinds of violence: between, say, the violence of the BBC series of Shakespeare history plays on television, *Age of Kings*, and that of *77 Sunset Strip, Wagon Train, Whiplash and Gunsmoke.* Such distinctions are impossible without some attention to questions of style and treatment. We shall have to understand the different qualities expressed in these programmes, trying to decide how they work as dramatised experiences, and what their psychological impact is.

First, then, in general terms, so far as television is concerned, we are faced with problems of timing and volume. What is suitable for adults in the late evening may not be considered suitable for young children in the afternoon – always supposing that the television providers are alive to their educational responsibilities here, and that a time limit or boundary can be established. When, in a debate on the issue in Parliament in 1962, the Postmaster General said that the BBC assumed children were in bed by nine o'clock, a wise but unidentified backbench voice commented, "They're wrong". As for sheer volume, the Pilkington Report remarked simply that "there was too much violence on television". Few would disagree with this.

When an incorrect programme balance is combined with the general effects of repetition, the judgement is strengthened. Repetition is crucial. The steady networking of badly produced low-level dramatised series – many of them American in origin or feeling – is one aspect of this saturation process. The "competition" between the BBC and ITV for the peak viewing figures is probably another. Both the Nuffield Report (1958) and the Pilkington Report (1962) present disturbing evidence on this score.

Although it seems that only the child who is already emotionally disturbed will actually learn violence from a particular television programme (the evidence on this score seems fairly conclusive, in both *Television and the Child* and the comparable American study *Television in the Lives of our Children*), it is certainly true that we gradually become habituated to certain attitudes and situations if they are repeated often enough. The danger here is that we develop a permissive attitude towards the existence of violence in the world, come to regard it as a "natural" solution to difficult social problems, or accept it as part of the background to life. This is what the Pilkington Report meant by the danger of a "callous indifference". The fear is strengthened when the whole balance is wrong, and when counter-images and attitudes, which enhance life or ennoble gentleness, kindness and love, are so difficult to evoke and often appear so trite and banal set beside the tension and vigour of the rougher scenes.

As the *Guardian* observed in an editorial: "An isolated murder which strikes the viewer with horror is less corrupting than the incessant suggestion that murder is a bagatelle". But the programmes in which this "incessant suggestion" is made are those in which nothing seems to exist on the screen except the moment of violence – many of the television crime serials, for example, in which characters are, at most, two-dimensional stereotypes, the settings simply a procession of expensive penthouses, and the only visual moments of climax those when bodies slump to the floor. As the Pilkington Report commented:

"Many submissions recorded the view that it [violence] was often used gratuitously, that it often did little or nothing to develop plot or characterisation and that it was, presumably, thrown in 'for kicks'. Another common opinion was that it was often unnecessarily emphasised by being shown in close-up and by being lingered over. The damage was not necessarily repaired by ensuring that, in the end, the good were seen to win and the bad to lose, and that crime did not pay: conventional endings of this sort did not penetrate to the level at which the portrayal of violence had its emotional effect. What mattered was that violence provided the emotional energy, the dramatic content of the programme.''

STUART HALL and PADDY WHANNEL

Newspapers

Newspaper organisation

Over the past forty years British newspapers have come to be divided into two broad categories: popular (or tabloid) and serious. Control of the press has altered during the same period. Between the wars the newspapers were owned and controlled by wealthy individuals, frequently referred to as "press barons", like Lords Beaverbrook, Northcliffe and, more recently, Thompson; now they have generally been swallowed up into large corporations, most notably oil companies, whose primary interests lie outside the press.

In the same period also the diversity of political affiliations of the press has largely disappeared, until now there is only one newspaper which consistently supports the Labour Party (the *Daily Mirror*); most of the others support the Conservative Party. All British newspapers, even the one or two more or less independent ones, maintain a fairly rigid editorial line, establishing limits beyond which their journalists cannot step.

The structure within which journalists work is discussed by the journalist Eamonn McCann in an article entitled "The British Press and Northern Ireland", included in *The Manufacture of News*, edited by Cohen and Young:

Those who have ultimate control over what is printed and what is not are drawn from a relatively tiny segment of society — the owners of big business. Generally speaking, what is printed tends to support their interests.

One of the qualifications for editorship is, naturally, a general acceptance of the owners' attitudes. This is reflected in the editorial "line" of every paper and it filters through to reporters, sub-editors, etc. A journalist who has covered Northern Ireland for a British daily paper explains:

"You must remember that every journalist wants what he writes to appear, and in practice all journalists know pretty well what their paper's line is, what is expected of them. There is a fair amount of self-censorship. This happens without thinking. No journalist I have met writes what he knows will be cut. What would be the point? If he has a story which he knows will cause controversy back at the newsdesk he will water it down to make it acceptable."

Most journalists rely heavily on "official" sources. This explains the some-times striking similarity of coverage. Stories from "official" sources will, of course, be eminently acceptable. Moreover, as a former *Mirror* employee writes:

> "In a situation like Northern Ireland our people would have to keep in close touch with the Army Press Office. It would be more or less part of their job to get to know the army press officer as well as possible and that in itself would affect their judgement a bit. Then one of their biggest pre-occupations is not to be scooped by a competitor. No one on the *Mirror* would be sacked because he didn't come up with a carefully authenticated and researched piece, written from local hard work. You do get sacked if the rival has a sensation about the IRA."

Even if a reporter does send through copy which is critical of the estab-lishment and its representatives (eg. the army), it is at the mercy of the news editor and the sub-editors. These are likely to be the most conservative of all the journalistic staff, with years of grinding practice in what is acceptable to the editor and the management. The average senior sub-editor will, as a reflex action, strike out any sentence which jars his sense of propriety.

McCANN

The influence of newspapers

How influential is the press in affecting the attitudes of its readers? To what extent does a newspaper merely respond to the expectations of the readership at which it is aimed? Contrasting views on the question of newspaper influence are represented in the following two extracts.

The first offers a general view of the British press, arguing that the content of newspapers is dictated largely by the nature and attitudes of their readers. It is taken from a book called *The Politics of the Media* by John Whale.

The tastes of a body of readers may alter over the years. They change as the prevailing climate of ideas changes. They change as a result of what they discover to be appearing in rival newspapers. The *Daily Mirror* would never have begun (in the 1970s) to show photographs of naked women, or to lead the paper with stories like "I married the monster who raped Miss X", if the *Sun* had not led the way after its change of ownership in 1969. Once the *Sun* had demonstrated that its readers liked that kind of approach, the *Mirror* adopted it too, and the decline in the *Mirror's* circulation was at least checked. Yet it was not an expedient which was open to *The Times*, struggling for new readers at much the same time. Existing readers of *The Times* would have been outraged at being addressed in that way. The loss would have far outweighed the gain.

It is readers who determine the character of newspapers. The *Sun* illustrates the point in its simplest and saddest form. Until 1964 the *Daily Herald*, and between 1964 and 1969 the broadsheet *Sun*, had struggled to interest working people principally through their intellect. The paper had declined inexorably. Murdoch gave up the attempt and went for the baser instincts. Sales soared. It was an owner's decision, certainly; but it would have meant nothing without the enthusiastic ratification of the readers.

That, in the end, is the answer to the riddle of proprietorial influence. Where it survives at all, it must still defer to the influence of readers. The policy of *The Daily Telegraph*, its selection and opinion of the news it reports, is decided by the editor and his senior colleagues. But there is a regulatory force which keeps the paper's policy from straying too widely or suddenly from pre-ordained paths; and that force is not the proprietor but the readers. They chose the paper for qualities they expect to see continued.

The press is thus predominantly conservative in tone because its readers are. If any substantial number of people seriously wanted the structure of society rebuilt from the bottom, the *Morning Star* would sell more copies than it does. The reason why national newspapers fall tidily into two bundles – popular and posh, with the popular ones all physically smaller than the posh (since the *Daily Express* joined the other tabloids in January 1977) but selling five times as many copies – is that British life remains similarly and obstinately divided. The steady lessening of the economic differences between classes has done nothing to narrow the cultural gap. Certainly there are people who read both a posh and a popular paper, just as there are gradations between the popular papers: both the *Mirror* and the *Sun* aim at readers who are more squarely working-class than the *Express* and the *Mail* do. These things show the complexity of the class pattern, without denying its general lines. The broad shape and nature of the press is ultimately determined by no one but its readers.

WHALE

The second extract argues a more positive influence by newspapers on readers' attitudes. It is taken from a book called *News Limited* by the journalist Brian Whittaker.

There are numerous examples of strange effects induced by the media. Probably the most famous was the panic caused by an American radio dramatisation of H G Wells' *The War of the Worlds* in 1938. But that was the result of people mistaking the play for reality. On another occasion, as an experiment, British astronomer Patrick Moore pretended to have seen an Unidentified Flying Object near his home. The story he told to his local paper was entirely fictitious but when it was published several "witnesses" came forward to confirm the "sighting". At a more down-to-earth level, a British newspaper once warned of the possibility of a salt shortage within a few months. The prophecy was fulfilled immediately as people rushed to the shops to stock up.

No self-respecting person admits to being easily influenced. If you were asked: "Do you believe everything you read in the newspapers?" the only sensible answer would be "No". And yet what alternative have we but to believe? We all rely very heavily on newspapers and television for our knowledge of what is going on in the world. So how do we decide what to believe and what not to believe? Partly, it is a question of credibility: does it seem likely that an event has actually happened in the way it is reported? Also, it is a question of reputation: we regard some sources as more reliable than others — often without any good reason. A survey in 1973 showed that only 27 per cent of people who said newspapers were their main source of news also believed newspapers were the most accurate and trustworthy source of news.

Also — rather illogically — we tend to become less sceptical about news reports the further they are removed from our personal experience. So factory workers may dismiss newspaper reports of a dispute in their own factory as a load of rubbish, but not question stories in the same paper that say the Social Security provides a life of luxury for immigrants.

Stories about "scroungers" and Social Security fiddlers, for example, are common in the popular press. These papers are read by vast numbers of ordinary people, and they influence ordinary people. Stories about "scroungers" can be effective in several ways. They can:

(a) make people more willing to accept work for low wages rather than stay on the dole;
(b) get popular support for keeping state benefits at a low level;
(c) create divisions between the employed "taxpayers" and the unemployed;
(d) encourage people to inform on fiddlers.

And by the simple repetition of such stories, the public begin to accept that "scroungers" are a major drain on public resources. But if the papers' real purpose was to save money, they would concentrate on the much more serious problem of tax evasion.

WHITTAKER

The appeal of the popular press

The "tabloid revolution" was begun by the *Daily Mirror* in the mid 1930s. Stuart Hall and Paddy Whannel, in their book *The Popular Arts*, trace and analyse this phenomenon, with quotations from writings by the former *Mirror* editor, Hugh Cudlipp.

In this first book, *Publish and Be Damned*, Hugh Cudlipp described the tabloid revolution led by Guy Bartholomew:

One Monday morning in 1935 the readers were informed, just as they had been in 1934, 1933, 1932 and 1931, that the swans on the lower reaches of the Thames were mating. Three weeks later they picked up their *Mirror* to learn that Queen Ena of Spain had shocked the guests at a dinner at the Savoy by using a toothpick after the succulent savoury and before the dreary orations; furthermore, that an actress had found it absolute hell to dance at the Dorchester Charity Ball because of her screaming corns. Her husband, a famous actor, threatened to horsewhip the columnist.

From Bath and Bournemouth came letters of protest; from Cardiff and Newscastle guffaws of delight.

The subject-matter of the new *Mirror* was unchanged — queens and duchesses, famous actors and actresses, the Savoy and the Dorchester. What had changed was the slant, the angle of presentation.

We can break the *Mirror* style down into a number of elements. First of all there is the paper's abiding interest in "life" – in human-interest stories drawn from the marginalia of human existence. Whatever else is happening in the paper, the hum of human gossip is an unmistakable sound in the background. All "events" in the *Mirror* take place against this backdrop. No deep pre-occupation with human nature is reflected here – the technique of the "human-interest story" is essentially fragmentary, and consistently works against depth of treatment. The style reflects its earlier antecedents – the "tit-bit" journalism pioneered by Newnes, Northcliffe and Pearson, the magic ingredient of "Tit-Bits", "Answers" and "Pearson's Weekly". Cudlipp has described those papers as consisting of ". . . the same formula; short paragraphs, half a dozen lines instead of half a column, scraps of jumbled news and information of the 'Fancy That' variety, competitions with prizes, answers to readers' queries, coloured cover, free railway insurance."

This is a style designed to mirror life's incessant surface flow. "In the hurrying years," Cudlipp writes, "the *Mirror* began to reach out and take up strange handfuls from the brantub of life."

To the brantub of life was added those other "human interests" – sex and crime – which have lived in very close proximity to the "human-interest" story in popular journalism. The third element was the typographic – a revolution in newspaper layout which the *Mirror* pioneered:

> First eye-opener was the transformation of the news pages. Sledge-hammer headlines appeared on the front page in black type one inch deep, a signal that all could see of the excitements to come. Human interest was at a premium, and that meant sex and crime.

Relentless personalisation is central to the paper's technique, a method which tends to reduce all kinds of news to the level of the "human-interest" story, and to familiarise all world figures, whatever may be their true interests, spheres of work or achievement.

"It was a cheeky pup of a paper", Cudlipp remarks of the *Mirror* in its formative years. "In a popular paper we are bound to write of politics in terms of persons not of principles", he once wrote in a letter to Churchill.

In the mind of the *Mirror*, this liveliness is closely related to the paper's reputation as "provocative and controversial". "Controversy and the *Mirror* were inseparable . . . That was its secret."

> "A popular paper has to be more than merely interesting; it must be alarmingly provocative in every issue and abundantly confident of its own prowess and importance."

STUART HALL and PADDY WHANNEL

The Falklands crisis in 1982 was an issue on which all newspapers were forced to take sides. The *Daily Mirror* was initially opposed to armed conflict whilst the *Sun* took the opposite line with a vengeance! The following extract from *Gotcha! The Media, the Government and the Falklands Crisis*, by Robert Harris, traces the *Sun*'s handling of the Falklands Crisis, and draws some conclusions about the nature of the popular press, and its significance as a vehicle for news in the 1980s:

When three national newspapers opposed the Government's handling of the Suez crisis in 1956, they lost readers heavily. The *Guardian* lost 30,000 in a matter of days, though it later recouped them. *The Observer* lost 30,000 in a week, fell behind *The Sunday Times* for the first time and never caught up again. It was the *Daily Mirror* itself which fared worst, losing 70,000 readers. The lesson appeared clear. Supported by Rupert Murdoch, the *Sun* moved swiftly to corner the market in patriotism and to label its rival firmly as a disloyal defeatist.

The *Sun* had already attacked "the sinking *Daily Mirror*" as a "paper warrior" on 2 April, the day of the invasion. On 6 April it struck again. "At home the worms are already coming out of the woodwork," taunted the *Sun*.

> "The ailing *Daily Mirror*, which tried to pretend that there was no threat to the Falklands until the invaders had actually landed, now whines that we should give in to force and obligingly settle the islanders. But our whole experience with dictators has taught us that if you appease them, in the end you have to pay a far greater price."

"Youths demonstrated outside the Argentinian Embassy in London last night," reported the *Sun* on 3 April. "They sang 'Rule Britannia', ending with 'Don't Cry for me, Argentina, We're going to Nuke you'." "Sack the guilty men!" ran the paper's editorial on the same day, "What the hell is going on at Britain's Foreign Office and Ministry of Defence?" To oppose sending the task force was to be "running scared"; on 7 April "The *Sun* Says" fired this salvo:

> "Out of the woodwork, like the political termite he is, crawls No. I Left-winger Tony Benn to demand the evacuation of the Falkland islanders
> . . .
>   And of course, he immediately wins backing from the whining namby-pamby ultra-Left, who always run scared at the first sign of a crisis."

The following day, the *Sun* printed a two-page spread of photographs of British marines surrendering on the Falklands. "LEST WE FORGET" was the headline. "This is why our lads are going to war."

> "These were the first moments of humiliating defeat for our brave Falklands few. It was a black moment in our history . . . a wound we cannot forget. But now our troops are on their way . . . to wipe out the memory and free our loyal friends."

The *Sun*'s attitude to a negotiated settlement was summed up in a five-word headline on 20 April: "STICK IT UP YOUR JUNTA". "We urge every housewife NOT to buy corned beef produced in the Argentine" was the theme of an early campaign. Two days later the *Sun* reported that "all over the country, families blacked the 'bully' beef to show the South American bully boys what they thought." "Angry Sonia Lewis of Hockliffe, Beds", was reported as saying: "Refusing to buy corned beef is one way we Brits can show the flag."

Argentinians were "Argies", a good target for humour. A daily series of "Argy-Bargie" jokes was instituted, and soon the *Sun* was able to tell its readers, "Your very own gags have been pouring in". "They are so funny that we have decided to give £5 for every reader's Argy-Bargie joke published. Plus a can of Fray Bentos 'non Argentinian' corned beef. Today's joke was told to us by Titus Rowlandson, 9, from Brighton . . ." (Titus earned £5 for a joke about two British soldiers wiping out hundreds of "Argy" soldiers.)

The *Sun*'s promotions department was equally busy. On 7 April, "to give the lads a big morale-booster", the paper began distributing free badges bearing the legend: "The *Sun* says Good Luck Lads".

"THE SUN SAYS KNICKERS TO ARGENTINA!" was the banner headline on 16 April. "Britain's secret weapon in the Falklands dispute was revealed last night . . . it's undie-cover warfare." The article revealed that "thousands of women" were "sporting specially made underwear embroidered across the front with the proud name of the ship on which a husband or boyfriend is serving." Even Prince Andrew had "bought several pairs of battle-briefs . . . . But Palace officials are keeping mum about who will get them as a Royal gift." Alongside the story was the inevitable picture of "delightful Debbie Boyland . . . all shipshape and Bristol fashion" in her "nautical naughties" embroidered with the name of "HMS *Invincible*."

From 11 May every front page bore the slogan "THE PAPER THAT SUPPORTS OUR BOYS". The comic-strip headlines continued. "AGRY JETS SHOT DOWN" (13 May), "OUR PLANES BLITZ ARGY SHIPS, HOW OUR TOUGH GUYS HIT PEBBLE ISLAND" (17 May), "ARGIES BLOWN OUT OF THE SKY" (24 May), "PANICKY ARGIES FLEE BAREFOOT" (3 June), "HERO BAYONET TROOPS KILL FIFTY" (14 June). Following their peace initiative, the "contemptible, treacherous Irish" joined the *Sun*'s gallery of hate-figures: "Don't buy Irish golden butter . . . . Don't holiday there this summer. It's not much but it's better than giving succour to our new enemy." The names of all thirty-three Labour MPs who voted against the Government on 20 May were printed as a "Roll of Shame". "Enemy quail at the touch of cold steel," reported the Sun on 14 June. "The Argies had no stomach for closequarters combat and crumbled before the Task Forces full-blooded assaults." The level of abuse was kept up to the end, even spilling over on to the sports pages during the coverage of the World Cup. "ARGIES SMASHED . . . They strutted, they cheated and, afterwards they bleated. That was the arrogant Argentines last night. They swaggered on as world champions, and crawled off, humiliated by little Belgium . . ."

Yet if the *Sun* hoped by such coverage to improve circulation, there was no evidence of that by the end of the war. Throughout the country as a whole there was only a tiny rise in the total circulation of all Fleet Street papers: from 14.9 million per day in March to 15.2 million in May (when fighting was at its height), falling back to 15 million in June – an overall increase of less than 1 per cent. In the same period, the *Sun* actually lost sales of 40,000 a day, while the *Mirror* added 95,000. "We put on 100,000 thanks to a promotional campaign just before the war started," says Molloy, "and we managed to keep most of them." Peter Stephens agrees: "I don't think anyone prospered or suffered as a result of the war."

Bearing in mind the precedent of Suez, this was, from the *Mirror*'s point of view, an impressive performance. Why was this? The Falklands war was, after all, a much more popular venture than Suez. If papers opposed to military action lost readers in 1956, surely they should have done even worse in 1982?

It seems almost certain that the explanation lies in the expansion of television over the past twenty-five years. At the time of Suez there were less than 6 million television licence holders in the United Kingdom; today there are around 18 million. By 1971, a BBC Audience Research Unit report found that 86 per cent of the population found television a "trustworthy" source of news; only 30 per cent "trusted" newspapers.

The Falklands crisis rammed home the lesson of how powerful a means of communication television has become. When the Ministry of Defence spokesman appeared "live" on television to announce the latest news from the South Atlantic, the night editor in Fleet Street was receiving the information no more swiftly and in no different a manner from his readers sitting at home. Voice reports from the television correspondents with the task force were arriving back hours, sometimes days, ahead of written dispatches. Throughout the war, as the *Daily Mail* pointed out in its evidence to the Commons Defence Committee, "most of Britain's national newspapers were largely dependent on taking notes from Brian Hanrahan and Michael Nicholson."

Given this immediacy, fewer people care any more what the *Sun* or the *Mirror* says. With bingo, the mass-circulation papers of Fleet Street are ceasing to be "newspapers" in the traditional sense. As bingo can apparently lead half a million readers to change their newspaper in a matter of weeks, it is scarcely surprising that the editorial pages are fast turning into wrapping paper for that day's lucky numbers. Add to this the fact that in recent weeks the *Sun* has sometimes had seven pages of sport and a further five of advertising in a twenty-eight page paper, and the reason why the Falklands war hardly touched circulation may well stand explained.

HARRIS

Themes for Discussion

What is the political affiliation of each of the British daily and Sunday national newspapers?

Do you think it would be better if there was greater political diversity in the British press?

Do you think that most people take a paper's political affiliations into account when choosing a paper?

Do you think the press would be improved if journalists had greater freedom to report and write what they wanted?

How far do you think newspapers respond to the perceived attitudes of their target readership, and how far do they set out to influence readers' attitudes?

How, and to what extent, do you think papers succeed in influencing their readers?

Why do you think the *Daily Mirror*, followed by all the other tabloid papers, adopted the sensationalising approach analysed by Hall and Whannell? Why haven't the "serious" papers followed suit?

What do you think is the appeal of the kind of "human interest" stories favoured by "tabloid" newspapers?

Why do you think the *Sun* treated the Falklands Crisis in the way illustrated? What is your view of this kind of journalism?

Do you think the *Sun*'s Falklands coverage is likely to have influenced a large number of readers?

For what reasons do you think the *Sun* is Britain's largest selling daily newspaper?

What is your opinion of the general standard of the press in Britain?

Research suggestions

Write a report on the work of each of the following:

(*i*)   staff reporters
(*ii*) correspondents
(*iii*) news agencies

Write a report on the ways in which a) national and b) local newspapers are financed.

Group Assignments

The best way to carry out group research on newspapers is probably to have available a full range of a particular day's papers to work on, individually or in small groups, one paper per person or group.

Here are a few suggestions for analytical work on newspapers:

1. Compare the main front page headlines in each paper, and consider what they reveal about the paper's priorities. Then compare the other front page headlines. This is best done over a number of days, if a significant picture is to emerge.

2. Look at the main front page story in each paper. With a ruler, count the number of column inches devoted to each of the following: the total item; the headline; the photograph; the story itself. Then work these out as a proportion of the total number of column inches of the page. Discuss the differences between the papers in this respect, and their significance.

3. Compare the main front page stories in each of the papers, and decide, as a group, which has the greatest national or international importance. Look for this story in each of the other papers, and discuss its position in the paper and the amount of space devoted to it, and the significance of your findings.

4. Look at a lengthy news story on the front page of each paper, and make brief notes, with illustrations, on the following: lengths of words; lengths of sentences; lengths of paragraphs; general style. Discuss the differences which emerge between the papers.

5. Read the front page stories in your paper, and list the stories in the order in which they interest you personally. Compare lists and discuss the significance of your discoveries.

6. Work through the paper, marking each news story **H** or **S**, according to whether it deals with "hard" or "soft" news. ("Hard" news is that which is concerned with political or economic affairs or social welfare, or which affects a large number of people; "soft" news is that which deals with events which have no broad significance, such as revelations about private lives of celebrities, or crime stories.) Work out the percentage of the paper devoted to "hard" news.

7. Work through the paper, looking for, and marking, each example you can find of each of the following categories:

   national political news and background;
   international political news and background;
   financial and industrial news;
   crime stories;
   "human interest" stories;
   gossip stories about celebrities;
   entertainment and the mass media;
   the arts;
   science and technology;
   sport;
   special features;
   photographs;
   advertisements.

   Roughly work out the percentage of space in the paper occupied by each category. Compare the percentages in all the papers, and discuss the significance of your findings.

8. Look at one or two political news stories, and one or two editorials, in your paper, and draw what conclusions you can about the political line taken by the paper, and the depth of political analysis it contains. Discuss your findings about each of the papers.

9. Read through your paper and write down examples of emotive language and clichés. Compare the papers in this respect.

10. Analyse the way the news is slanted in the different papers by looking at the position of particular news stories and the space devoted to them, biased uses of language and the use of photographs and interviews.

(Some of these assignments could be extended to take in foreign newspapers as well, if the class contains linguists.)

Television

Television in Britain

Television as a mass medium is a phenomenon of the post-Second World War era. Its importance can hardly be overestimated. It has penetrated to all but the remotest areas of the globe, and has been largely responsible for the present American cultural domination over much of the non-communist world. The saddest effect of this has been to open the eyes of many of the Third World's poor to a lifestyle and level of affluence to which they can never aspire.

Yet television has developed in very different ways in different countries. The development of British television is closely related to the nature of British society, according to Richard Hoggart, in the following extract from his essay "Mass Communications in Britain".[1]

In Russia and China the mass media are substantially arms of government, with positive and comparatively single-minded functions. In different democracies their use differs, according to the structure and underlying assumptions of each society. We can say roughly that in America the main emphasis is on the commercial use of the means of mass communication — they tend to be aids to selling, or profit-making organisations in their own right. In Britain, which is both a stratified society with a responsible and still fairly powerful Establishment and yet a commercial "open" democracy, the use of mass communications reflects this piebald character. The British like to use direct governmental controls as little as possible, but their strong tradition of public service and public responsibility causes them (where it is not possible or relevant to support existing voluntary agencies) to establish semi-autonomous chartered bodies under regular, but not day-by-day, government surveillance. This tradition helped to ensure that, once broadcasting had begun to show its powers, in the middle 1920s, a new chartered body was created — the British Broadcasting Corporation — charged with the responsibility for public service broadcasting. After the appearance of television there was considerable pressure for a commercial channel — strengthened by the country's increased prosperity — and so in 1954 the Independent Television Authority was created, to run a second channel from the proceeds of advertisements.

RICHARD HOGGART

The coming of ITV forced the BBC to reconsider its approach to television broadcasting. The main effect was to create competition between the BBC and ITA over audience ratings, so that programmes with a minority appeal were moved to off-peak times, and popular serials, scheduled at the same time each week, became an established feature of the television diet.

The creation of BBC 2 in 1964 provided the BBC with the opportunity

1. From a chapter of *The Pelican Guide to English Literature*, Vol 7: "The Modern Age", edited by Boris Ford (Penguin, 1964).

to expand its service to take in minority and more experimental programmes again, since the second BBC channel was not expected to compete so strenuously for a share of the television audience.

The TV critic Peter Black, in his book *The Biggest Aspidistra in the World*, discusses the BBC's view of its role after the creation of BBC 2:

The BBC's share of the audience remained what it had been, roughly 50–50; for as Attenborough[2] declared, if its share ever rose above sixty to seventy per cent or beyond, it would signal failure, not triumph. It would mean that the BBC was failing to take advantage of its freedom to balance its output between serving minorities and majorities. "It would be clear that the schedules were not enterprising enough to devise innovations which initially might be unpopular, nor daring enough in its catering for minority tastes."

Advertising tends to dominate television in some countries, most notably the USA. In Britain an attempt was made to avoid this danger when commercial television was introduced, as is shown in James Curran and Jean Seaton's book *Power Without Responsibility*:

The American system of programme sponsorship, in which advertisers pay for individual programmes, was rejected when commercial television started in Britain on the grounds that it gave advertisers direct power over programme content. Instead, only "spot advertising" was permitted. Advertisers could only buy time slots between or within programmes. At first, advertisements were limited to an average of six minutes per hour. Later, when it was seen that this led to an accumulation of advertisements in peak viewing times, which had above average amounts of advertising, it was decided to limit advertisements to no more than seven minutes in any one hour.

The decision to adopt restricted spot advertising had been hailed as a victory for public service broadcasting. Spot advertisements were seen as guaranteeing the independence of programme making from the influence of advertisers. Spot advertising would protect the editorial integrity of commercial television. "Advertising will be an asset worn as a bright feather in the cap of free TV," Sir Robert Fraser wrote, "not as a soiled choker around the throat."

The dream machine

If it is used with intelligence and discrimination by producers and public, television is uniquely equipped, in the immediacy and vividness of its sensory appeal, to help break down the barriers of misunderstanding between peoples. In Marshall McLuhan's much-quoted phrase, it has turned the world into a "global village". It can even have a significant impact on the course of world events. The day-by-day American television coverage of the Vietnam War, in the 1960s and 1970s, exposed the

2. David Attenborough, then Head of BBC 2, writing in 1972.

carnage and horror of that war with such stark vividness that the war became unacceptable to a large body of the American people.

Used without intelligence, however, television tends to produce inertia or worse. It enslaves millions of undiscriminating addicts. It can even, at its most insidious, blur the line between reality and fantasy. These negative aspects of television are discussed in the following extracts from Peter Conrad's book *Television: The Medium and its Manners*:

Commercials

As well as enticing us to lust for hardware instead of human bodies, consumerism boasts of its victory over economic necessity by striving to make us hungry when we don't need to eat. This is why television has so charmed a generation with the junk food it advertises. We watch television between meals, when we oughtn't to be thinking about food, but the medium exploits our suggestibility by encouraging us to slaver at the chocolate bars, potato crisps and popcorn it's selling. Consuming these unnutritious victuals isn't eating so much as the repletion of a bored and querulous vacancy, as indeed is watching television. One of the mixtures of toffee and chocolate advertised on British television presents as its chief virtue the time it takes to chew. Disconsolate queuers at a bus stop snap at their chocolate bars and gobble them up at once. The chap armed with the correct brand is still contentedly toiling over his when – presumably hours later – the bus arrives. This is a kind of eating which, like gaping at television, is a substitute for doing anything, a condition of inane passivity. The original technological revolution was about saving time, shortcutting labour; the consumerism which is the latest instalment of that revolution is about wasting the time we've saved, and the institution it deputes to serve that purpose is television. The ads are always admonishing us to stop working. A dishwasher volunteers to relieve us of our chores, saying, "Sit, America – we'll do the washing up". But what do we do while we're not washing up? Television's answer is smugly self-referring: we watch television, and on it we see the dishwasher uncomplainingly toiling on our behalf.

Soap Operas

Stardom on television is experienced by its beneficiaries as a limitation and an ignominy not, as in the movies, an access of monarchical power or an ascension to the company of divinity. The television star is someone who has been made the victim of a stereotype, and who feels cramped and depreciated by its strictures. He longs to shed the image which has supererogated his own reality, and battles frantically to break out of the box. Henry Winkler, donating the Fonz's scuffed leathers to the Smithsonian, resents the programme to which he owes his celebrity and irritably corrects infants who yell, "Hi Fonzie!" at him, explaining that his name is Winkler.

The type may, as in the case of *Dempsey and Makepiece*, seem benign, but the stereotype is malignant, and its most pathetic victims are the actors on the soap operas. They're required by their contracts to conduct their private lives as extensions of the fiction: morality clauses empower the producers to dismiss a performer if he or she violates the sudsy probity which the serials defend. Yet at the same time they're punished in their own persons for the malfeasances of the characters they play. The soap actors have a sorry history of bruises and buffetings, administered by a censorious public. Margaret Mason, when playing Linda in *Days of Our Lives*, had a carton of milk poured over her in a supermarket by a consumer outraged at the character's perfidy; Eileen Fulton, playing the bitchy Lisa in *As The World Turns*, was clubbed with a handbag by another viewer who shrieked while beating her, "I hate you!" Paranoia is an occupational ailment for these people. When Rachel Ames as Audrey was flirting extra-maritally in *General Hospital* she was accosted and abused by a man who claimed that his wife had been so upset by her vicious goings-on that she'd almost suffered a heart attack. When her character was on trial for murder, Rachel Ames was convinced that shop assistants were punishing her by refusing to wait on her. In spite of their protests, these actors have been subsumed by their roles.

News

Television's deftest alteration of content to match its hermetic, transistorised form occurs with the news. As we watch, reality is remade as televisual fiction. For, rather than reporting the news, television's presumption is to invent it. The news on television isn't hearsay, relayed to us by an impartial messenger. It happens at the medium's instigation, for the cameras are no longer obsequious witnesses but agents of provocation. The demonstrators raise their voices and their clenched fists when the cameras arrive. The newsman won't scruple to incite a media event if it seems reluctant to occur. Gary Paul Gates – in his account of CBS television news, *Air Time* – describes an adventurer who, hastening to New Jersey to film what he hoped would be a prison riot, found only a mild ruckus, which had already been pacified. The prison authorities at first refused to admit the cameras, knowing they could easily reignite the protest. Eventually they relented, but still would not allow the crew direct access to the prisoners. The news team therefore went sedately about its business, preparing to film some indifferent and inactive convicts. Then, when all was ready, the reporter in charge signalled to the prisoners with a raised arm and a single extended finger in a gesture of scabrous disdain. They of course co-operated by staging a noisy riot for the cameras.

PETER CONRAD

Television news

Whilst a "tabloid" newspaper can present a trivial but titillating discovery about the private life of a popular entertainer as its main front page feature, national television news generally concentrates on events of genuine significance. Nevertheless, selection is a vital part of the television news presentation, since only half a dozen or so items can be dealt with in any single news bulletin. Peter Golding and Philip Elliott researched the criteria for television news selection in four different countries for their book *Making the News*, from which the following extracts are taken:

Drama:

New stories are, as the term suggests, stories as well as news. Good ones exhibit a narrative structure akin to the root elements in human drama. To recall Reuven Frank, former President of NBC news in America, "joy, sorrow, shock, fear, these are the stuff of news". The good news story tells its tale with a beginning, a middle and an end, in that order.

Dramatic structure is often achieved by the presentation of conflict, most commonly by the matching of opposed viewpoints drawn from spokesmen of "both sides of the question". The audience is here felt to be served by being given the full picture as well as an interesting confrontation.

Importance:

The most frequently cited reason for including a particular item in news bulletins is its importance. This is usually taken to mean that the reported event has considerable significance for large numbers of people in the audience. Most often importance is cited to explain the inclusion of items which might be omitted on the criteria of other audience-based news values. That is, items which may be boring, repetitive or non-visual must still be included despite audience disinterest. The item refers to something the audience needs to know. This news value is rooted in theories of the social role of journalism as tribune of the people. In broadcasting it has the further support that state-authorised corporations are expected to behave responsibly, informatively and educatively. Importance is often applied to political and foreign news. Both are assumed to be of greater interest to journalists than to their audience. Both are included, however, because of their unquestioned importance.

Proximity:

The criterion of proximity derives partly from considerations of the audience, partly from problems of accessibility. Proximity has two senses, cultural and geographical. Stories are culturally proximate if they refer to events within the normal experience of journalists and their audience. They are the kinds of events which require a wide range of common language and shared cultural assumptions. For this reason they are normally, but not necessarily, domestic stories. Cultural proximity can be applied to stories by, for example, putting foreign news into a domestic context to explain its importance or significance.

Geographical proximity refers to the simple rules of thumb that suggest the primacy of domestic news and the allocation of news from the rest of the world according to their nearness to the audience. Several Nigerian sub-editors adopted a three-tier news geography: Nigeria, Africa, the world. In other countries, too, there was a sense of concentric spheres of influence. This design was of course totally disrupted by the availability of material. The geographical criterion thus moderates to two rules. Either, the further away an event the bigger it has to be, or, nearby events take precedence over similar events at a distance.

Negativity:

Bad news is good news. As is often observed there is little mileage in reporting the safe arrival of aircraft, the continued health of a film star, or the smooth untroubled negotiations of a wage settlement. News is about disruptions in the normal current of events. In the literal sense it is not concerned with the uneventful. The concentration on negative events, that is events perceived or presented as damaging to social institutions, is not the result of a mischievous obsession with misery or discontent among journalists, but the outcome of the history of their occupation. News began as a service to groups directly concerned for the uninterrupted flow of commercial life. Interruptions included loss of merchandise at sea, financial upheavals in mercantile centres or, of course, war. These events remain paradigm instances of bad news.

It is for this reason that news is described as a social surveillance, registering threats to the normal fabric of society and explaining their significance. It is worth noting that negativity is not a universal primary news value. What western journalists often see as the tediousness and irrelevance of broadcast news in eastern Europe has much to do with the conventions in many of these countries of presenting positive news (industrial production achievements, the award of honours, etc.) while excluding accidents, violence, crime and other negative categories prominent in news elsewhere.

Elites:

News values emphasise that big names are better news than nobodies, major personalities of more interest than ordinary folk. There is an obvious circularity in this in that well-known personalities become so by their exposure in news media. It is this that leads us to root this news value in production rather than in audience interests. Clearly audiences are interested in major rather than minor figures, people they all know about rather than the acquaintances of a few.

Elites are covered to the extent that their activities are accessible and to the extent that these activities match other news values. Thus the political circus is a prime focus of attention, while economic and financial élites remain shrouded. It is those élites whose activities fit, or who choose to be accessible and visible, which make news.

PETER GOLDING and PHILIP ELLIOT

Since its foundation, the BBC has maintained a reputation for providing an exceptionally unbiased news service. In her essay "Fourth Channel: Third World", from which the following extract is taken, J Ann Kammit considers this claim with reference to British television news coverage of Third World affairs:[3]

Television tends to be interested in the stories, not the issue. Therefore most programmes and reports on the developing world are eye-catchers focusing

3. Included in *What's This Channel Four? An Alternative Report*, edited by Simon Blanchard and David Morley (Comedia Publishing Group, 1982).

on the drama of disasters — floods, famine, earthquakes and disturbances such as wars and coups. This is further accentuated by the news, which normally only refers to the Third World when there are catastrophes or political conflicts. This gives an extremely negative impression of developing countries and their populations.

The real drama affecting Third World countries is the drastic poverty and exploitation which forms the permanent economic and social context for the mass of the population, who are only occasionally affected, if at all, by the more newsworthy hurricanes. But the many programmes which deal with the immediate effects of such disasters naturally concentrate on those most affected — the poor — helping to establish the overall impression that all Third World people are desperately poor. Those of us who have benefitted from travel or study know this not to be the case. As in our own society, most underdeveloped countries do have wealthy, sometimes very wealthy, élites and often a sizeable middle class. This is not to argue of course that we should not be concerned most with the poor and oppressed, but that we should see their poverty in context.

However, media treatment, like many development policy documents, tends to make frequent reference to Third World countries or nations rather than particular social groups. This is an effective means of depoliticising issues, leaving aside crucial questions about the simultaneous existence of extreme poverty and substantial wealth, and the social, political and economic structure which explain that poverty.

The view of "the Third World problem" which underpins the perceptions and analyses of most programme makers, and particularly news reporters, reflects the ideological structures of our own society. Thus TV programmes are informed by the dominant model of so-called development theory, which still holds sway in most of academia and schools education. This model of the causes (ignorance, ill health) of Third World poverty, and of the remedies (modernisation, increased aid) has been persistently challenged within development studies over the last decade.

Cable television

Cable television is likely to widen viewing choice enormously. It has been available in North America for many years. In his book *Television in the Eighties* Rex Moorfoot describes cable television in the USA, and discusses its possibilities for Britain.

The cable viewer has his choice extended — he can choose from relays of the networks, local stations and locally produced community programmes and access programmes. The local programmes will range from earnest features of one kind or another to the most risqué access programmes, for example, in New York regular interviews conducted in the nude, men and women sitting comfortably on a hearth rug in front of a blazing fire. For the remainder of channels, the cable operator, wherever he is, will select a dozen or so of the forty programme services distributed by satellite to the whole nation. Most are 24-hours-a-day services: four news channels, one sport, one weather, three religious, one black, one Spanish, and one Jewish; three popular music channels, three cultural channels, specialist channels for women, children and health; and "super-stations" such as WTBS, Ted Turner's 24-hour independent channel from Atlanta, Georgia, which provides family entertainment based on feature films and sport. These cable services come free to the viewer, supported for the most part by advertising.

There is little doubt that the development of cable television, based on thirty channels and available in half the homes in Britain, would have profound effects on the acquisition and scheduling of programmes. It could lead to "generic" television, national channels distributed by cable for local relay, not by satellite as in America. These could include a news channel, a sports channel, a weather channel, a "pop" channel, a music and arts channel, an educational channel, and others. New organisations could come into being to provide these generic services.

MOORFOOT

Themes for Discussion

The Television Act (1964) requires "that nothing is included in the programmes which offends against good taste or decency or is likely to encourage or incite to crime or to lead to disorder or to be offensive to public feeling". Do you think there is too much sex and/or violence on British television? Can you think of any programmes which you have seen recently which infringe any of the prohibitions in the Act?

Do you think the distinction between the behaviour of heroes and villains in crime series is clear enough? Does it matter?

Do you think British television is sufficiently broad and enterprising in its scope? What kinds of programmes would you like to see more, and less, of?

Do you think Channel 4 has broadened the scope of television?

Do you see any advantages in the British system of financing television programmes partly through licence fees rather than wholly by advertising? How would you feel about the BBC introducing advertising?

The avowed purpose of television in Britain is "information, education and entertainment" (Television Act). How much of each is reflected in a typical evening's viewing? How much of each do you think the typical viewer watches? Do you think most people discriminate sufficiently in their television viewing?

To what extent do you think television increases passivity and unsociability?

Are there any television programmes that you try never to miss? What are they?

What is the appeal of "soap operas"? Do you consider any of them to be successful artistically? Why do you think some people become involved in the lives of "soap opera" characters to the extent illustrated by Peter Conrad?

Do you think British television presents the news in an unbiased way? Do you think it is too parochial in its choice of news items?

Do you think news bulletins should be more positive, and concentrate more on success stories (e.g. good industrial relations) and less on conflict (e.g. strikes)?

Why do you think television (and the mass media generally) fails to follow up situations once their initial news value has waned? Do you think it ought to produce more follow up items?

In what ways do you think poor people in the Third World are influenced by seeing television programmes showing life in the West?

Do you think television could/should do more to educate people about the crisis in the Third World and the global environment?

Would you welcome the advent of cable television?

Questionnaire

After reading the guidelines for preparing and presenting a questionnaire on page 76, it could be of value to produce a questionnaire on television viewing habits. Here are some specimen subjects on which questions might be set:

the number of hours television watched each week on average;
whether a television programme or a book is preferred on a particular theme, such as an adventure story;
whether TV is watched mainly for amusement, relaxation or education, or for no special reason;
if radio is ever preferred to TV in the evenings, and the sort of radio programmes listened to;
if there are any TV programmes which the interviewees try never to miss, and what they are.

(Some of the questions could be correlated, to work out, for example, if people who watch large amounts of television discriminate as much as those who watch less.)

Assignments

1. With the help of several copies of *Radio Times* and *TV Times* for a particular week, work out the proportion of broadcasting time in the evenings devoted to "Serious" and "Light" programmes, following discussion to establish the distinction. This could be undertaken in groups, working on different channels and blocks of time. The findings can be correlated, and percentages worked out.

2. Using *Radio Times* and *TV Times*, draw up a chart of the number of hours per day or evening, over the period of a week, which each channel devotes to each of the following categories of programme:
   news and news magazines;   "soap operas";
   current affairs;   comedy;

documentaries;
drama;
music;
films;

quiz shows and other light
entertainment;
sport.

Work out percentages for each channel, and draw conclusions.

3. Watch an instalment of a "soap opera" or an episode of a weekly
   crime or drama series, and make notes on each of these features:
   The characters: Were they convincingly drawn, or merely stereotypes?
   Were their reactions to situations realistic on the
   whole?
   Were you able to get involved with the characters and
   situations?
   The dialogue: Was it convincing?
   The story: Was it realistic, amusing or exaggerated?
   Did it contain any interesting insights into life?
   You should note down any episodes or incidents which particularly
   illustrated any of these features, positively or negatively.

4. Make a study of fictionalised violence on television, over several days,
   noting the number and instances and the types of violence portrayed.
   The best way to organise this work would be for students to volunteer
   to watch particular programmes advertised in the *Radio Times* or *TV
   Times*, so that the entire range of programmes in which fictionalised
   violence is likely to feature is covered.

5. Watch the evening news bulletin on each channel, over a period of 3 or
   4 days. List each item, and work out the proportions of domestic and
   international news on each channel. Work out the proportion of items
   involving conflict, and involving violence. Compare the selection of
   items on the different channels. Were you aware of bias in any of the
   news coverage?

Advertising

Social effects of advertising

Advertising is massively big business, and is the only mass medium from
which no one in the Western world can escape. A whole new pseudo-
science of "motivational analysis" has grown up over the past few
decades, seeking ways of persuading us to buy one company's product
rather than another's. Since for all practical purposes there is nothing to
choose between different brands of toothpaste, soap powder, petrol and
thousands of other consumer items, advertising is inevitably concerned
largely with the creation of imaginary differences between brands, which
in turn lead to all kinds of distortion and deception on the part of the
advertisers. As J A C Brown put it: "It is obviously impossible to appeal
to common sense by truthful advertising which relies on giving factual
data if the brands from which the customer is expected to choose are alike

in all essential qualities."[4] What are the implications of this?

The psychological and social effects of advertising in Western society are discussed by Frank Whitehead in a chapter of the book *Discrimination and Popular Culture*, edited by Denis Thompson.

In recent years the advertising world has turned increasingly to the twin techniques of market research and motivational research, in order to make more efficient its empirically-gained knowledge of how best to work upon human frailty.

It can be argued that the constant appeal to discreditable impulses is unlikely to have much effect except on those who are already abnormally susceptible. We may agree that it is the self-indulgent who will respond with most alacrity to slogans about chocolates with "less-fattening centres", or to the stomach-powder manufacturer's encouragement to "Eat what you like – without suffering for it". On the other hand advertising agents are united in their conviction that sheer weight of repetition can be amazingly effective (hence the remarkably long life meted out to such slogans as "Players Please" or "Guinness is Good for You"); and it should be remembered that what we are exposed to is a combined assault by many different advertisers, all converging to direct their appeal to a small number of well-proved human weaknesses. Thus although it may be only the exceptional motorist who falls in at all fully with the implications of the invitation to "Put a Tiger in your Tank", nevertheless this particular extreme example works in consort with a host of other advertisements for petrols, cars, and motoring accessories to establish an unquestioned assumption that what every motorist longs for above all (on our overcrowded roads) is speed, engine-power, and acceleration. Road safety is not apparently considered a strong selling-point for motor-cars.

For the most part, advertising acts (and is content to act) as a reinforcement of already existing tendencies, but even so it seems likely that the multiplicity of small pressures work together to effect significant shifts in the total pattern of socially-accepted values. In countless ways often unnoticed we are led to accept as common ground a world in which the key to happiness is the possession of the newest model of car, dining-room suite, refrigerator, and television set, in which any malaise can be neutralised by recourse to a branded anodyne or laxative, and in which the chosen reward for a hard day's work is to "treat yourself" to a luxury you can't afford because you feel you "deserve" it – or even "owe it to yourself".

The tendency to reinforce impulses which are socially undesirable is only part of the problem. Even more insidious may be the advertiser's growing ingenuity in linking his product with ideas and images which are in themselves innocuous, pleasurable, even commendable. In consequence of this the concepts of sexual love, manliness, femininity, maternal feeling are steadily devalued for us by their mercenary association with a brand-name – as though the real human values they represent can be purchased by

4. J A C Brown, *Techniques of Persuasion* (Penguin, 1963).

rushing out and buying a new shaving lotion, a new deodorant, even a new washing-machine. Mother-love seems to be the target most favoured by practitioners of this tactic, and the following example is only a little more nauseating than most of its kind:

> "When there's love at home, it shows. It shows in the smile of the mother who gives it. It shows in the happiness of her family who are secure in it . . . . It shows in the fact that she chooses Persil for their clothes."
>
> WHITEHEAD

The rationale of advertisers

Advertising costs large companies millions of pounds. How can the expense be justified? In an essay entitled "Understanding Advertisers"[5] Kathy Myers reveals some of the underlying assumptions, approaches and justifications of the advertising industry:

For a product to become a brand it needs to establish and maintain a position in the market over a defined period of time. Market stability ultimately depends upon repeat purchases.

Ralph Horowitz put the case for manufacturers' investment in advertising as follows: "The role of advertising is to diminish uncertainty. Advertising sets out to secure a predetermined level of demand for a given future and to diminish fluctuations around that predetermined level." The ability to predict total revenue from advertised products is crucial if manufacturers are to accurately plan future output, product development and capital investment.

It is therefore the need to take the trial and error out of selling that motivates advertisers to create a clear picture of the audience they are selling to and what role or function the product could play in people's lives.

Attention to the "needs" and "desires" of the consumer informs every level of marketing strategy: the design of the campaign, the kind of media exposure given, the amount of exposure, the choice of packaging, distribution, etc. The advert which we see is only one part of this highly co-ordinated marketing offensive.

From the advertiser's point of view, women's magazines are a highly reliable way of reaching the female consumer. Readership profiles are available for each magazine on the market.

One unquantifiable benefit to advertisers is that magazines provide a "hospitable environment" for the digestion and assimilation of advertised information. Glossy, colourful and eye-catching, women's magazines are reputed to have a "keep" value. They may be read at leisure, used for reference, shown to friends or left about the house. Publishers and advertisers believe that these magazines provide a source of information, advice, solidarity and companionship, and that women have grown to trust the opinions voiced. It is a credibility jealously guarded by editors and highly

5. Included in *Language, Image, Media*, edited by Howard Davis and Paul Walton (Basil Blackwell, 1983).

valued by advertisers, for both groups feel that some of the journalistic credibility is carried over into the advertisements. The magazine environment as
an essential ingredient of advertising success was the message of an IPC
advert for their Women's Group of magazines. The copy quoted a Saatchi
and Saatchi spokesman on the subject of Anchor Butter:

> "While our TV advertising is promoting the use of Anchor Butter in the
> family, we are looking to posters and women's magazines to reinforce our
> branding for us. We want the housewife to be absolutely certain that
> Anchor is the name she can rely on for real butter goodness, and we are
> confident that in the relaxed, intimate environment of women's maga-
> zines our message carries complete conviction."

Conflicts within agency strategy are reflected in the system of beliefs
which validate the industry as a whole. On the one hand, members of the
advertising profession see advertising mythically as consistent with the needs
of a democratic egalitarian society: it helps to make the consumer aware of
available market "choices"; it "educates" the consumer into "product
benefit" and so on. But the vision of advertising as a democratic
information service is distorted by the fact that it is the job of each individual
agency to promote one product at the expense of competing products. The
apparent contradiction between these two aspects of commercial philosophy
is rationalised in terms of the "Darwinian" survival of the fittest product. In
the Western economy, where 95 per cent of the new products introduced
onto the market each year fail to maintain a market position, successful
marketing and advertising is felt to be essential to give products a
competitive chance.

MYERS

Themes for Discussion

Why do companies spend so much money on advertising?

How do you think people in general are influenced by advertising?

Can you think of any ways in which you personally have been influenced
by advertising?

What influence do you think advertising has on people's lifestyles,
attitudes and aspirations? How important a part does it play in Western
culture?

Do you think that advertising has a tendency to cheapen and debase
language?

Are there any aspects of advertising which you feel should be legislated
against?

Research topic

Write a brief report on the advertising code of practice in Britain.

Assignments

1. Collect a range of newspaper and magazine advertisements and analyse the appeal of each. Try to find an example of an advertisement appealing to each of the following basic urges and anxieties:

   greed   security
   ease and comfort   maternal feelings
   snob appeal   fear of nonconformity and urge
   identification with famous   for acceptance
      people   health fears
   sex appeal

2. Analyse some of these advertisements in more detail. Consider:
   The picture: Is it appropriate to the product? If not, what urge is it
                           appealing to?
   The slogan: Is it a logical, verifiable statement?
   The copy: Does it concentrate on presenting facts which will help the
                        reader make an informed decision? Does it make any
                        claims or statements which cannot be verified? Does it use
                        inappropriate pseudo-scientific language? Does it use an
                        inappropriate or exaggerated style?
   Does the advertisement as a whole link the product with irrelevant drives, and make questionable statements?

3. Decide what kind of people the advertisement is appealing to, on the basis of your analysis.

4. Look at a selection of recorded television commercials. Analyse the appeal of each, in similar terms to those suggested above.

5. List the commercials in order of effectiveness, and discuss what makes an effective television commercial.

6. Make a collection of advertisements from each of the following: a "quality" Sunday newspaper colour supplement; a "tabloid" newspaper; a women's magazine. Look at some of the advertisements in each, and try to draw some conclusions about the kinds of appeals and audience each is aimed at.

7. Look at a range of advertisements for the same type of product, e.g. cosmetics, cars, beer, chocolates, shampoo. Decide whether the basic appeal is similar in each, and if not, why not.

8. Make a collection of advertisements which link products with irrelevant urges.

9. Make a collection of meaningless slogans and statements in advertisements.

10. Make a collection of inflated, inappropriate phrases used in advertisements.

Film, Video and Censorship

For centuries censorship has been a contentious issue. In Britain, all films
have to be passed for public exhibition by the British Board of Film
Censors. In the extracts which follow, from an interview in a 1982 issue
of *Screen* magazine, the Secretary of the Board, James Ferman, discusses
film censorship and the dangers of video "nasties":

When I joined the Board in 1975, censorship was extremely controversial.
The Board was going through a difficult period largely as a result of a
number of contentious films which came out in the early 1970s − *Straw
Dogs, Last Tango, Emmanuelle, The Devils* . . . . And there had of course
been a sudden trend for sex films, beginning with sex education films in the
early 1970s and going on to soft porn films of which *Emmanuelle* is the most
obvious example. This meant that the local authorities suddenly found themselves involved in a very controversial business, while the newspapers found
that there was a lot of good copy in censorship. The film industry in its turn
− to be fair to the newspapers − often traded on that, because controversy
was good for the box office.

It has generally been thought that the OPA[6] refers only to pornography,
but it's not just hard-core pornography, it's anything that may be depraving
and corrupting to a significant proportion of those who are likely to see it. It
includes the advocacy of drug-taking, the portrayal of horror or violence as a
"turn-on". In other words, there may be something which is not porno-
graphic in the common sense of the term, in that no genital organs are on
display on the screen, but the wicked behaviour portrayed is presented as a
"turn on", an encouragement to behave in an anti-social or seriously
harmful manner.

There is a tradition in this country that, on the whole, we restrict seriously
offensive or potentially offensive sexual material by confining it to clubs or
semi-private situations. This is the British solution. It's not a solution which
any other country has developed, but if we can accommodate the club
licensing system to that tradition then on the whole it will prove more acceptable, and clubs and public cinemas could still retain their character as
different social spaces.

I think the Board's view has always been that there was room in our
society for a kind of film which would not be widely shown but shown only
to those who seek it out. Provided that it did not encroach on the consciousness of those who had no wish to know about it, through indecent or disturbing advertising − advertising is very important, the ads for *Driller Killer* on
video are very worrying, and advertising also affects how people come to see
the film or video itself − and provided it was not depraving or corrupting.

I think it's fair to say that no film made before 1970 had a serious tendency
to deprave and corrupt by today's standards. But since then there has been a
tendency to indulge in an exploitation of evil for its own sake: "We are now
going to show you the nastiest, most unpleasant thing you've ever seen −

6. Obscene Publications Act.

and if this isn't strong enough for you, next week we'll show you something even stronger," putting the idea into people's mind, that is, actually inciting them to find evil attractive, saying, "We want to put you in the position of the rapist, we want you to watch this from the standpoint of a man who is enjoying participating in it."

The problem is that the way films work is not necessarily a direct incitement. The law talks of a tendency to deprave and corrupt, which is exactly what it is. There's very little evidence that if you see one rape film, it will incite you to rape, but if you see two, six, ten? Out of 402 films in 1976 we had 58 which included scenes of on-screen rape. Some were quite serious films, but most were exploitation trying to make the audience enjoy the rape as male spectators. I don't think you can say that any one of those films is a direct incitement, but they gradually erode the taboo against it, they gradually teach a male audience − at least American porno films do − that women don't really mind rape, that they will respond to it as a liberating experience. I think it's a tendency, the cumulative impact of a whole genre of film.

In a *Newsweek* programme on pornography, Gene Abel, the New York researcher, found that in showing rape images to normal men, measuring their physiological sexual response, the erotic content was the main factor and the physical response decreased when the violence factor was increased. With convicted rapists, on the other hand, it was the other way around; and this is the problem with these recent "slasher" films − which are in fact all heavily censored in Britain, more than the critics notice − that violence and rape itself is presented as a "turn on".

And, again, I think we must remember that films are not isolated experiences, people go to the cinema repeatedly. The generation 16 to 25 used to go a couple of times a month, or used to when they had money. Now they're hiring video, and seeing far worse things, with the added factor that they don't even have to see the "film as a whole" − they can just skip the boring dialogue and spool through to the rape or the brutality, and see it again and again.

Discussion points

Do you think that scenes of explicit sex and ultra-violence should be banned from the cinema? How would you draw the line between what is acceptable and what is not?

Why do you think people watch "video nasties"? Do you see them as a reflection of any trends in our society? What do you think is the probable effect of films which present rape and other forms of sadistic cruelty as a "turn on"?

Essay Titles

(a) "Advertising and affluence are closely related."

(b) "A good newspaper is a nation talking to itself." What are your views on what constitutes a good newspaper?

(c) "Sir Brian Young of the Independent Broadcasting Authority has been quoted as saying: 'It's better violent than cosy.'" What is your opinion of this view of television broadcasting?

(d) The freedom of the press.

(e) "The prime concern of the popular newspaper is entertainment, not news." Discuss.

(f) How far do newspapers influence views in society and how far do they merely reflect them?

(g) In what respects do you think standards in television may be in decline?

(h) Consider the treatment by the mass media of any *one* important recent issue.

(i) To what extent do national newspapers reflect all shades of public opinion?

Bibliography

Black, Peter. *The Biggest Aspidistra in the World: a personal celebration of fifty years of the BBC*, British Broadcasting Corporation, 1972

Cohen, Stanley, and Young, Jock. *The Manufacture of News: Deviance, Social Problems and the Mass Media*, Constable, 1976

Conrad, Peter. *Television: The Medium and its Manners*, Routledge and Kegan Paul, 1982

Curran, James, and Seaton, Jean. *Power without Responsibility, the Press and Broadcasting in Britain*, Methuen, 1985

Glasgow Media Group. *Bad News*, Routledge and Kegan Paul, 1976. *More Bad News*, Routledge and Kegan Paul, 1980

Golding, Peter, and Elliott, Philip. *Making the News*, Longman, 1979

Hall, Stuart, and Whannel, Paddy. *The Popular Arts*, Hutchinson, 1964

Harris, Robert. *Gotcha! The Media, the Government and the Falklands Crisis*, Faber & Faber, 1983

Moorfoot, Rex. *Television in the Eighties: The Total Equation*, British Broadcasting Corporation, 1982

Smith, Anthony. *The Newspaper: An International History*, Thames and Hudson, 1979

Thompson, Denis (ed). *Discrimination and Popular Culture*, Penguin, 1964

Whale, John. *The Politics of the Media*, Manchester University Press, 1977

Whittaker, Brian. *News Ltd: Why You Can't Read All About It*, Minority Rights Group, 1981

Williams, Raymond. *Communications*, Penguin 1968

Advice on Writing: Choosing a Question

The right choice of question on a language essay paper is of fundamental importance. If you realise after half an hour that you do not know enough about your chosen subject to continue writing authoritatively about it, then you cannot expect to do well. A reasonably detailed plan, with a paragraph scheme, should prevent this from happening. Your plan should enable you to establish quickly whether you can write convincingly about the subject for the length of time allocated. Scrapping an essay after five minutes' unsuccessful planning is better than struggling to think of ideas when it is too late to start a different essay. During the planning stage, you should try to think out exactly what the examiner is looking for, and make sure that you have sufficient information and ideas about the topic you have chosen to write an effective answer. We will look at some specimen essay questions, and consider how you can decide when a question is best avoided.

It is quite likely that at least one of the questions on a general language essay paper will concern a comparatively current issue. We will look at one or two such questions, and discuss what the examiners will be likely to be expecting. The issue of terrorism, for example, was prominent in the news in 1986. Let us therefore take the question: "Can terrorism ever be justified?" If you have read newspaper reports and analyses of the Libyan terrorist attacks, and the American response to them, then this might be a good question to attempt. However, if this is the only example of terrorism which you can think of, then your answer is likely to be too narrow. A discussion of the situation in Northern Ireland, for instance, would show that you are aware of the wider issues of terrorism. Furthermore, if you have only a vague knowledge of the situation involving Libya and America, then you are unlikely to be able to write convincingly about it. You would be expected to be aware of arguments about "state terrorism", as well as the horrors of isolated bomb attacks. You would also be expected to show some understanding of the justifications (however dubious) for terrorism, and not assume that terrorists are simply lunatics who enjoy killing people.

Similarly, an issue which was current in the early 1980s was that of the subsidisation of public transport. If the question was, "The case for or against a heavily subsidised public transport system", you would be expected to show some awareness of the arguments presented, for instance, by the Greater London Council for subsidising public transport in London, and the reasons why the policy was declared illegal. If you argued hypothetically, as though subsidisation was merely an idea, which had never been put into practice, you would be unlikely to score very highly. The problem of hunger strikes was another topical issue in the early 1980s. In answer to the question, "The problems posed by hunger strikes", some knowledge of specific situations, such as the IRA hunger strikes which ended with the death of Bobby Sands, would be expected. In this case, simply a review of different hunger strikes, without discussion of the various problems which resulted, would score poorly.

Vagueness is one of the most serious failings in language essays. If you write in generalities when the question invites specific illustration, you will lose quite a lot of marks. If the question, for example, was, "Do we owe a greater debt to the artists than to the scientists?" you would be expected to cite a reasonably wide range of both. If you can only think of one or two writers whom you happen to be studying in literature, then you will merely be displaying your ignorance. Again, if the question was, "Given a Time Machine, to which past age would you like to return, and why?" you would be expected to display a fairly detailed knowledge of life in your own chosen era. If your historical memory is sketchy, then it would be best not to attempt the question. Similarly, if the question was, "Modern dramatists apparently enjoy expressing violence; they should look for more positive values in our society", then you would be expected at least to display a knowledge of the works of a variety of dramatists who express violence, and ideally be able to cite one or two whose messages you consider positive.

Vagueness can be a fatal flaw in essays on the press. To answer a question which reads, "To what extent do national newspapers reflect all shades of public opinion?", you would be expected to be aware of the political affiliations of the main national papers; an answer which did not refer to specific papers would be bound to lose marks. Likewise, the question, " 'A good newspaper is a nation talking to itself.' What are your views of what constitutes a good newspaper?" could not be answered adequately without some analysis of at least one specific paper.

You must make sure, therefore, that you fully understand the implications of a question before attempting to answer it, that you can discuss it in depth, and that you can illustrate your answer adequately, if illustrations seem to be called for.

11
Four Themes in Brief

In this chapter, four more themes are suggested, in addition or as alternatives to the eight already explored in depth. Written exercises and ideas for planning a discussion or debate are provided on each. The themes are: politics; the nuclear debate; youth, marriage and old age; and drugs.

1. Politics

With a topic as wide as this, all that can usefully be done is to suggest a few approaches to discussion. First, a comprehension.

Read the following passages, and answer the questions below them. You are advised to spend about one hour on this exercise.

A *The identity of conservatism*

1 Running through the varieties of conservatism is the theme of inequality. Conservatives stress the benefits to society of a ruling class whereby a rich and powerful minority guide can restrain the conduct of a majority. Conservatives, then, advocate a class or hierarchical society where authority
5 issues from an economically and politically ascendant élite to the mass of people.

The conservative defence of inequality is conducted on three grounds. First, human beings are said to be naturally unequal in their possession of skills and energies. Social, economic and political inequalities do not signify
10 the exploitation of the poor by the rich: they simply mirror the immutable facts of human biology. Even should socialists construct their egalitarian paradise, argued Bernard Braine in *Tory Democracy* (1948), former social distinctions would quickly emerge: "Within a very short space of time this new equality will have vanished into the mist. Some men will be rich, some
15 will be poor. Some will be masters, some will be servants. A few will lead, the rest will follow." Far better, on this view, to defer to human nature than to embark upon a misconceived plan of social levelling.

Conservatives suggest, second, that egalitarian policies contain the seeds of totalitarianism. A programme of social engineering which overturns
20 natural inequality is not merely an abortive enterprise: it is likely to engender a tyrannical and dictatorial regime which stifles diversity and crushes individual freedom. Any government which makes equality its primary

objective, conservatives believe, treads a slippery slope towards the kind of regimented society said to be found in Eastern Europe.

25   Finally, inequality is said to benefit rich and poor alike. Social distinctions enable the talent for leadership to be channelled into the provision of wise government and a sound economy. Society, deprived of the initiative of its talented minority, would drift into political muddle and economic stagnation. Everyone would then suffer.

30   The conservative case for inequality has been stated with particular clarity by Harold Macmillan:

> "Human beings, widely various in their capacity, character, talent and ambition, tend to differentiate at all times and in all places. To deny them the right to differ, to enforce economic and social uniformity upon them,
> 35 is to throttle one of the most powerful and creative of human appetites. It is wrong, and it is three times wrong. It is wrong morally, because to deny the bold, the strong, the prudent and the clever the rewards and privileges of exercising their qualities is to enthrone in society the worst and basest of human attributes: envy, jealousy and spite. It is wrong practically . . .
> 40 because it is only by giving their heads to the strong and to the able that we shall ever have the means to provide real protection for the weak and for the old. Finally it is wrong politically; because I do not see how Britain, with all its rich diversity and vitality, could be turned into an egalitarian society without, as we have seen in Eastern Europe, a gigantic exercise in
> 45 despotism."

For conservatives, then, there is nothing either just or laudable in the spurious demand for an egalitarian society.

ROBERT ECCLESHALL

B   *What is socialism?*

1 All forms of socialism comprise three basic components: a critique, an alternative, and a theory of transition; that is, they reveal defects in a society, suggest better arrangements, and indicate how these improvements are to be achieved. Although there is a great variety in socialism, it is none the less
5 possible to outline a few general characteristics.

    In the case of the critique there is invariably a grounding in some form of egalitarianism. Capitalism, which has historically been the main target of socialists, is usually seen as a fundamentally unequal society, concentrating wealth and power in the hands of a minority and condemning the majority to
10 absolute, or relative, poverty and impotence. Socialists stress the unacceptable differences between life chances in such divided societies. In capitalist societies, socialists argue, equality exists only at the formal constitutional level, and they echo Anatole France's oft-quoted remark that "The law in its majestic equality forbids the rich as well as the poor to sleep under bridges,
15 to beg in the streets, and to steal bread."

    A second common feature is a critique of societies which undermine or stifle sociability and co-operation. Capitalism, for example, is criticised for the isolated, selfish characters it tends to create; too little care is shown for

others, most of whom are seen as either irrelevant to one's "private" sphere,
20 and therefore not worthy of genuine concern, or as competitors, and as such
a threat. The result is a stunted individual unable to achieve the humanity
that only flows from a genuine community. Socialists agree with the words
of John Donne:

"No man is an island entire of itself: every man is a piece of the continent,
25 a part of the main: . . . any man's death diminishes me, because I am
involved in mankind: and therefore never send to know for whom the bell
tolls: it tolls for thee."

Socialists, third, have a conception of freedom which makes them highly
critical of many conventional formulations. They highlight, for example, the
30 contradictory and shallow classical liberal definition of freedom as absence
of constraint. It is contradictory because the liberty of the "free" market
undermines the freedom formally enshrined in social and political rights; the
market produces poverty and poor individuals cannot be fully free. Marx,
for example, says of freedom in capitalist societies:

35 "the practical application of man's right to liberty is man's right to
private property . . . . The right of man to private property is, therefore,
the right to dispose of it at one's discretion . . . without regard to other
men, independently of society, the right of self-interest?"

Or using David McLellan's paraphrase, "it was no use having the right of
40 access to the Grill Room at the Ritz if you couldn't afford the bill." It is
shallow in that genuine liberty is not mere freedom from external pressures
but freedom to develop fully as an individual among other free individuals:
to be not a mere isolated unit ("free" from all that is most satisfying) but a
well-rounded, fulfilled human being, delighting in the free use of all one's
45 faculties. In their critique, socialists have therefore echoed, and concep-
tualised in their own particular way, the great rallying call of the French
Revolution – liberty, equality and fraternity.

VINCENT GEOGHEGAN

Note: Your answers should be *in your own words* as far as possible.

(a) Explain the phrase "the immutable facts of human biology" (line 10)
as used in passage A. (2 *marks*)

(b) Explain, in your own words, what would happen according to
Bernard Braine "should socialists construct their egalitarian
paradise" (lines 11 to 12). (4 *marks*)

(c) Why would Conservatives argue against "a programme of social
engineering which overturns natural inequality" (line 19) according to
passage A. (5 *marks*)

(d) Explain the point of Harold McMillan's reference to "envy, jealousy
and spite" (line 39). (3 *marks*)

(e) Consider the relevance of the quotation from Anatole France to the
argument in favour of "egalitarianism" in passage B. (4 *marks*)

(*f*) Explain why, according to the "second common feature" of the socialist critique, "socialists agree with the words of John Donne" (line 22) quoted in passage B. (*5 marks*)

(*g*) Explain how the quotations from Marx and David McLellan shed light on "the contradictory and shallow classical liberal definition of freedom as absence of constraint". (lines 30 – 31) (*5 marks*)

(*h*) Give the meaning of the following words as they are used in the passage:
  (i) hierarchical (line 4);
  (ii) totalitarianism (line 19);
  (iii) relative (line 10);
  (iv) classical (line 30);
  (v) constraint (line 31); (*5 marks*)

(*i*) Briefly comment on any *one* idea in either passage with which you strongly agree or disagree. (*7 marks*)

(*Total:* 40 *marks*)

There are plainly any number of approaches to a discussion of politics. Exploring particular issues can be a valuable way of developing a political perspective, but the goal of being able to read political reports in newspapers with some degree of understanding is probably as valuable as any. The suggestions which follow have this end in view.

British politics
A debate, in which individuals or pairs present a general case for the main British political parties' current policies.

A discussion of the different parties' policies with relation to specific issues, such as defence, privatisation and nationalisation, workers' participation in industry, law and order, etc., following research by individual students.

Research and/or discussion of current political vocabulary, such as: "left" and "right" in a party and general political sense; mixed economy; monetarism; Keynesian economics; proportional representation; Marxist; capitalist, etc.

World politics
A discussion of the major world political systems: anarchism, capitalism, centralist communism, democratic socialism, fascism. A useful approach might be to take a political map of the world, and discuss the political systems in operation in different areas and countries.

A discussion concentrating on the differing political systems in selected areas, e.g.: Central America, the Far East. In the former case, individual students could research the current politics of Nicaragua, El Salvador, Honduras and Costa Rica; in the latter the systems in India, China, Indonesia and Taiwan could be discussed and compared.

As a follow up or an alternative to this kind of approach, discussion could centre on more general political abstractions such as: the meaning and value of "democracy", the concepts of "freedom" and "liberty", the uses and limitations of bureaucracy, etc.

Essay Titles

(a) "Power tends to corrupt, and absolute power corrupts absolutely. Great men are always bad men."

(b) "When people contend for their liberty, they seldom get anything by their victory but new masters."

(c) In pursuing higher living-standards, do we overlook the quality of life?

(d) Discuss the case for the complete revision of the electoral system in Great Britain.

(e) "As society becomes more complex we have more government and less freedom." Is this inevitable?

(f) "Liberty must be limited in order to be possessed."

(g) "The principal concern of politics is the allocation of resources." Discuss.

(h) Is "equality of opportunity" attainable or is it only an ideal?

(i) "Democracy is the tyranny of the majority." How far do you respond to this assertion?

2. The Nuclear Debate

The issues both of nuclear weapons and nuclear power lend themselves very well to full-scale classroom debate. Since information and theories about nuclear weapons crop up constantly in serious newspapers, as well as in periodicals, pamphlets and books, there is plenty of material to assemble and construct your own argument for debate.

As an introduction to the issues, and also as an exercise in note-taking and analysis, here are two extracts on the question of deterrence, or "mutual assured destruction", from opposite sides of the nuclear fence.

Nuclear weapons

What would happen in the event of a nuclear strike against Britain? . . . The principal effects of nuclear weapons are very intense heat, blast and radio-active emissions. Within a certain distance of the centre of the detonation all houses, cars, clothes, the hair on dogs, cats and persons, and so on, will spontaneously ignite, while at the same time the blast will bring the houses tumbling down about the cubby-holes . . . .

The acceptance of such human sacrifice has become part and parcel of nuclear "deterrence". The current chatter about "theatre" or "tactical" nuclear war is not a sophisticated variant of the old vocabulary of "deterrence"; it is directly at variance with that vocabulary. For it is founded on the notion that either of the superpowers might engage in a "limited" nuclear war which could be kept below the threshold at which retribution would be visited on its own soil.

Thus it is thought by persons in the Pentagon that a "theatre" nuclear war might be confined to Europe, in which, to be sure, America's NATO allies would be obliterated, but in which immense damage would also be inflicted upon Russia west of the Urals, while the soil of the United States remained immune . . . . While the Generals make their plans for a European "theatre" war the advocates of civil defence are offering a corresponding political initiative.

These advocates wish to hurry the British people across a threshold of mental expectation, so that they may be prepared, not for "deterrence", but for actual nuclear war.

The expectations supporting the theory of deterrence are in the final analysis that deterrence will *work*. Deterrence is effective, because the alternative is not only "unacceptable" or "disagreeable": it is "unthinkable".

Deterrence is the posture of MAD (mutual assured destruction), not of menace. It does not say, "If we go to nuclear war we intend to win": it says, "Do not go to war, or provoke war, because neither of us can win". In consequence it does not bother to meddle with anything so futile as "civil defence". If war commences, everything is already lost.

Those who have supported the policy of deterrence have done so in the confidence that this policy would prevent nuclear war from taking place. They have not contemplated the alternative, and have been able to avoid facing certain questions raised by that alternative . . . .

But the argument of civil defence advocates are designed to hurry us past these questions without noticing them. They are designed to carry us across a threshold from the *unthinkable* (the theory of deterrence, founded upon the assumption that this must *work*) to the *thinkable* (the theory that nuclear war may happen, and may be imminent, and, with cunning tactics and proper preparations, might end in "victory").

More than this, the arguments are of an order which permit the mind to progress from the unthinkable to the thinkable *without thinking* – without confronting the arguments, their consequences or probable conclusions, and, indeed, without knowing that any threshold has been crossed.

It has never been true that nuclear war is "unthinkable". It has been thought and the thought has been put into effect. This was done in 1945, and it was done upon two populous cities. It was done by professing Christians, when the Western Allies had already defeated the Germans and when victory against the Japanese was certain in the longer or shorter run. The longer run would have cost some thousands more of Western lives, whereas the short run (the bomb) would cost the lives only of enemy Asians. This was perfectly thinkable. It was thought. And action followed on.

What is "unthinkable" is that nuclear war could happen to *us*. So long as we can suppose that this war will be inflicted only on them, the thought comes easily. And if we can also suppose that this war will save "our" lives, or serve our self-interest, or even save us (if we live in California) from the tedium of queueing every other day for gasoline, then the act can easily follow on. We *think* others to death as we define them as the Other: the enemy; Asians; Marxists; non-people. The deformed human mind is the ultimate doomsday weapon − it is out of the human mind that the missiles and the neutron warheads come.

Within the logic of "deterrence", millions are now employed in the armed services, security organs and military economy of the opposing blocs, and corresponding interests exert immense influence within the counsels of the great powers. Mystery envelops the operation of the technological "alchemists". "Deterrence" has become normal, and minds have been habituated to the vocabulary of mutual extermination. Local crises are survived and it seems as if the decisive moment − either of war or of peace-making and reconciliation − has been postponed and pushed forward into the future. But what has been pushed forward is always worse. Both parties change for the worse. The weapons are more terrible, the means for their delivery more clever. The notion that a war might be fought to "advantage", that it might be "won", gains ground. There is even a tremor of excitement in our culture as though, subconsciously, humankind has lived with the notion for so long that expectations without actions have become boring. The human mind, even when it resists, assents more easily to its own defeat. All moves on its degenerative course, as if the outcome of civilisation was as determined as the outcome of this sentence: in a full stop.

E P THOMPSON

If we could abolish all arms then the world would *ipso facto* be a more peaceful place. Unfortunately that option is not available. We are talking only about less − perhaps substantially less − arms, which is quite a different thing and certainly not synonymous with more peace. *There is simply no direct correlation between arms spending and incidence of war . . . .*

Let us look at some uncomfortable facts. The millions of people killed in wars since 1945 have, with notable exceptions, not been victims of the world's larger military powers; they have not been killed by hyper-expensive and super-sophisticated weapons but rather by mundane, small arms of the sort that could have been used in previous generations and even centuries; and they have resided in the poorer regions of the world. Where the arms race has been at its most intense and where there is the greatest concentration of advanced weaponry − Central Europe − there has been relative peace, stability and prosperity. Along the Sino-Soviet border deep antagonism and large military deployments have co-existed. One can detect enthusiasm for war declining (unfortunately not to zero) in the Middle East with the accumulation of those weapons that would ensure that a future war would be even more deadly than those of the past.

Thus relationships of mutual deterrence can develop, in which aggressive motives are suppressed because of the fearful costs that would probably be incurred in war. These relationships can often be fragile and they are not a particularly sensible way to manage human affairs. But we are not designing a new world − only attempting to survive in the one that exists. So if we can identify relationships of mutual deterrence we should approach them with care and dismantle them only if we can be sure this will not trigger off the very process we wish to avoid.

This may be particularly true in Europe, where many would blame East-West tension and the concomitant arms race both for placing mankind in danger of extinction and for the neglect of the problems of the Third World. Fundamental to European security is the stand-off between the two great alliances that dominate the continent. This stand-off has been achieved, and is maintained, at human and financial cost and substantial risk. *Yet it has resulted in a period of peace which has contributed to prosperity which has in turn generated funds, albeit insufficient, for development aid.* The alliances and the consequent peace are not wholly the responsibility of judicious deployments of military power. But nuclear weapons have instilled caution and circumspection into the leaders of the major powers which has prevented crises, such as those over Berlin or Cuba, turning into war.

There is much to be said for reducing the role of nuclear weapons in international affairs, but in the short-term at least this could involve an increased dependence on conventional forces which happen to be much more expensive. Most important of all, if the alliance structure within Europe collapsed, the result would probably be the resurgence of old conflicts – in the Balkans, over Germany – rather than an all-pervading amity. I am not trying to assert the opposite of the conventional view: that somehow arms races have inevitably peaceful consequences and that we interrupt them at our peril. Rapid re-armament is as worrying as rapid disarmament. Any dramatic shift in military balances, one way or the other, can be profoundly unsettling. Thus the attempt by both super-powers to establish new military positions in Africa and Asia makes local politics more turbulent and dangerous.

Obviously there are many instances where military build-ups have been responsible for those evils attributed to them – international distrust and war, as well as being a gross waste of resources. But our focus should be the avoidance of war rather than military spending per se. *Where international stability benefits from a balance of military power then disarmament for its own sake can be positively harmful.*

LAWRENCE FREEDMAN

1. Summarise, in note form, the arguments of each writer about "deterrence". (Each set of notes should contain 8–10 headings.)

2. Decide which of the two writers you most agree with, and use your favoured writer's arguments to make a case against the other.

Suggestions for debate

Suitable motions might be:

1. The only sane nuclear policy for Britain is one of unilateral nuclear disarmament.

2. To go "naked to the conference table" is to invite destruction.

Research

Students who are interested might undertake private research, either to assist in the discussion, or to report back to the class, on the following:

"theatre" nuclear war	fallout shelters
cruise and pershing missiles	radiation effects
sea-based missiles	"overkill"
neutron bombs	the defense budget
"star wars" weaponry	Greenham Common
the "balance of terror"	"nuclear winter"
"first-strike capacity"	

Further reading

Since new information and developments in the nuclear weapons debate occur so frequently, it is impossible to provide an up-to-date bibliography. Here are a few basic titles:

Chant, Christopher, and Hogg, Ian. *The Nuclear War File: Weaponry, Strategy, Flashpoints, the Balance of Power*, Ebury Press, 1983
Freedman, Lawrence. *Britain and Nuclear Weapons*, McMillan, 1980
Hersey, John. *Hiroshima*, Penguin, 1972
New Statesman. "New Statesman Report 3: Britain and the Bomb", *New Statesman*, 1981
Rogers, Paul, Dando, Malcolm, and van den Dungen, Peter. *As Lambs to the Slaughter: the Facts about Nuclear War*, Arrow Books, 1981
Schell, Jonathan. *The Fate of the Earth*, Pan Books, 1982
Thompson, E.P. *Protest and Survive*, Spokesman Books, 1980

Pamphlets can be obtained from a wide range of sources, such as "Peace Through NATO" (the multilateralist case) and CND (the unilateralist case).

Nuclear Power

Once again, a considerable body of information about and arguments for and against the use of nuclear energy is readily available. The simplest way to prepare for a debate on the topic is to send off for leaflets. There are several organisations which would be happy to send you propaganda for their point of view, if you explain why you want it. Here are a few:

The United Kingdom Atomic Energy Authority Information Services Branch 11 Charles II Street LONDON SW1Y 4QP	The Conservation Society 12 London Street Chertsey Surrey KT16 8AA

British Nuclear Forum
1 St Albans Street
LONDON
SW1Y 4SL

Friends of the Earth
377 City Road
LONDON
EC1V 1NA

The Central Electricity Generating
    Board
Press and Publicity Office
Sudbury House
15 Newgate Street
LONDON
EC1A 7AU

Nuclear Information
PO Box 11
Godalming
Surrey

British Nuclear Fuels
Information Services Department
Risley
Warrington
WA3 6AS

Socialist Environment and
    Resources Association (SERA)
9 Poland Street
LONDON
W1V 3DG

Essay Titles

(a) "In a war of ideas it is people who get killed."

(b) Nuclear power – bane or boon?

(c) Unilateral versus Multilateral Disarmament.

3. Youth, Marriage and Old age

This may seem a rather artificial linking of what are in reality separate themes. They can of course be treated separately, but since each is in itself a relatively minor social issue in terms of a written English language examination, it may be convenient to deal with them all in a single discussion session. A comprehension on the family will serve as the preliminary written exercise.

Read the following passage, and answer the questions below it. You are advised to spend about one hour on this exercise.

1   The most neurotic, the most difficult marriages, those with a lot of anger and frustration, are not those that dissolve most easily. In fact, outwardly bad marriages often last till death. It is the easy marriages, those with less pathology, that often separate so smoothly they scarcely seem to have been
5   joined.
      In fact, marriage until death seems an absurd route to choose for an easy life. An absurd route to choose for other goals – not necessary for sex, indeed in the long term inimical to it; very difficult for equal and mutual growth; deep relationships are quite possible outside it (one of the messages
10   of Ingmar Bergman's "Scenes from a Marriage" was that the couple could only be genuine friends once they were apart. Only then did they understand

each other). Indeed, one quite possible explanation of the state of marriage today is that a great many people are entering it who are quite unsuitable to something so strenuous. A hundred years ago far fewer people were able to
15   marry, largely because of their financial situation. About one-third of adult women under forty-four, for example, were not married in the Victorian era. Today about 95 per cent of males and females have been married by the time they reach forty-five.

What then is the point of monogamous marriage till death? Guygenbuhl-
20   Craig, the Swiss Jungian psychiatrist who made all these observations, derived the facts from the married people he treated in his practice. In his book *Marriage − Dead or Alive*, he looks at an archetypal marriage, that of Hera and Zeus. To the Greeks, this was marriage. It was extremely stormy −
25   usually about Zeus's incessant infidelity (though Hera was by no means faithful herself). At one time Hera tied Zeus up so completely that helpers from Tartarus had to free him. At another, he had her hung from the rafters of heaven. She was furiously jealous and would exact appalling revenge against his lovers. When he seduced Io, Hera turned her into a cow. This wasn't enough, so she loosed upon Io a gadfly, a gigantic insect whose stings
30   drove her mad. In complete panic, raving with fear, Io as cow raced through large parts of the world. Many wives must have longed for such powers.

This myth holds a clue to what marriage is about. It is about the Jungian view of salvation.

Salvation is distinct from well-being. Well-being means comfort, freedom
35   from anxiety, sexual relief, companionship. Salvation has to do with the meaning of life far beyond comfort. It is about facing up to suffering and death. Jungians have a word to describe the search for salvation − "individuation". Guygenbuhl-Craig says that individuation can be described exactly, in detail. This is not true. It is a mystical concept which is rather
40   fuzzy and that is its strength. It can only be described in terms of the kind of things it involves, and by reference to myth and metaphor. It means not just finding out about, but working through, the forces in our subconscious: in a man, the powerful aspects of the feminine which are part of him; in a woman, the active masculine aspects; dark forces of destruction and cruelty
45   which are also part of our natures. This last is particularly difficult, and all ages try and avoid it (putting it on to the devil, for instance, or, like us, on upbringing or social forces or "capitalism", "communism"). This process is, in fairy stories, a journey. But individuation is both the journey and the goal − the process of working through the self and the achieved reconcilia-
50   tion. It is like the life of Christ, where the life and its end were together the message.

Marriage till death is a pathway to salvation, a process of individuation. Because there is no avenue of escape it is an extremely unusual path. Here it resembles the strictest of enclosed mediaeval orders, or the vocation of a
55   hermit. "In this partially uplifting, partially tormenting evasionlessness lies the specific character of this path." It is absurd to expect that marriage should be "happy". It is the way of salvation, and in myth the road to heaven leads through hell. Because it is a way of salvation marriage is an endless series of exalted high feelings and deep low ones, a continuous belt of

60 ups and downs. It has happy moments of course, many of them, but also suffering and sacrifices.

Sacrifice always plays a major role in the myths of salvation. It is true that with Abraham and Isaac, God accepted a goat, but many myths have a tendency to comfort. The point was that Abraham had to be ready to
65 sacrifice. In Christianity, the central myth of the last 2,000 years, sacrifice is cardinal. In any road to salvation there is a profound need to sacrifice oneself, a feeling one should pay the price. It goes without saying — you have only to look — that great sacrifices are demanded by marriage. The long-term confrontation of marriage is only possible if one or both partners
70 renounce something important. This sacrifice is necessary to the personality. It is quite wrong for friends or therapists to say no one should have to go on giving affection to someone cold, no one should have to make such sacrifices. That situation is the marriage. Their sympathy is misplaced. Dante crossed hell, but he reached heaven. The successful marriage, the
75 endured marriage, leads to the deepest kind of existential satisfaction.

JONATHAN GATHORNE-HARDY

Note: Your answers should be *in your own words* as far as possible.

(*a*) Consider the meaning of the sentence "It is the easy . . . seem to have been joined" (lines 3 – 5). (*2 marks*)

(*b*) Explain, in your own words, what the writer means by saying "marriage until death seems an absurd route to choose for an easy life" (lines 6 – 7). (*4 marks*)

(*c*) Why do you think the writer mentions the myth of Hera and Zeus? (*3 marks*)

(*d*) What do you understand by the term "individuation"? (*4 marks*)

(*e*) Consider the significance of the references to: (i) the devil and (ii) the life of Christ. (*5 marks*)

(*f*) What do you think that the writer means by saying that marriage "resembles the strictest of enclosed mediaeval orders, or the vocation of a hermit" (lines 54 – 55)? (*5 marks*)

(*g*) Why is the "sympathy" of "friends or therapists" in the final paragraph "misplaced", according to the writer? (*4 marks*)

(*h*) Give the meaning of the following words and phrases as they appear in the passage:
(i)   inimical (line 8);
(ii) strenuous (line 14);
(iii) incessant infidelity (line 24);
(iv) myth and metaphor (line 41). (*6 marks*)

(*i*) Briefly comment on the view of marriage expressed in the last three paragraphs. (*7 marks*)

(*Total:* **40 marks**)

A discussion of the theme of youth may usefully take in youth culture. Here are some forms of preparation:

A history of post-war fashions and ideologies amongst young people might provide an enjoyable project to undertake.

A more time-consuming but more creative approach to youth culture would be for a group of students to present a history of rock music since the mid-50s. A cassette could be prepared, illustrating the changes in popular music, to be accompanied by an analysis of the movements and trends in fashion and philosophy which went with these musical styles. Different students might perhaps work on different eras. A strict time limit must be established at the outset, however, if this project is not to last for ever! The following books might be useful for research into the music and movements of the 1950s and 1960s:

Cohn, Nic. *Awopbopalubopalopbamboom: Pop from the Beginning*, Paladin, 1970

Gillett, Charlie. *The Sound of the City: The Rise of Rock and Roll*, Souvenir Press, 1983

Melley, George. *Revolt Into Style: The Pop Arts in Britain*, Penguin, 1970

More formal discussion might take in such questions as inner-city riots, the effects of unemployment on young people, or, on a more personal level, young people's experiences of the "generation gap" and the problems of adolescence. Four books which deal with these issues through the eyes of teenagers are the following:

Cashmore, E. Ellis. *No Future*, Heinemann, 1984

Fisher, Susie, and Holder, Susan. *Too Much Too Young?* Pan Books, 1981

Lawton, Anthony. *Parents and Teenagers*, Allen and Unwin, 1985

McCormack, Mary. *The Generation Gap: the view from both sides*, Constable, 1985

Any discussion of the family will inevitably enable you to talk from personal experience. The theme can be considered purely on a personal level, without any prior preparation, dealing with such questions as:

What is the best age at which to marry?

Should marriage be a lifelong commitment?

Under what circumstances should partners consider divorce?

Are extra-marital affairs ever right?

Should both husbands and wives work if they have young children?

Should children be brought up in a strict or a liberal family environment?

Research can again be useful to back up discussion of the family. It may be interesting to look up comparative divorce statistics, and statistics of the ages at which men and women married in different eras and areas. More detailed research could be undertaken on such subjects as alternative methods of child rearing (such as the Israeli Kubbutz system) and differing concepts of marriage in different countries. The following books may be of interest:

Bernard, Jessie. *The Future of Parenthood*, Calder and Boyars, 1975
Gathorne-Hardy, Jonathan. *Love, Sex, Marriage and Divorce*, Jonathan Cape, 1981
Skynner, Robin, and Cleese, John. *Families and how to survive them*, Methuen, 1983

The magazine *New Society* frequently carries articles on the family.

Old age is becoming an increasing social problem in western society, and, once again, research will considerably aid discussion. An illuminating exercise would be to compare the numbers of people over retirement age in Europe, with those under school-leaving age in Latin America or other areas of the Third World. A discussion of the significance of these statistics would provide a useful introduction to the problem.

Further research could be undertaken into such matters as the National Health Service provisions and services for old people, methods of preparing people for retirement, and the problem of senility.

A more personal response to growing old might be evoked from reading stories about old people, such as "Uncle Ernest", in Alan Sillitoe's *The Loneliness of the Long Distance Runner* (Granada, 1985) or listening to songs such as "Bookends" (and the accompanying, "Voices of Old People") from Simon and Garfunkel's *Bookends* LP (CBS, 1968). A collection of stories and extracts about old people is to be found in a book called *Old Age*, in the Routledge and Kegan Paul *Themes* series, published in 1972.

Books of general interest on the theme are as follows:

Greengross, Sally (ed). *Ageing, an Adventure in Living*, Condor, 1985
Hellie Huyck, Margaret. *Growing Old: Things you Need to Know About Ageing*, Prentice Hall, 1974
Hobman, David (ed). *The Social Challenge of Ageing*, Croom Helm, 1978

Essay Titles

(a) "Fashion dictates the way we live."

(b) Is there a "generation gap"?

(c) "The old-fashioned respect for the young is fast dying out."

(d) Is the family out of date?

(e) "Love and marriage . . . go together like a horse and carriage."

(f) It used to be said that it was a woman's business to get married as soon as possible, and a man's to keep unmarried as long as he could. Is this a fair view of marriage?

(g) The duties, responsibilities and pleasures of the family.

(h)   We do not respect the old; they are no longer wise.

(i)   How will we cope with the problems of living to an average age of one hundred years?

(j)   "Most older people have forgotten the important things in life." Discuss.

4. Drugs

This is obviously one of the most sensitive of all social problems to discuss in a class situation. The passage which follows serves as a historical introduction to the subject, as well as a précis exercise.

Write a summary of the following passage in not more than 230 words (the passage contains about 680 words). Your summary should be in clear, connected English, and the number of words used should be indicated at the end. You are advised to spend about one hour on this exercise.

Even if heroin and cannabis could have been banished, it had become clear by the 1970s that they would immediately have been replaced by other drugs. Some had already established themselves – occasionally with the active help of governments, or of the medical profession, or both.

When the amphetamines – "pep pills" – were first marketed in the 1930s, doctors had begun to prescribe them for patients who felt tired or lethargic; and later as a slimming aid. During the war they proved a help to men in the forces who were required to stay alert on duty; and when it ended, vast quantities of them, surplus to requirements, were dumped on the open market . . . . But then it was realised that, injected intravenously, the amphetamines could produce an explosive bout of euphoria; and as they were cheap and easily available, they were soon being extensively used for that purpose, with destructive effects on the health of some of the addicts, ranging from brittle finger-nails to ulcers, chest infections, liver disorders, and cerebral haemorrhages. Governments banned sales, except on prescription; but so many people had acquired the habit of taking the drug, and so many doctors were willing to indulge them, that the black market was rarely short of supplies. Taking amphetamines, in Brecher's estimation, ranked "among the most disastrous forms of drug use yet devised" – particularly in Sweden, where the attempt to impose total prohibition led only to a rise in the price, encouraging illicit manufacture and smuggling, and leading to a spectacular growth in the number of addicts . . . .

Cocaine also made a come-back. "Sniffing" had enjoyed a vogue in the United States in the 1920s; in his *Drugs and the Mind*, Robert S. de Ropp surmised that the original "dope friend" peddled cocaine, rather than heroin. But it was expensive; the amphetamines, far cheaper and more easily obtainable, for a while replaced it. When the amphetamines proved an unsatisfactory substitute, cocaine began to return to favour in American cities. Its high price was less of an impediment to sales than it had been in the depressed 1930s, and provided an incentive to smugglers. With the raw materials, coca leaves, abundant and cheap, this left an ample margin to perfect smuggling techniques, and to bribe Customs or police. Once the cocaine had been brought in, there was no difficulty in selling it. What Plate called the iron law of drug marketing, "supply determines demand", came into operation; whenever it was available, cocaine became . . . the drug of choice, not only among whites but ever increasingly among affluent black drug users as well . . . . Among Latin Americans in New York, cocaine is often the preferred drug of entertainers, expensive prostitutes, very successful businessmen, and certain religious sects for whom cocaine use is literally an act of faith. And among white drug users, cocaine is especially popular with rock stars, writers, younger actors and actresses, and stock-brokers and other Wall Street types . . . .

And even if all these drugs could have been brought under some control — by, say, the discovery of some instrument on the lines of a geiger counter, capable of infallibly detecting them — it would not have solved the problem. Apart from synthetic variants, there were numerous substances which, though not sold as drugs, could be used for that purpose — and frequently were. Benzine and glue had long been sniffed "for kicks", and with the advent of the aerosol can, it was found that there were endless alternatives; "literally hundreds of easily accessible sources", the Le Dain Committee found, including paints, paint removers, lighter fuel, and dry-cleaning fluids: 'it was recently observed that thirty-eight different products containing such substances were available from the shelves of a service station's highway store in Ottawa''. In the circumstances, the Committee pointed out, effective restriction was hardly practicable, "except at considerable inconvenience to a large segment of the population"; and, as the large segment of the population was unlikely to accept that inconvenience, the existence of these "substances" created a problem "which clearly calls into question the potential of the crimino-legal system in controlling drug use''.

BRIAN INGLIS

Further reading

Inglis, Brian. *The Forbidden Game: a Social History of Drugs*, Hodder and Stoughton, 1975
Lamour, Catherine and Lamberti, Michael R. *The Second Opium War*, Allen Lane, 1972
Manning, Mary. *The Drugs Menace*, Columbus Books, 1985
Nowlis, Hellen. *Drugs Demystified*, Unesco Press, 1975
Wyatt, John. *Talking About Drugs*, Wayland Publishers, 1973

Newspaper and periodical articles
"A generation on the main line to tragedy."
"The deadly traffic from no-man's land."
"Cuts that contribute to crime." Series by Paul Brown on p 11 of *Guardian* (3, 4, 5 January 1984)

"Smack City!" Helen Chappel. *Observer* (24 June 1984, p 37)
Addiction a challenge to Society. Griffith Edwards. *New Society* 70.
 (25 October 1984, pp 133–5)
Britain's 50,000 heroin addicts: the people who believed they'd never get
 hooked. Liz Donnelly and Brandon Farrell. *Listener* 113.
 (10 January 1985, pp 10–14)
Now the cocaine threat. Paul Eddy and Justine Picardie. Sunday Times
 (3 March 1985, pp 17–18)
Can a war on drugs succeed? Gerry Stimson. *New Society* 74. (15
 November 1985, pp 275–278)

Films
A variety of films are available on drug abuse and its dangers. There are
police officers in most areas of Britain who can be contacted to show
drug films at schools and colleges, and this may be the best visual
approach to the issue.

Essay title

The abuse of drugs.

Advice on Writing: Over-emphasis on a Limited Aspect of an Essay Question

In Chapter 4, the danger of irrelevance in the language essay was
discussed. One form of irrelevance which was touched upon there was the
mistake of limiting your discussion to a specific issue when a more general
treatment is called for. We will now consider this type of error, and the
resolution of it, in more detail, with reference to the issue of nuclear
weapons.

It is possible that, having thoroughly studied the vexed question of
nuclear weapons, you find a question in your examination on armaments
in general. You *can* quite possibly answer the question by concentrating
heavily on the nuclear issue, but great care will be needed to relate your
discussion satisfactorily to the question.

Let us look at both a successful and an unsuccessful attempt to plan an
essay round the nuclear issue, when the question is not specifically related
to nuclear weapons. Here are two plans for the same essay:

"Weapons of war are obsolete. We should abolish them."

1. Paragraph 1 – introduction:
  Existence of wars since beginning of recorded time
  Current world balance of terror
 Paragraph 2:
  Difference between earlier weapons and nuclear weapons
  Danger of worldwide holocaust from nuclear weapons build-up

Cruise missiles: danger of theatre nuclear war obliterating most of
  Europe
Paragraph 3:
  In this situation, unrealistic to talk of abolition of all weapons.
    Suggestions: strengthen conventional forces to avoid invasion;
    work towards phasing out nuclear weapons. Discussion of
    question of unilateral disarmament as way of achieving
    multilateral nuclear disarmament.
Paragraph 4:
  Discussion of alternative weapons of mass destruction, e.g. germ
    warfare.
  Practical difficulties involved in abolishing all weapons: nuclear
    knowledge will remain when weapons phased out; some weapons
    largely undetectable.
Paragraph 5 conclusion:
  Ultimate hope: work towards concept of brotherhood of man —
    state of mind whereby people don't want to destroy one-another.

2. Paragraph 1 — introduction:
   Existence of wars since beginning of recorded time
   Current world balance of terror
Paragraph 2:
   Explanation of nuclear weapons' capacity for destruction
   Danger of worldwide holocaust from nuclear weapons build-up
   Cruise missiles: danger of theatre nuclear war obliterating most of
     Europe
Paragraph 3:
   Suggestion: work towards phasing out nuclear weapons. Discussion
     of question of unilateral disarmament as way of achieving
     multilateral nuclear disarmament.
Paragraph 4:
   Discussion of alternative weapons of mass destruction, e.g. germ
     warfare.
Paragraph 5 — conclusion:
   Unilateral/multilateral disarmament is only hope for future of
     mankind.

The two plans are obviously similar, yet the first could form the basis of
an excellent answer to the question, whilst the second would have to be
treated as more or less irrelevant. Before reading on, try to work out why.
   Both plans concentrate heavily on the nuclear weapons issue, but the
second fails to make the few crucial references to the issue of the
abolition of *all* weapons, by which the first is linked to the question. The
second essay would therefore *merely* be a discussion of the abolition of
nuclear weapons. The first plan builds carefully towards the conclusion
that the best that mankind can hope for at present is the abolition or
reduction of nuclear weapons, whilst the ultimate abolition of all weapons

is a goal for the distant future. Thus, in this plan, the speculation in paragraph 4 about new forms of mass destruction can be made to develop directly from the arguments about the abolition of current weapons, and the whole issue of weapons abolition generally can be brought neatly back into focus. In the second plan, on the other hand, paragraph 4 seems to be included merely because the writer has learnt about nerve and germ warfare and wants to fit it in somewhere.

Clearly, then, however much you know about a subject, and however well you write about it, you will fail if you do not relate your material precisely to the question. There is no simple answer to the problem of irrelevance. All you can do is practise plans and essays, and, while you are writing them, as was suggested in Chapter 4, think constantly about, and actually look back frequently at, the title, asking yourself whether what you are writing actually *is* relevant to it.

As a way of developing expertise in essay writing, the occasional quarter-hour spent writing an essay plan can be valuable. You might try writing a plan for an essay with this title: "The nation that neglects its defences is courting disaster."

12
Literary Style

All discussions of writing up to this point in the book have been concerned with the presentation of argument and explanations. In this final chapter we will consider writing in its more imaginative aspects, and look at some of the essential techniques by which writing can be invested with special vividness and resonance. A study of literary technique is obviously essential for those who are studying literature as well as language; it should also prove useful for those whose exam contains a "creative" essay option. Even a formal discussion essay can be enlivened by imaginative uses of language.

The purpose of the chapter, therefore, is to explain, illustrate and analyse the main literary techniques. We will separate them into two main divisions: figures of meaning and figures of sound.

Figures of Meaning

Simile

A comparison between two distinctly different things, indicated by the word "like" or "as".

> e.g. Sometimes I might get drunk,
> Walk like a duck and smell like a skunk.
> > Bob Dylan ("I shall Be Free")
>
> The child was like ice in her womb.
> > D H Lawrence ("Odour of Chrysanthemums")

Comparisons are used to clarify ideas by appealing to our imagination. The similes in the Bob Dylan song appeal directly to our senses, creating a vivid momentary picture in our mind's eye. The line from the D H Lawrence story also creates a powerful sense impression, of extreme physical coldness, capturing a sense of the mother's emotional coldness towards the baby inside her, far more vividly than any literal explanation could.

Metaphor

A direct statement of identity between two distinctly different things, *without* using "like" or "as".

e.g. But at my back I always hear
      Time's winged chariot hurrying near;
      And yonder all before use lie
      Deserts of vast eternity.

Andrew Marvell ("To his Coy Mistress")

      Life's a long song,
      But the tune
      Ends too soon
      For us all.

Ian Anderson ("Life's a Long Song")

The pair of metaphors in the Marvell extract heighten, and make more imaginatively compelling, the contrast between the intensity and brevity of earthly life, and the infinite nothingness of death. By comparing the rapid movement of earthly time with a "winged chariot hurrying", a powerful sense of speed and urgency is created, and this forms a vivid contrast with the impression of everlasting barrenness captured by the metaphor of "deserts". The images are largely visual. The idea of the shortness of life is also suggested in the lines from the Ian Anderson song, though here the metaphorical comparison of life with a song which "ends too soon" has a direct, non-visual appeal.

Personification

An inanimate object or an abstract concept is spoken of as though it were endowed with life or with human attributes or feelings:

e.g. The yellow fog that rubs its back upon the window-panes
T S Eliot ("The Love Song of J Alfred Prufrock")

Pale flakes with fingering stealth come feeling for our faces
Wilfred Owen ("Exposure")

In these two images, fog and snow are given the force of living presences by the use of personification. A gentle, quite benign quality is given to Eliot's "yellow fog" by the human comparison, whereas Owen's "pale flakes", though also gentle, are made to seem much more sinister and malign, by the comparison with a blind person's fingers feeling for the faces of the soldiers in a First World War trench.

Though not strictly personification according to the conventional definition, the attribution of human qualities to non-human living creatures has much the same effect:

e.g. . . . the hens twitch and grieve for their tea − soaked sops
Dylan Thomas (*Under Milk Wood*)

Thomas's description of the hens in terms of human beings in a state of nervous anxiety might well be considered to be an example of personification.

Symbol

A word or object which is both literal and which also signifies something beyond itself.

Some symbols are widely recognised in Western culture, for example, the peacock as a symbol of pride and vanity, the eagle as a symbol of heroic endeavour. Leonard Cohen uses the former in this symbolic sense in "Story of Isaac", a song about the dangers of self-glorification, which ends:

The peacock spreads his fan.

Other symbols are more personal to a particular writer and work. The old priest in James Joyce's story "The Sisters", for instance, is literally paralysed, but he also becomes, in his *physical* paralysis, a symbol of the *spiritual* paralysis of Ireland's religious life, of which he is a representative. Whether or not symbolism is present in a work depends on personal interpretation; sometimes it is obvious, sometimes subtle and uncertain.

Figures of Sound

Alliteration

The repetition of consonants in a sequence of words:

e.g. Only the stuttering rifles' rapid rattle
Can patter out their hasty orisons.
Wilfred Owen ("Anthem for Doomed Youth")

Figures of sound produce sound colouring, designed to add emphasis to ideas and emotions, and to create and reinforce tone and feeling.

The lines from "Anthem for Doomed Youth" capture the sound and rapidity of rifle fire in wartime, an effect which is created partly by the repeated, relatively harsh "r" consonant. The line from "Exposure", by the same poet, quoted in the section on personification, also employs alliteration. The effect here is quite the opposite. The repeated soft "f" sounds help to capture a sense impression of the gentle, slow, unremitting, deathly penetration of snowflakes in a trench in wartime, killing the soldiers who are exposed to them more slowly, but more certainly, than bullets.

Sibilants

Alliteration using "s" sounds:

e.g. As he slowly drew up snake-casing his shoulders.
D H Lawrence ("Snake")

The sound and motion of an uncoiling snake, lithe and leisurely, and hissing, is here captured partly by the use of repeated "s" sounds.

Assonance

The repetition of vowel sounds in a sequence of words:

> e.g. Heaps of entangled weeds that slowly float
>
> George Crabbe ("Peter Grimes")

The sound colouring of a passage is largely dependent on the juxtaposition of vowel sounds. If a particular vowel is repeated, it gains special emphasis, and tends therefore to be the dominant sound. In the line from "Peter Grimes" there are two pairs of identical vowel sounds. Both are long vowels, helping to emphasise the impression of slow, meandering movement of the "heaps of . . . weeds"; the repeated long "o" sound at the end of the line creates an especially heavy, sombre effect. The sentence from the D H Lawrence story, quoted in the section on simile, also employs assonance. The key word "ice" receives great emphasis from the repetition of the same long "i" sound in the words "child" and "like", investing the line with an "icy" feel. The chilling effect of the line is enhanced still further by the dark, heavy sound of the final word, "womb". In the line from "Anthem for Doomed Youth", which is quoted above to illustrate alliteration, assonance is also used, in the words "rapid rattle/can patter", the sharp, hard short "a" sounds adding to the violent, mechanical impression of rapid gunfire.

Onomatopoeia

A word, or sequence of words, whose sound seems to resemble the sound it denotes:

> e.g. And *droning* shells *burst* with a hollow *bang*.
>
> Siegfried Sassoon ("The Redeemer")

The line is intended to capture the sound of shells in flight, and exploding. A similar onomatopoeic effect is created by the lines from Owen's "Anthem for Doomed Youth", in the word "stuttering" and in the cluster of words discussed in the section on assonance.

Passages for Literary Analysis

Let us now see how these techniques can be used by a skilful writer for atmospheric and dramatic effect.

The Birds

The passages which follow are from "The Birds", a short story by Daphne du Maurier. "The Birds" is a horror story (which was freely adapted by Alfred Hitchcock for his famous film). It explores the reactions of a Cornish farm labourer, Nat Hocken, and his family and neighbours, to regular, concerted attacks on people and their homes by birds, whose aim, as the story gradually reveals, is the destruction of the human race!

The first three passages illustrate the use of literary devices to create atmosphere: the first, of the restless movement and the abnormality of the birds' behaviour, at the beginning of the story; the second, of cold and desolation, and the third, of a more relaxed atmosphere, as normality seems to have returned. The fourth passage is both atmospheric and dramatic, as Nat watches the birds mass over the sea for an attack, and the final passage is a climactic description of birds swooping down on Nat as he rushes across the fields towards his home.

1.

Black and white, jackdaw and gull, mingled in strange partnership, seeking some sort of liberation, never satisfied, never still. Flocks of starlings, rustling like silk, flew to fresh pasture, driven by the same necessity of movement, and the smaller birds, the finches and the larks, scattered from tree to hedge as if compelled. Nat watched them, and he watched the sea-birds, too. Down in the bay they waited for the tide. They had more patience. Oyster-catchers, redshank, sanderling and curlew watched by the water's edge; as the slow sea sucked at the shore and then withdrew, leaving the strip of seaweed bare and the shingle churned, the sea-birds raced and ran upon the beaches. Then that same impulse to flight seized upon them too. Crying, whistling, calling, they skimmed the placid sea and left the shore. Make haste, make speed, hurry and begone; yet where, and to what purpose? The restless urge of autumn, unsatisfying, sad, had put a spell upon them and they must flock, and wheel, and cry; they must spill themselves of motion before winter came.

2.

The sky was hard and leaden, and the brown hills that had gleamed in the sun the day before looked dark and bare. The east wind, like a razor, stripped the trees, and the leaves, crackling and dry, shivered and scattered with the wind's blast. Nat stubbed the earth with his boot. It was frozen hard. He had never known a change so swift and sudden. Black winter had descended in a single night.

3.

She said nothing of the birds. She began to push and struggle with another little girl. The bus came ambling up the hill. Nat saw her on to it, then turned and walked back towards the farm. It was not his day for work, but he wanted to satisfy himself that all was well. Jim, the cowman, was clattering in the yard.

4.

He got up and went out of the back door and stood in the garden, looking down towards the sea. There had been no sun all day, and now, at barely three o'clock, a kind of darkness had already come, the sky sullen, heavy, colourless like salt. He could hear the vicious sea drumming on the rocks. He walked down the path, half-way to the beach. And then he stopped. He could see the tide had turned. The rock that had shown in mid-morning was now covered, but it was not the sea that held his eyes. The gulls had risen.

They were circling, hundreds of them, thousands of them, lifting their wings against the wind. It was the gulls that made the darkening of the sky. And they were silent. They made not a sound. They just went on soaring and circling, rising, falling, trying their strength against the wind.

5.

As he jumped the stile he heard the whirr of wings. A black-backed gull dived down at him from the sky, missed, swerved in flight, and rose to dive again. In a moment it was joined by others, six, seven, a dozen, black-backed and herring mixed. Nat dropped his hoe. The hoe was useless. Covering his head with his arms he ran towards the cottage. They kept coming at him from the air, silent save for the beating wings. The terrible, fluttering wings. He could feel the blood on his hands, his wrists, his neck. Each stab of a swooping beak tore his flesh. If only he could keep them from his eyes. Nothing else mattered. He must keep them from his eyes. They had not learnt yet how to cling to a shoulder, how to rip clothing, how to dive in mass upon the head, upon the body. But with each dive, with each attack, they became bolder. And they had no thought for themselves. When they dived low and missed, they crashed, bruised and broken, on the ground. As Nat ran he stumbled, kicking their spent bodies in front of him. He found the door, he hammered upon it with his bleeding hands. Because of the boarded windows no light shone. Everything was dark. "Let me in," he shouted, "it's Nat. Let me in." He shouted loud to make himself heard above the whirr of the gulls' wings. Then he saw the gannet, poised for the dive, above him in the sky. The gulls circled, retired, soared, one with another, against the wind. Only the gannet remained. One single gannet, above him in the sky. The wings folded suddenly to its body. It dropped, like a stone. Nat screamed, and the door opened. He stumbled across the threshold, and his wife threw her weight against the door. They heard the thud of the gannet as it fell.

DAPHNE DU MAURIER

If we look again at the first passage, we can see clearly how figures of meaning and sound are used to create atmosphere. The predominant consonant in the first paragraph is "s", the sibilants emphasising the restlessness and the nervous energy of the birds. The simile in the second sentence reinforces this sensation. Again, in the second paragraph, sibilants feature prominently; in the long fourth sentence the sound of the words is combined with the rhythm of the prose to suggest an impression of the sound and movement of the sea; the separated syllables of "the slow sea sucked" create a slow rhythm which is enhanced by the "s" consonants and the long, heavy vowel sounds; but the rhythm of "at the shore and then withdraw" is faster, and the whole effect is to suggest the movement of a wave itself, rolling in, breaking, and rushing out again. Similarly, rhythm and sound combine in the last part of the sentence, the alliteration of "raced and ran" adding emphasis to the rushing rhythm of the words. Some of the sound colouring and the rhythmic movement of this passage are in fact too subtle for any simple analysis in terms of recognisable technique to be possible.

You could now look at some or all of the remaining passages from "The Birds" to find examples of the various literary techniques we have considered, and try to explain and assess their purpose and effectiveness. You could also consider the rhythm of the prose; you will notice that the more dramatic passages contain a greater variety of sentence lengths. It should be easy enough to work out why.

Death

Not only fiction and poetry use figurative language of course. It can be equally suitable for some kinds of factual writing. We will conclude this discussion of style by looking at a piece by the American novelist, essayist and journalist Norman Mailer, which describes an actual event. It is a description of a world championship boxing match which took place in the early 1960s, between Emile Griffith, the challenger, and Benny Paret, who was the current world champion, a fight which had a tragic ending.

After reading the passage you might attempt a full stylistic analysis, selecting and discussing images and phrases in the passage which you consider particularly effective.

The rage in Emile Griffith was extreme. I was at the fight that night. I had never seen a fight like it. It was scheduled for fifteen rounds, but they fought without stopping from the bell which began the round to the bell which ended it, and then they fought after the bell, sometimes for as much as fifteen seconds before the referee could force them apart.

Paret was a Cuban, a proud club fighter who had become welterweight champion because of his unusual ability to take a punch. His style of fighting was to take three punches to the head in order to give back two. At the end of ten rounds, he would still be bouncing, his opponent would have a headache. But in the last two years, over the fifteen-round fights, he had started to take some bad maulings.

This fight had its turns. Griffith won most of the early rounds, but Paret knocked Griffith down in the sixth. Griffith had trouble getting up, but made it, came alive and was dominating Paret again before the round was over. Then Paret began to wilt. In the middle of the eighth round, after a clubbing punch had turned his back to Griffith, Paret walked three disgusted steps away, showing his hindquarters. For a champion he took much too long to turn back around. It was the first hint of weakness Paret had ever shown, and it must have inspired a particular shame, because he fought the rest of the fight as if he were seeking to demonstrate that he could take more punishment than any man alive. In the twelfth, Griffith caught him. Paret got trapped in a corner. Trying to duck away, his left arm and his head became tangled on the wrong side of the top rope. Griffith was in like a cat ready to rip the life out of a huge boxed rat. He hit him eighteen right hands in a row, an act which took perhaps three or four seconds, Griffith making a pent-up whimpering sound all the while he attacked, the right hand whipping like a piston rod which had broken through the crankcase, or like a baseball bat demolishing a pumpkin. I was sitting in the second row of that corner – they were not ten feet away from me, and like everybody else, I was hypnotised. I had never seen one man hit another so hard and so many times.

Over the referee's face came a look of woe as if some spasm had passed its way through him, and then he leaped on Griffith to pull him away. It was the act of a brave man. Griffith was uncontrollable. His trainer leaped into the ring, his manager, his cut man, there were four people holding Griffith, but he was off on an orgy, he had left the Garden, he was back on a hoodlum's street. If he had been able to break loose from his handlers and the referee, he would have jumped Paret to the floor and whaled on him there.

And Paret? Paret died on his feet. As he took those eighteen punches something happened to everyone who was in psychic range of the event. Some part of his death reached out to us. One felt it hover in the air. He was still standing in the ropes, trapped as he had been before, he gave some little half-smile of regret, as if he were saying, "I didn't know I was going to die just yet", and then, his head leaning back but still erect, his death came to breath about him. He began to pass away. As he passed, so his limbs descended beneath him, and he sank slowly to the floor. He went down more slowly than any fighter had ever gone down, he went down like a large ship which turns on end and slides second by second into its grave. As he went down, the sound of Griffith's punches echoed in the mind like a heavy axe in the distance chopping into a wet log.

Paret lay on the ground, quivering gently, a small froth on his mouth. The house doctor jumped into the ring. He knelt. He pried Paret's eyelid open. He looked at the eyeball staring out. He let the lid snap shut. He reached into his satchel, took out a needle, jabbed Paret with a stimulant. Paret's back rose in a high-arch. He writhed in real agony. They were calling him back from death. One wanted to cry out, "Leave the man alone. Let him die". But they saved Paret long enough to take him to a hospital where he lingered for days. He was in coma. He never came out of it. If he lived, he would have been a vegetable. His brain was smashed. But they held him in life for a week, they fed him chemicals, and made exploratory operations into his skull, and fed details of his condition to The Goat. And The Goat kicked clods of mud all over the place, and spoke harshly of prohibiting boxing. There was shock in the land. Children had seen the fight on television. There were editorials, gloomy forecasts that the Game was dead. The managers and the prize fighters got together. Gently in thick, depressed hypocrisies, they tried to defend their sport. They did not find it easy to explain that they shared an unstated view of life which was religious.

MAILER

Essay Titles

Here is a set of titles for stories or other varieties of creative essay:

Horizons	Flattery
Paths	Wounded pride
A sense of failure	Revenge
The power of ridicule	Betrayal

Bibliography

du Maurier, Daphne. *The Birds and Other Stories*, Longman, 1980
Mailer, Norman. *The Presidential Papers*, Penguin, 1968

Advice on Writing: The Creative Essay

Your English language examination may offer the option of writing a "creative" essay. If you enjoy writing stories, and are adept at inventing dialogue and creating atmosphere and the other features of the narrator's art, then the "creative" essay option may well be worth considering. Personal, descriptive and discursive essays may also sometimes be valid approaches to the more open kind of essay title. Story writing, it must be said, holds more potential dangers than any other variety of essay, and tends to produce the weakest answers in advanced English examinations; if it is handled skilfully, with flair and imagination, it can also produce the best.

Before briefly considering some of the essential features of an effective story let us look at the possible alternative approaches to essay titles. The majority of titles will, in fact, offer no alternatives to the formal discussion essay. Obviously enough, titles which ask you to "discuss" or "consider" or "argue a case for or against" something, or are posed as questions, require arguments. On the other hand, open titles, such as "The right to strike", "In defence of discipline and order", "Privilege" or "The problems posed by hunger strikes", while most obviously encouraging discussion essays, could also be treated as titles for stories, unless you are specifically told in the general instructions to write a discussion essay. More obviously "creative" titles are often open to a variety of treatments. Titles like "The power of ridicule", "A sense of failure", "Flattery" or "Revenge", could be treated as discursive or personal as well as narrative essay titles. A title like "Night" could lend itself to a descriptive approach.

Generally, the least promising of these approaches is the discursive essay. Essays of the "There are many varieties of . . ." type, in which half a dozen different kinds of "flattery" or "failure" or whatever are described, are almost invariably dull to read. The main danger with the personal approach is triviality. If the most vivid experiences of failure which you can think of are on the level of failing an examination that you expected to pass, for instance, you are unlikely to produce a very interesting or thoughtful personal essay in answer to the title: "A sense of failure". Unless you have genuinely amusing or intense or unusual experiences to relate, it is probably best to avoid this approach. Personal and narrative essays, of course, are often indistinguishable, and a story about a single personal experience which is relevant to the title can make a very effective essay. Extended descriptive essays tend to ramble and run out of steam, and are probably best avoided.

If you decide to write a story in answer to one of your examination questions, certain essentials must be borne in mind. Most of the points which follow will be obvious to anyone who writes fiction at all regularly, but are, it is to be hoped, worth making, so that disaster may be averted!

The most obviously disastrous error is the failure to make it clear how the story is relevant to the essay title. The title theme *must* be an integral part of the story, and must not just be loosely fitted in somewhere. However effective a story may be otherwise, if the reader cannot work out fairly early on how it relates to the title, it will fail badly.

A successful story requires careful construction, and for this reason is more difficult to produce successfully within a narrow time limit than any other kind of essay. Starting a story before you have got a clear idea of the story-line and the climax is almost certain to lead to weaknesses of construction and, at worst, incoherence. A well-constructed story usually has a single climax, towards which everything that happens in the story builds up. It certainly doesn't need to have a wealth of incident to be interesting, as long as the climax itself is made vivid in some way. Often the most memorable stories are those which lead the reader to anticipate a certain ending, and then provide an unexpected "twist" at the climax. The opening of a story should be as vivid as possible, and a lengthy introductory explanation of the situation and characters is a poor way to begin. A passage of dialogue, or an arresting incident well into the story, followed by flashbacks clarifying the situation, and telling the story from the beginning up to that point, are far more effective.

A successful story must appeal to the reader's imagination. Characters and places must be introduced in such a way that the reader can easily visualise them, without clogging the story up with excessive detail. Dialogue is a very effective way of bringing characters to life, though it is essential that the rules of punctuating dialogue are accurately followed. It is important, of course, that you see and hear the incidents and characters clearly in your own mind; if you cannot do this, then it is probably best not to attempt a story.

Finally, you must pace yourself especially carefully if you are writing a story, and make sure you do not include so much incidental detail that you rush the ending. A rushed climax is likely to be unconvincing, and may even spoil the whole story.